D0397369

The
Future Belongs
to
Freedom

Eduard Shevardnadze

The Future Belongs to Freedom

Translated by Catherine A. Fitzpatrick

THE FREE PRESS · *A Division of Macmillan, Inc.* · *New York*

MAXWELL MACMILLAN CANADA · *Toronto*

MAXWELL MACMILLAN INTERNATIONAL
New York · *Oxford* · *Singapore* · *Sydney*

Copyright © 1991 by Eduard Shevardnadze, Будущее принадлежит свободе
Published by permission of Rowohlt Verlag Gmbh, Reinbek b. Hamburg.
English translation copyright © 1991 by The Free Press
A Division of Macmillan, Inc.
All rights reserved. No part of this book may be reproduced
or transmitted in any form or by any means, electronic or mechanical,
including photocopying, recording, or by any
information storage and retrieval system, without permission
in writing from the Publisher.

The Free Press
A Division of Macmillan, Inc.
866 Third Avenue, New York, N. Y. 10022

Maxwell Macmillan Canada, Inc.
1200 Eglinton Avenue East
Suite 200
Don Mills, Ontario M3C 3N1

Macmillan, Inc. is part of the Maxwell Communication
Group of Companies.

Printed in the United States of America
Designed by REM Studio, Inc.

Library of Congress Cataloging-in-Publication Data

Shevardnadze, Eduard Amvrosievich.
The Future belongs to freedom / Eduard Shevardnadze : translated
by Catherine A. Fitzpatrick.
p. cm.
Translated from the Russian.
ISBN 0–02–928617–4
1. Shevardnadze, Eduard Amvrosievich. 2. Soviet Union—Foreign
relations—1985- 3. Statesmen—Soviet Union—Biography.
4. Reformers—Soviet Union—Biography. I. Title.
DK290.S54A3 1991
947.085'4'092—dc20

[B]   91-29334
                                                             CIP

Contents

Introduction

Why Did I Write This Book?

The history of any cause is always the story of an individual. Our causes share our personal destinies, and this book is no exception. It has its own story, mirroring the events of my life in recent years. By itself, my life would not have been of great interest had it not been fated to coincide with a crucial period in my country's history and in world affairs. Thus the story of the book itself is worth retelling.

In April 1990 Rowohlt Verlag in Germany, made contact with me through Novosti Press Agency[1] to ask permission to publish a collection of my speeches and articles on foreign policy.

Someone once said that a man must perform four duties in his lifetime: plant a tree, build a home, raise a child, and write a book. I doubt that every person is capable of writing a book. Someone else said that a man's life contains at least one novel, although many lives do not even amount to a short story.

I would not be telling the truth if I said that my life held too few events to fill a book. But while I had planted quite a few trees,

---

[1] Renamed Novosti Information Agency in July 1990.—Trans.

had built a house in the country, and had raised my children, I had never written a book. There was never enough time. I have always liked the saying that a line is worth writing only if it is worth reading. I detest the practice of churning out books assured of publication merely because the authors are high-ranking officials.

In all these years, I had never accepted any offer to publish a book. Now, for the first time, I gave my consent because the timing seemed right to me. The book would appear when much of what we had been thinking about and aiming for in foreign policy in the past five years had already been achieved in some way, or would be soon. The irreconcilable antagonism of the two worlds and the cold war were receding into the past. East and West were moving from confrontation toward cooperation. Europe was gravitating toward integration, and the two Germanys were about to be united. We were at the threshold of a pan-European summit, which would bring profound changes into the Helsinki process.[2]

But meanwhile certain trends began to make themselves felt, sending tremors through the seemingly stable process of our joint efforts to build a new, reasonable world order. Areas of world affairs that we had thought were already settled were not running as smoothly as we would have liked.

The book was to be a collection of already published material, which, according to international publishing regulations, was already in the public domain. I was pleased to think that my ideas and views about international relations would reach a wider audience. After all, the concepts, principles, and practices of the new political thinking, which shaped Soviet foreign policy after April 1985, were intended for the world.

I had another strong motivation, relevant to the situation inside the Soviet Union. I was increasingly aware of the discrepancies between the new political thinking and its practice. The priorities disseminated so widely abroad were increasingly clashing with events on the home front. It was as if two different brands of policy were being generated in two incompatible dimensions.

---

[2] The Final Act on Security and Cooperation in Europe, known as the Helsinki accords, was signed in 1975 in Helsinki, Finland, by thirty-five nations in Western and Eastern Europe as well as the Soviet Union and the United States. The agreement provides for regular review conferences on arms control, human rights, environment, and other bilateral issues, and has come to be known as the "Helsinki process."

The "export" version of the new thinking was greatly in demand abroad. But at home it was being pressed into old molds.

My colleagues and I in the Foreign Ministry were facing growing opposition. How it was manifested is a story in itself. It was a matter not of isolated cases, but of a definite trend. Glasnost was being haunted by a "shadow" political struggle. The idea that political means are preferable to the use of force was falling victim to violence, and the principle of freedom of choice was reverting to imperial diktat.

When I mentioned the danger of an impending dictatorship in my resignation speech, many people racked their brains to guess who was meant. They demanded that I name names and speculated as to the political coloration of the putative dictators. Both then and now, I might have quoted a Soviet political scientist who said that dictatorial force has no face and no home address. Rather, it is a question of method and style. Lies, provocations, and crooked politics are always at the service of whoever chooses them. Soon, it is no longer a question of "who" but "why" and "what for," a matter of a means to an end.

The ends of the new thinking began to encounter stiff opposition from certain powerful interest groups. Foreign policy had served their interests before, but no it longer did so. The new foreign policy line now found itself under siege. Since an organized political force always tries to personify any trends hostile to it. I was made the scapegoat. A creature and guardian of the system myself, who had risen to the top by using it, I was now a deviant, slated for ruthless treatment.

By the spring and summer of 1990 the attacks had swelled to a well-orchestrated offensive. The first direct blows delivered at the February 1990 Central Committee Plenary Session had crescendoed into a campaign by the Twenty-eighth Party Congress in March. The handwriting was on the wall, and the pressure would only increase.

In the book I was planning, intended for Soviet publication as well, I wanted to describe how I came by the views I upheld while in office and, most importantly, to defend the principles of the new thinking. I wanted to bring home their importance for the country and the world both to my fellow citizens and to readers abroad.

Everything comes down to three major issues:

First, do we want our country to be a civilized state, ensuring all its citizens an all-around decent existence and defending their civil and human rights in accordance with the highest world standards?

Second, do we want to see our country among the leading nations, advanced in income level, scientific and technological progress, and the quality of life of its citizens and the nations of the Union?

Third, do we want to live in complete confidence that we can guarantee peace and security for ourselves and cope with all present and future dangers?

I began writing my book during vacation in August of 1990 at the Barvikha resort outside Moscow. I sifted through material accumulated over five years, throwing out what was clearly outdated, and made some additions. My work was constantly interrupted. I had left for vacation immediately after my meeting with James Baker in Irkutsk, but on August 2 Iraq invaded Kuwait. Baker and I met the following day at Moscow's Vnukovo Airport to issue a joint Soviet–American statement.

The political process never takes a vacation, and the people caught up in it do not have the luxury of relaxing. In the days that followed, German Foreign Minister Hans-Dietrich Genscher came to Moscow for our eleventh meeting, if we count from the time when the "two-plus-four" mechanism was conceived in Ottawa in February 1990.[3]

Preparations were set in motion for a September conference of the six leaders in Moscow. My foreign colleagues were constantly phoning me at the resort. Iraqi representatives came to Moscow for talks. Under such conditions work on a manuscript might have seemed overwhelming, but, surprisingly, it was not. Instead, it exactly filled the remaining holes in my schedule, and it dovetailed with my current preoccupations. The writing tied together past and present, and shored up my sense of the wisdom of our foreign policy. More aware now of the thrust and continuity of our political line, I rethought many things in a new light, going over the whole course from the beginning, and I found answers to many of the questions that had continued to worry me.

---

[3] The "two-plus-four" mechanism for resolving the question of German reunification involved West and East Germany and the four powers that had divided Germany at the end of World War II: the United States, Great Britain, France, and the Soviet Union.—Trans.

People were absolutely right to claim that up until a certain time, the Soviet Union's foreign policy was an island of national consensus in a stormy sea of internal upheavals. But we were still far from the day when our fiercest critics would liken foreign policy to a "sacred cow," immune from whips and birch switches. They preferred to see it as a milk cow, more profitable if tethered in its old, cramped stall.

Naturally, that was not the way I would put the case in public; I would try to make my arguments more dignified. My critics soon convinced me that they had no use for my arguments. But that was still to come.

In the summer of 1989, the U.S.S.R. Supreme Soviet unanimously confirmed my appointment as Foreign Minister. But by October 15, 1990, several deputies were accusing me of allegedly damaging the interests of national security.

Why was foreign policy attacked internally at that particular juncture, and why did this coincide with the rise of right-wing forces within the country? No one had previously questioned our chief national objective: to create the maximum favorable external conditions needed in order to conduct internal reform.

From the outset, it was clear to all that the old methods of confrontation and the elevation of ideology above politics and law were no longer suitable. By remaining stuck in the old positions, we would not stop the arms race, which was bleeding our already anemic country, or reestablish cooperation with the West, or cease our involvement in regional conflicts, primarily in Afghanistan, or normalize relations with China. We had to build new relations with the Third World, to search for a new world economic order, and to prevent the dangers of global crises.

To achieve this, we had to rebuild confidence, convince the world of the absence of a Soviet threat, and reassure our partners that our intentions were pure and sincere. In time, we marshaled convincing arguments with the policy of new thinking.

On numerous occasions, both at home and abroad, I was asked what "the new political thinking" really meant. I would reply with a question: Can a person think and act in the old way in conditions that absolutely rule out any reasonable possibility of doing so? Now I know that, paradoxically, it is more than possible, if the new conditions are adverse—if they threaten to strip him of authority and the privileges of power and influence, or

remove him from top management positions with all their privileges.

While new thinking was eliminating the old barriers in our
relations with the West, people were somehow placated. Although
during the early stages certain ideas were debated by some of our
high-ranking ideologues, on the whole no one dared to refute them.
Perestroika was understood to be universally applicable and could
not be guided by a double standard. If you start democratizing
your own country, you no longer have the right to thwart that
same process in other countries. If you reject a resort to "tank
philosophy" in relations with neighboring countries, at the very
least you ought not to conceive of your own country in those terms.

All well and good, but the moment the new thinking touched
the old shackles that held the Soviet Union together and kept it
dominant in its spheres of foreign influence, the situation changed
drastically. That occurred when Article 6 of the Soviet Constitution, on the "leading and guiding role" of the Communist Party in
the life of the state, was about to be repealed. The amendment
immediately faced resistance. Groups that feared the loss of their
one-time omnipotence rallied together. They hastily contrived a
new "profile of the enemy," an indispensable element for an army
preparing for battle. A battle-tested weapon was dredged up from
the past: a vocabulary for back-stabbing and discrediting politicians and statesmen, who were accused either directly or indirectly of collaboration with the "adversaries" of the state.

The new political thinking was harshly indicted for the separatism in the republics; inter-ethnic clashes; the "loss of the *cordon
sanitaire*," i.e., the countries of Eastern Europe; the "collapse of
the socialist camp"; the unification of Germany; and "concessions"
to the West. As noted already, Soviet foreign policy or, more
precisely, the Soviet Foreign Ministry was the main target. That
meant, lest there be any doubt at all, the Foreign Minister.

I probably ought to explain my own attitude toward these *ad
hominem* attacks, and tell about my feelings, if only because many
people said the reason for my resignation was "exaggerated sensitivity to criticism." I have my own ideas of dignity and honor, of
course, but I have never sacrificed the cause to them. I view any
criticism as normal, provided it is specific and well-reasoned. I
have a keen sense of guilt, and I know when I have wronged
someone. It would be foolish to suppose I did not understand that,

given the stakes, I cannot avoid having enemies. Naturally, there are people who regard me as their adversary, but I have always refrained from naming them. That is not because I don't know who they are. Far from it. My upbringing, my life experience, and my profession have taught me to make dialog my first priority, both in my work and in private life. For me, it is both a means and an end. Dialog requires impartiality and lack of prejudice, regardless of the partner. Even if I feel uneasy with my counterpart, I suppress my dislike. I know all too well that to stereotype a person as a personal enemy is fatal to the cause. Regarding your opponents as enemies is irrational, unproductive, and imprudent; you only increase their numbers by loftily snubbing them. When conducting policy on the grand scale, that is a luxury no one can afford.

When I am treated roughly, I do not respond on the principle of "an eye for an eye." But I won't budge an inch if I believe I am right. I will not back down unless someone convinces me I am wrong.

It was a tragedy for all of us that with the power monopoly in the Soviet Union, dialog was rejected as a political device. A system based exclusively on order and obedience leaves room only for the monolog of the hierarch. Totalitarianism presumes the pronouncement of ideas raised to an absolute, and a ruthless battering of countervailing views. It is more convenient to crack an opponent's head than to crack the ideas he comes up with. This has been so deeply instilled in us that we have forgotten how to converse normally with each other.

I experienced something like this in the way I was treated. Frankly, it hurt, but not much. So intense was the pace of work occasioned by the year's events, and so much time and energy were required to solve the problems that arose every minute, that I could not let the business of absorbing and parrying attacks distract me. Long ago, I made it a rule that when I concentrate on one matter, I push aside anything unrelated that may interfere. And if I was trying to set a standard in the Ministry for freedom of expression, and was encouraging my staff to escape conformity imposed from above, did I have the right to express displeasure at criticism directed my way?

True, I did occasionally catch sight of the latest journalistic lampoon out of the corner of my eye, or of a banner waved by protesters in front of the Foreign Affairs Ministry, or overhear some parliamentary deputies and a few of my comrades in the Party leadership, or observe their behavior. But it would strike me more and more how distorted our notions of democracy are—unconsciously distorted, or perhaps altogether deliberately. I couldn't help thinking that freedom without decorum and responsibility was mutating into anarchy fraught with chaos, and would someday become unmanageable. I recalled the idea so beautifully expressed by a great Russian writer: In a democratic, civilized society, freedom is nothing other than well-regulated liberty.

I concluded that the freedom that rejects order and decency is in fact nonfreedom of conscience and action. It can be regulated only by nonfreedom, that is, coercion. And then it's all over.

In other words, as I watched the mounting offensive on our foreign policy, I was alarmed, but not for my own future. My antagonists had taken everything into account, except for the way a person of my Georgian background operates. Since childhood, I have never allowed any encroachments upon my own notions of duty. Under the rules of the system's power monopoly over the individual, you must bear without a murmur all attacks upon yourself and must accept as your due the diktat of the political patriarchate, which arrogates to itself the right to decide your fate. While it decides what to do with you, sit tight, do your work, and take advantage of the privileges and benefits offered to you. Don't try to yank the fish hook out of your mouth, or it will be certain death.

Only those close to me knew that I wasn't clinging to any post, except for the sake of our political future. Although I had said publicly time and again that nothing would keep me from leaving office if I found it impossible to follow my conscience, few people took me seriously. This was unfortunate, of course. At any rate, I was inwardly protected by my conviction of my own correctness and my freedom to act as I saw fit. But outwardly, it was different. My colleagues and I outwardly defended the cause, but really we were losing hope. The threats to unseat the Foreign Minister were heard not somewhere out on the streets, but in the corridors of power. Worse, they were not challenged by those whose business it was to respond. The parliamentary chambers were opened to the free distribution of disinformation. Some highly placed representatives watched impassively as the facts were distorted and the Foreign Ministry was cast in a false light. Top officials in other ministries also remained silent, although they shared equal responsibility with the Foreign Ministry for some of the foreign policy decisions and had given their consent. While conducting negotiations abroad, I kept stumbling on discrepancies in positions I thought had been agreed upon at the highest level.

It was very hard to work normally in such an atmosphere, but we managed. We were regularizing foreign policy aspects of German reunification, concentrating on ensuring Soviet security as a priority. We prepared and signed agreements with Germany and other major European powers, creating for the Soviet Union the maximum favorable conditions for cooperation in the new Europe. We worked hard to find mutually acceptable solutions at the Vienna talks on reduction of troops and conventional arms, from the Atlantic to the Urals. We called for a European summit to lay the groundwork for new continental security structures, now that the division of Europe and the cold war were over. We continued the traditional agenda with our American partners, where problems of strategic offensive weapons cuts and regional conflict resolutions were discussed along with the task of enlisting political and material support for perestroika at home. We had some success in seeking foreign sources of credit, both monetary and otherwise, for our crisis-ridden country. Iraq's invasion of Kuwait, a dangerous precedent of aggression in the emerging nonconfrontational world order, put an additional strain on Soviet diplomacy.

The year 1990 was equivalent to several decades. We lived through it without pausing for breath, preoccupied with numerous external worries and constant internal pressure.

But what about the book? The typed manuscript had been sent back to me by the publishers and languished in a bottom drawer. I had neither the time nor the inclination to touch it. Now that it's all in the past, and I'm not likely to hurt the publisher's feelings, I can say that I was no longer happy with the book. In the first place, the swift march of events had meant considerable additions to the body of the text, and I wasn't certain that they were sufficient. Second, the editors had departed from their initial idea of publishing the material in its original form. Instead, they had reworked the material by topic: the new thinking, European affairs, global problems, and so forth. I didn't feel that this was the best way of doing it. Torn from the actual context where they had been articulated, my ideas had lost their original currency and had become abstract and academic. A few insertions of a personal nature hadn't saved the manuscript.

With all the daily crises, the book went on the back burner again. Events between September and December 1990 forced me to realize that it was impossible to remain in the post of Foreign Minister. What was left of the policy of new thinking was diminishing before my eyes. The gap was widening between the policy's logistical support at the rear and the proclamations on the foreign policy front. I had a growing premonition that events would soon destroy our achievements, which had been made largely because my foreign partners had trusted me personally. I kept in constant touch with them, doing all in my power to persuade them to support perestroika. The credit line of trust was still open. But at times it was hard for me to look them in the eye. I could not explain to them, for example, the sudden complications and reversals, clearly stage-managed by someone in order to jeopardize agreements we had already reached. Suddenly, I would find out that people were manipulating things behind my back, damaging our hard-won reputation as a reliable partner, and undermining our diplomatic successes. Our chosen course was in trouble, facing an uncertain future.

I could cite many examples but will limit myself to the story of the military hardware moved beyond the Ural Mountains. Legally, it seemed right. But it was not right that one of the top leaders of the country had to learn about this "maneuver" from the Western press, and when the Soviet Foreign Minister had to explain this wrinkle after the fact to foreign partners who were already suspicious of any cover-ups or traps.

The "shadow" government had been battling to recover lost territory. Now it had come out of the shadows and fought in the open. Only the rallying of democratic forces buttressed by law and order, in both the political and the legal sense, could stop it. But, regrettably, the moment for that was lost.

I had foreseen this turn of events and had spoken openly to people of like mind. But our agreement on principles didn't translate into unity of action. I had no other choice but to resign. There was no room for any other move except the one I made on December 20, 1990.

But even on that day and in the days to come, my thoughts did not return to the book. Even after I announced my resignation, I continued to perform my duties for nearly a month. One can imagine the state I was in. Each day I would pick up gossip, speculation, and accusations, each more absurd than the last. I kept mum. The Baltic crisis broke out in January, then war was unleashed in the Persian Gulf. A new flood of filthy insinuations, mixed with ultra-right "patriotism" and old ideology, inundated me. Now they claimed I had stepped down because I didn't want to face up to supposed failures in foreign policy. Their "evidence" and "proof" mounted. I struggled to remain silent.

A joint Central Committee and Central Party Control Commission plenary session was called in January 1991. As a Central Committee member, I was supposed to participate, but I fell ill. Several days later, when I read the minutes of the plenary session in *Pravda*, I pulled the manuscript folder out of the bottom drawer. After leafing through it, I decided to get down to work. I brought in my close aides, Teimuraz Stepanov and Sergei Tarasenko, men who shared my views. Without them this book would never have been finished.

Why did I pick up the book again after all that? Mainly, I wanted to reply to those who were trying to bury perestroika at the plenary session and elsewhere. They had crawled out of their foxholes and had signaled to the reactionaries to attack the considerably weakened positions of democracy and glasnost. They made their intentions and demands very clear: dump the policy of new thinking, and reject its achievements and victories. Essentially, they were directly challenging the 28th Congress mandate to make human life the highest value and chief aim of social development. Instead, they were resurrecting the dogma of the primacy of class interests over universal human values, which they said "did a disservice to the socialist idea." They tried to prove that new thinking had outlived its usefulness, destroying the old order without creating the new.

They rejected the notion of removing ideology from intergovernmental relations, which, in the opinion of the commanders, "sacrificed socialist interests, purposes, and values to bourgeois ones." They restored the language and ideas of the era of irreconcilable antagonism, a system based on permanent military tension, with the Soviet Union doomed to lag behind, isolated from the rest of the world.

All of this took place in the presence of the President and

leader of the Party who had begun perestroika. Now they were telling him to his face that perestroika had failed and that his policy was to blame. The seasoned debater, who had persuaded the Party and the country that democracy and innovation were vitally needed, kept silent. They were burying his main life's work before his very eyes, saying his ideas were worthless, and it was necessary to go back to the old but still fearsome artillery.

There is nothing more pathetic than an idea whose time has expired. But were perestroika, democracy, human rights, freedom of choice, and equal security for all outmoded ideas? Having known Gorbachev long and well, I am certain that he did not think so. I can imagine why he did not speak up; a politician has to size up the actual situation and the balance of forces. As matters stand now, those considerations cannot be discounted. But back in the early days of perestroika, while acknowledging the existence of an opposition, he wasn't afraid to go against the grain. He appealed to the people and won their support. All the more boldly, he hammered out the credo of the new thinking and put it into action. He was so single-minded that some of the domestic critics he and I have in common complained that foreign policy was getting too far out in front, cutting itself off from the home front. But, in fact, domestic policy was trailing behind, deliberately stalled. New social forces that could have created the necessary base for a bolder program were ignored. Antiperestroika circles were trying to rein in foreign policy. We moved too slowly and timidly at home. Yet even here, I refuse to take the role of a critic of Gorbachev, because I bear equal responsibility. My internal disagreement with some of his decisions is of no account now if I didn't openly oppose them at the time.

Nevertheless, there is still the question of mistakes.

Did perestoika's architects design the reconstruction of the building so as to prevent it from buckling? Is it perhaps not so far-fetched to claim that perestroika's strategic planners overlooked some flaws?

I recall a book I read in the 1960s by Leonid Volynsky, *Colors of the Caucasus*, which had the following line: "The architect would rather pronounce the words 'will be' than 'is.'" Obviously, the author was talking about a Soviet architect; even his most brilliant design is at the mercy of numerous vicissitudes—the state of the construction industry, for example, or the quality and selection of materials. Ultimately, he depends on the aesthetic culture, resources, possibilities, and notions of the client.

By analogy, the architects of politics must also cope with an enormous number of variables. In the Soviet Union, it's a question of whether certain things are present—or, more frequently, absent. If hardly anyone doubted perestroika's necessity, there was a glaring absence of the will, desire, and ability to realize it in many social circles. This became especially obvious with the reactionary assault upon the active fighters for political reform at the Twenty-eighth Congress.

It was said that the pace of change was too slow, that crucial measures were taken too late. That is correct. But the truth is, you cannot proceed rapidly and confidently toward a goal without glancing over your shoulder at the people who are trying to thwart you. If you don't factor that in, you can lose everything. You should not lose sight of the most decisive yet most fragile link, which is called "the individual." It doesn't matter whether it's Ligachev or Shevardnadze. What's important is the tendency he embodies, and whether he is strong and resilient.

Once you appeal to the human factor, deliberately summon it to life, and grant it the right to active self-expression, then you simply have no right to ignore it, even in the form of opposition. A man is not a machine that can be turned on or off at the press of a button. If he shines, don't get in his way, make use of his light. If he sows darkness, try to make those around you aware of it. But you can no longer just turn him off at whim, as in the past. That is the theory, but in practice people continue trying to switch others off, sometimes successfully.

Now, as I encounter this more and more, I conclude that you cannot ignore the actions of forces trying to prevent you from reaching your goal. But you also cannot overlook the forces that want to help you. I cannot say that Gorbachev has ignored them. He has constantly had to choose among constituencies, and if one of them turned out to be weak and unreliable, then, willingly or not, he had to cast his lot with another that could guarantee him more stability. Some of his backers really were unreliable; others he himself alienated, and as a result, the old standbys, tested by "decades of struggle," rushed to fill the vacuum. But I fear they are not as reliable as they seem to Gorbachev.

I should warn that readers will be disappointed if they expect this book to be the sensational story of the "human factor" as exemplified by certain specific personages. This book is not a political memoir. The time has not yet come for that. Memoirs are a genre that belong to departures, and I do not intend to leave the scene. But neither is the book a confession, although I must make frequent use of the pronoun "I." For many reasons, this will be difficult for me. But I do not know how to tell a story in the first person without using "I."

Perhaps the reader would find a "history of the personalities of perestroika" much more interesting. But I would rather tell the story of the ideas of perestroika. It deserves to be told; the ideas are not outdated, and must not be replaced or forgotten. They need to be defended, because the individual and humanity must be defended. After all, the ideas were conceived and brought forth in their name. And finally, they must be defended because they are dear to me.

I should also explain how and why I came to these ideas. And for that, I must explain a little about my background. Perhaps the story will seem too long for some readers. If so, I ask forgiveness in advance. But it cannot be told otherwise. I and all my generation have traveled a difficult path; we have believed, we have blundered, but we have reached the truth at last.

The
Future Belongs
to
Freedom

CHAPTER ONE

My Home and the World

"In the eyes of your country, you are a son of your family; in the eyes of the world, you are a son of your people." My father spoke these words when I was a child, and for a long time I did not understand them. By a great stretch of the imagination, I could somehow see myself standing "in the eyes of my country." But before the "eyes of the world"? My world in those years was the village of Mamati, where I was born on January 25, 1928, and where I spent my childhood and adolescence. Green hills covered with waves of tea plantations descended to the marshy ravines of the Lake Colchis lowlands; the silver ribbon of the Supsa River sparkled; the beech trees ranged along the mountain crest. A house was built from beech trunks sawed into planks smooth as mirrors—two stories perched on pilings. To this day, I remember the whorls in the fresh-hewn boards, tracing an intricate pattern in the wood's texture.

My brother Akaky had built the house before he went into the army. All together, there were four brothers and one sister in our family. It was a large family, and it grew even larger as the home was constructed.

According to the local custom, every house was built by the entire village. We had a word for this kind of mutual aid—*nadi*. No sooner did Akaky announce a *nadi* than the entire village from oldest to youngest turned out to contribute to the work. Everybody sang the *naduri*, a popular work song. Each person had his voice, his part to sing, and together they made a rare harmony.

In this multiplicity of voices was a mystery that was more than I could fathom. Only later did I learn that having your own voice was not enough; you had to harmonize with others. Otherwise, there is no melody. In life, however, it was different. In our house, many very different voices sounded their notes, and often they were in discord.

Mamati is one of the numerous villages of Guria, and Guria is one of the many provinces of Soviet Georgia. In their ethnography, dialects, and natural and climactic features, these provinces are quite different from one another. But their historical destinies and aspirations combine in the same kind of melodious unity of multiple voices, with the leitmotifs of freedom and independence.

A brief glance at a map will illustrate this. Georgia is situated between the borders of both Europe and Asia, at the ancient crossroads of the most important routes of migration of peoples and civilizations, where the cultures, faiths, and strategic interests of the powerful of the world intersected and clashed, ensuring Georgia an enviable, glorious, but in many ways torturous fate. The choice of Christianity as the state religion in the fourth century destined Georgia to a struggle to preserve national identity and its main foundations: language, letters, and faith. She fought against powerful neighbors, whose designs on the strategically important territory were disguised under the banners of an alien faith. Georgia was subjected to forcible assimilation and the destruction of her culture and methods of farming. Her way of the cross is reflected in the first surviving Georgian literature, *The Martyrdom of St. Shushanik*, a hagiographic novel of the torments endured for the faith, which could not destroy the spiritual freedom of the soul. The novel was written in the fifth century, but Georgian letters had emerged even earlier, with an original alphabet, free from borrowing and influences, despite its proximity to the ancient and Hellenic world, with which Georgia had developed trade and cultural ties. The myth of the Golden Fleece of Colchis was not such a myth after all; it symbolized the allure of this beautiful and bounteous land. The sacred ram skin inscribed with magical letters was well worth fighting for. And fight they did, some setting sail aboard the Argo, others sending hordes of conquerors.

Not coincidentally, all the fundamental concepts having to do with the genesis of the nation found in the Georgian language have as their root the word "mother": earth, language, city, and homeland. In giving birth to the spirit of freedom and providing the sustenance to repel hostile forces, these words demanded filial devotion and implacable resistance to encroachments on the dignity and peace of the Georgian motherland. Similarly, the basic greeting in the Georgian language is not "be well," as in Russian, but "victory," since to be well meant to be victorious. The nation needed nothing else but a victory over the external threats and vicissitudes of its fateful history.

Even today the Cachetian grapegrowers and the Tushetian sheep-herders never part with their black felt caps. When I see them, I always recall that at one time they were not merely hats, but helmets—the farmer or shepherd had to be ready to exchange his work clothes for battle gear. The helmet was always at hand— that was the reality. This reality was also dominated by the vineyard, to which much of Georgian culture can be traced. Both ornamental motifs and the shape of Georgian letters evoke the vine. But more importantly, it is the source of the province's material abundance, the basis for popular independence. Invaders always headed first for the vineyard, chopping and burning it down like a live creature; hence the Georgian's feeling that his vineyard is like his own child.

In 1985, when I learned about the "anti-alcohol" laws then in preparation, I was horrified. Perestroika was off to a false start, fatal for our republic at least. The proclamation of a new war against an old evil threatened to devastate the wine industry, one of the mainstays of our national economy. This loss could have been foreseen and prevented. But no prognosis could have foretold the losses from the blow that the command system dealt to the concepts we held most dear.

I must confess that I did nothing to prevent this. All I did was look for ways to soften the blow to our vineyards and winemakers. I should say outright that I voted for these decisions, although inwardly I disagreed.

What was the matter with me? Was it just the discipline of a dedicated "soldier of the Party"? Yes, but not entirely. To this day, I can muster the determination to act in an uncompromising manner only after a long struggle with myself. I will not hasten to speak out until the right "critical mass" of willpower and thought spills over into a decision. This is a serious drawback for a politician, and for the cause, but I cannot hide it. There is no other way to explain how and why I took so long to reach my present stance.

When deliberating over what one cherishes and what one does not, the aggressiveness of those who disagree carries no weight. From childhood, I had been taught to respect the vineyard. My first thought was: Our people are going to call the initiators of the "anti-alcohol" laws by the same names they used for the medieval conquerors. I was not mistaken. One "campaigner for sobriety" claimed that he had not seen a bunch of grapes in his homeland for years, and therefore preference should be given to table grapes, to the detriment of grapes for wine. I could not see much difference between this psychology and the philosophy of an aggressor attacking alien principles of life. Authoritarian thinking, elevating its own rules to incontrovertible absolutes, is the same in any era.

The material damage suffered by the country from the "battle against alcoholism" topped 15 billion rubles. There was no profit gained. We only made our troubles worse.

Take away from someone everything that offends you and impose your own way. History has been made according to that scheme for centuries—with fire and sword, iron and blood. The justice of the strong has meant injustice for the weak. That was the way with Georgia, and even its rulers did not escape the fate of their subjects. Stripped of their kingdoms, they sought refuge in occupations seemingly incompatible with their royal titles. They tried to establish book-publishing in a foreign land or wrote poems. I think they were trying to invent the kingdom of free thought. Is that perhaps why it was said of the Georgians that their kings were poets and their poets kings? But for both, the dream of restoring lost statehood reigned supreme.

After the fall in the twelfth century of the mighty, enlightened kingdom that was Georgia, an endless chain of torments followed as it searched for outside support. The European monarchs had no wish to risk higher political interests for the dubious gains to be had from aiding a small Christian country. Georgia's neighbors controlled important trade routes, and the European powers preferred not to quarrel with them. Ideology—in this case considerations of the faith—counted for little. The alliance with the West did not materialize.

Only one hope remained, and it was to the North. Eyes turned ever more frequently toward Russia, a land of the same faith. It seemed that help could be expected only from this quarter. For several centuries, with varying success, emissaries from Georgia had beaten a path to Moscow. They settled in for the long run, put down roots, and founded villages. The Moscow streets named Bolshaya and Malaya Gruzinskaya (Big and Little Georgia) originated in those days. Sreten Church Cemetery at the Great Don Monastery also dates from that era; that is where the most zealous advocates of rapprochement with Russia, representatives of the Bagration dynasty, are buried. They suffered much here, but they never lived to see a free homeland.

Not until 1783 did emissaries of Catherine II and Heracles II, in Georgievsk in the North Caucasus, sign a treaty of alliance between Russia and Georgia. The great power to the north promised to protect the little country, but eighteen years later, with the manifesto of Emperor Alexander I, Georgia was annexed to Russia. The Georgian kingdom was abolished, and bureaucrats from Moscow ran its government.

By any standards, this was typical colonial politics. True, it did save Georgia from external threats by placing a barrier in their path, but it brought the imperial yoke down on the nation. Action provokes counteraction. The emerging Georgian national liberation movement made common cause with the struggle of the progressive public of Russia and other enslaved nations of the empire in order to overthrow the Tsar. For many in Georgia, it was a struggle for the rebirth of nationhood.

The year 1917 provided the chance they needed. Given the right to self-determination proclaimed by the revolution and the difficult circumstances following the signing of the Brest Peace Treaty, the leaders of the Georgian social-democrat and other national parties now had a real opportunity to create an independent republic. On May 26, 1918, the republic was declared. And it ceased to exist three years later, after Red Army detachments marched on Tbilisi.

In such a cursory review, many things appear simplified and glossed over. Many complex events remain unexplained. Personal assessments, perceptions, and opinions have been held in reserve. This would be unforgivable for a historian, but a historian of one's own life may be indulged. In order to explain certain things about myself, I must describe the environment in which I was raised.

The government that ruled Georgia from 1918 to 1921 was mainly social-democratic, and, in a certain sense, "mononational." I set this word in quotes, because although the government was completely homogeneous in its national composition, it included many people from Guria. There were quite a few Gurians in the Bolshevist wing, vigorously working to defeat their fellow Mensheviks.

How did this region become so politicized, with such vivid polarity in political views and programs? The reasons undoubtedly had to do with the difficulties of material existence in the marshlands of Colchis and the bare mountain ranges so unsuitable for effective farming. My ancestors on my mother's side, who possessed one hectare of land on the banks of the Supsa River, were considered very prosperous farmers. The scourge of land hunger chased the poor peasants onto the roads leading to the large cities of Western Georgia—Kutaisi, the ports of Batumi and Poti, and others—which became the centers of revolutionary ferment. The struggle to escape poverty, together with the traditional yearning for education, compelled them to seek out any sources of knowledge. The proximity of a hostile religion had great significance, as organization and weapons were needed to resist it. People kept guns in their homes. All of this molded an altogether unique, explosive nature, susceptible to rebellious free-thinking, which displayed itself in widespread insubordination.

The peasant uprisings in Guria were distinguished by their scale as well as the cruelty of their suppression. One of the most powerful rebellions during the revolution of 1905 went down in history as the Battle of Nasakiral. An armed peasant band was headed by my father's cousin, David Shevardnadze. After the rebellion was defeated, he disappeared into the mountain forests. A large sum was offered for his head. Surrounded by a punitive expedition, David and a handful of his comrades took the brunt of the onslaught. One of his comrades, his closest and most reliable friend, passed him something to drink in the heat of the crossfire. It was poisoned.

This sounds like a legend, but it actually happened. David's sons visited our home often. His eldest often spoke of him. Other names flashed through conversations about the past, and all of them are surrounded with an aura of self-sacrificing struggle for justice. Loti, my father's younger brother, died in 1918 while defending an Armenian family from a pogrom. I was born four years after the anti-Soviet uprising which is called the "Menshevik adventure" in the official historiography. My acquaintances included quite a few people who had fought on both sides of the barricades. They would debate whether it had been adventurism or a battle for freedom.

My father was Ambrosy Georgievich Shevardnadze, and my mother was Sofia Glakhunovna, née Pateshvili. My father's mother, Grandmother Sarla, tried with all her might to give us children a good education. After completing his studies in Batumi, my father returned to Askana, the birthplace of the Gurian Shevardnadzes, and began to teach in a school in the village of Dzimiti. It was there he met his future wife, my mother.

My father taught Russian language and literature. A list of the first Georgian subscribers to a prerevolutionary edition of the collected works of Leo Tolstoy was found recently in the archives of that era. My father's name was near the top of the list. People strove to push away the oppressive boundaries of their world and to come out on the open plains of the progressive ideas of the time. Along with the guns, people kept the Georgian classics in their homes: Ilya Chavchavadze, Akaky Tsereteli, Vazha Pshavela, and then later the books of Tolstoy, the Russian revolutionary democrats, the legal Marxists, Plekhanov, Kautsky.

My father and his relatives and my mother's brothers were no exception. Her eldest brother, Akaky Glakhunovich, a former officer of the Tsar's army who had fought in World War I, stayed loyal to the social-democratic world view to the end of his days. My father also sympathized with the social democrats but grew disenchanted with them and entered the Communist Party. He explained that the Mensheviks had not solved the main problem, aside from national sovereignty: They did not and could not create a healthy economy, which had led to enormous privations for the population. Chaos reigned in the country. Power was easily seized by the Bolsheviks. Akaky, a fierce antagonist of Stalin and Bolshevism, engaged in endless disputes with my father on that score. Konstantin, my father's brother, a person of similar experience and convictions, was also a former officer and social democrat with an unusually original, sharp mind. He would always find the most surprising ways of reconciling the views of the two opponents. His arguments always amazed us with their complex simplicity and logical resolution.

It was like a kind of multiparty system in one large, friendly family. It was friendly despite the differing political views of its members. I tried to sort them out, to make my own choice, but it was hard, because I loved them all equally. And if I inclined toward one opinion, I did not reject the opposing view out of hand, because I wanted to understand what was guiding a person dear to me, and why he put things one way, and not another. If you eat such bread in childhood, you will always have a taste for it.

Everyone around me spoke of class warfare and class enemies, and I asked myself: "Is this the class enemy—Uncle Akaky?!" And later in life, when a person was pointed out to me as a "carrier of alien views," I would remember my relatives and the people dear to me: They too could have been put in this category without much difficulty. Life taught me otherwise. Its lessons were not always easy, but that's probably how it is for everyone.

My father would come home from school, have dinner, and go out to hoe corn, train vines, and tend beehives. He would labor until late in the evening, when we were already asleep, and would rise the next day at dawn, light the lamp, and read his teaching notes in preparation for his lessons.

My mother had more worries with the five children. The eldest, Yevgraf, was stricken with polio and permanently crippled. In those years we often came down with malaria from living near the swamps. Then the taming of the Colchis Lowlands began, the marshes were drained, tea plantations were established, and the fever left us alone. My mother went out to pick tea leaves and took me along with her because there was no one to babysit. I picked my first pound of tea leaves at the age of six.

My brothers and sister helped my parents as best as they could. Even my brother Yevgraf, unable to get around, found a way of being useful. He decided to become a journalist and took to editing the district newspaper. Akaky came up with the idea of building a house, as I have mentioned, and provided us with a spacious, comfortable new dwelling in place of the old one-story, two-room house with the little shed used as a kitchen outside. My brother Ippocrat served as a model for me. He was a thoughtful, reasonable fellow, and also very energetic and kind. My sister, Venera, was like a second mother to us all, a rare, tender, considerate soul.

The beautiful thing about village life is its openness; the people and their affairs are all out in plain sight. It is good that in early childhood, in the most natural way, a person is drawn into the round of daily concerns and is acclimated, without coercion, to sensible, purposeful behavior. The result is always before your eyes; here, take it in your hands. No one ever said to me: "you have to . . . ." I knew what I had to do and felt joy when I did it. I shinned up the walnut tree, which was wrapped with vines of a rare sort of *chkhaveri* used to make a remarkable wine, and gathered the slightly crushed grapes, sticky from the juice, into a cluster of leaves. Then I crushed the grapes and poured off a thick stream into clay pitchers, and the liquid began to ferment. I ran to the mill to grind corn, anticipating the aroma of fresh-baked corn fritters, still steaming when broken in half. I knew the value of grain, because I knew the work that went into it, the sweat that must flow in order to bring it to harvest. In some parts of Guria, the cornfields ran up such steep slopes that farm workers had to tie themselves to trees to keep from falling. The bread was bitter, but also sweet. Anyone who has obtained his bread from working the land will understand me.

My father taught us how to tend the beehives, and the sight of dripping honeycombs still gives me pleasure. Many years later in Tskheti, a suburban resort town in the mountains above Tbilisi, on a government dacha plot, I planted a few vines and set up four beehives. As First Secretary of the Central Committee of the Georgian Communist Party, I had no need to raise food for myself in this way. Busy every day with a multitude of concerns, including agriculture, I was glad that the habits of working the land had not been lost. I could still talk shop on equal terms with a plowman or a shepherd, a winegrower or a beekeeper, a tea-picker or a construction worker. And to be completely candid, I still take pride in my ability to do something with my own hands.

One of my close relatives was the village mailman. The newspapers and letters had to be brought in from the district center. It was fairly far away from my village, and there was no public transportation. I knew a shortcut, but even that was a 12-kilometer hike

over a hilly trail. For an elderly and not very well man like my
uncle, it was hard to make the daily trip with the heavy sack of
mail. But for me, the trip was a joy, if only because of the thought
that I knew the shortest and most beautiful route, although not the
easiest.

I was ten years old at the time. Almost every day, I raced
along this path, then slowly trudged back, laden with the mail,
stopping to catch my breath and read the newspapers. Today, we
might argue about how informative they were, but they reflected
the basic trends and the tenor of life at that time. Endless homages
to Stalin and reports of the successes of the first five-year plans
were juxtaposed with accounts of subversion, terrorist acts, and
the intrigues of "enemies of the people" and world capitalism. The
voices of my relatives resounded within me, the truth which they—
each his own truth, each in his own way—upheld, raising doubts
and countless difficult questions, and all this, superimposed on
what I was reading, produced a complicated and contradictory
effect.

Not long ago a film crew from ABC visited my village home
and panned their cameras along a shelf laden with dog-eared books.
On the television monitor, I saw my favorite childhood novel,
David Copperfield by Charles Dickens. The magic of great literature has bred in me boundless faith in the printed line. The authority of the printed word was such that I believed what I read in
the newspapers. Even later, when it was not a line in a newspaper
but the fate of the people most dear to me that tormented my
child's heart, I retained this credulity. Only with the passing years
by learning to analyze, did I elaborate my own system of views,
which increasingly clashed with prevailing notions.

I am well aware that such admissions are dangerous. The
genre of the autobiographical sketch is deceptive. Even a very
sober, self-critical person capable of harsh self-examination feels
tempted to present himself, his positions, his acts, and his words,
as correct, to endow himself with more virtues, to forgive himself
more sins, and to play down his faults. A deep-seated instinct for
self-preservation is probably at work here. You defend your own
"I" in the desire to leave behind a good memory of yourself, so as
not to depart this life without a positive legacy.

I have no illusions about myself—I know everything I need to
know. People with whom I have crossed paths know just as much

about me as I do, if not more. By no means do all think and speak well of me. This is not pleasant, but it's logical: You will not be loved by everyone, especially those for whom your power of decision has caused discomfort or even pain. I know this heavy burden all too well. In offering this cursory self-portrait, I have tried to avoid self-flattery. I think I have succeeded, since my main purpose is to explain—perhaps to myself—how my views were shaped and transformed, and how I got to where I am now.

In the terrible days of April 1989 when I went to Tbilisi, after people had died tragically when force was used to disperse a demonstration, I said to my fellow countrymen: "You are already not the same people you were yesterday. But I, too, have changed."

I could be blamed for departing from my previous views—the general desire to stick with firm principles is natural. But I think that the mortal grip with which some people hang on to dead or dying dogmas is hostile to life itself, to its eternal, constant renewal.

To change means responding to life's challenges. I am not talking about fickleness, accommodation, cowardly adaptation, or spinelessness, but about the goal for which you conduct a ruthless inventory of your own positions and views. The problem of a goal is always a problem of choice, and if it is morally above reproach, then you must make it without fear, in the face of accusations of heresy and deviance.

My final choice was predetermined by everything that was good and bad in my whole life, and the life of my home, my family, and my people, with whom I may be at odds, but from whom I cannot stand apart. Processes and events occurred in my life and that of the whole nation that inevitably left their imprint on the formation and evolution of my philosophy. I shall now recount the most critical of them.

The year was 1937. People began to disappear from Mamati and the surrounding villages. They were the most respected and the most authoritative. A day did not go by without a rumor spreading through the village of the arrest of the latest "enemy of the people." The chairman of the rural soviet, the chairman of the collective farm, the agronomist, and the collective farm foremen were labeled "wreckers," "Trotskyites," "nationalist deviationists."

One day my father disappeared. A member of the Party since

1924, who had overseen the opening of a middle school in Mamati, he was both an enlightened and respected figure in the village. My mother withdrew into herself, refusing to answer our anxious questions, but her tears were more eloquent than any words. Outside my home, I sensed the chill of alienation around me. In school I had been considered a leader, I had been elected chief of my Pioneer club, the boys had always crowded around me, but now I was completely alone, no one approached me, no one called me over to play. I felt as if the label "son of an enemy of the people" was already stamped on my chest when I learned that I was not accepted for the rural Pioneer camp that summer. This was the first and greatest shock of my childhood.

Father was released some time later. Only later did I learn that a warrant for his arrest had been signed, but he escaped persecution thanks to one of his former pupils, an officer of the district NKVD.[1] His old student warned him of the impending arrest and recommended that he go into hiding and wait out the time of troubles somewhere in the forests. Many people took that option. The repressions of 1937 were so widespread that there was no one left to do the work, so in February and March of 1938 the machinery of terror slowed to a halt. At the time I didn't know that, and was glad that my father wasn't an "enemy of the people" after all. But for the first time I began to think about the reasons why families were divided and the harmonious choir of the rural community was splintered. The main reason was said to be class warfare, whose laws were elevated above those of kinship, human intimacy, and the simple and vital relations among friends and neighbors. They had loved me, had taught me kindness, and were good to me. They surrounded me with concern, affection, and warmth, and it was impossible to reconcile myself to the idea that they were enemies. I believed in their truthfulness and righteousness, but those times imposed different, more cruel judgments, which it was just as hard for a youngster not to accept.

A particularly convincing argument for me was the war, the attack of Nazi Germany on the Soviet Union. The thesis about a black force plotting to enslave our country turned out to be true. As a volunteer rural mailman's helper, I became a bearer of bad tidings. In my imitation leather mailbag, I carried to Mamati the

[1] Peoples Commissariat of Internal Affairs, or secret police.—Trans.

news of my fellow villagers killed in battle. People looked at me with horror and with hope—was there anything? Nothing?

Sorrow came to our own home. My elder brother Akaky, drafted into the army before the war, perished during its first days while defending the Brest Fortress. My other brother, Ippocrat, was also called up, and we were expecting his assignment to the front any day. My mother dressed in mourning for all present and future losses. So it went in almost every home. Out of 700,000 men called to war from Georgia (out of a population of 3.5 million), only about half returned.

The war with fascism became a personal battle for me. The fascists were attacking Communism, and Communism was my religion. The victory in that war became the victory of Communism, and that meant my own personal victory. The war shaped me as it did millions of my contemporaries. It formed my convictions and purpose in life. Thus I was drawn to politics at an early age. Rather, politics drew me to itself. In the seventh grade my classmates elected me chairman of the student committee. I had been raised by people close and dear to me, people who had different ways of looking at things, and I came to see things through others' eyes. But it would be more truthful to say I was raised in the spirit of the times, and it was a powerful, all-pervasive spirit.

I have always been impatient with a "methodology" that measures complex events with the crudest of instruments. Glaring mistakes are left out of the account or dismissed, but quite often they contained the truth. Whether for their own convenience or for that of someone else, critics of the past squeeze it into their own theoretical framework. But that is too confining for a human being! I feel cramped within a framework that comes down to this: We were stupefied, duped, manipulated, coerced. The truth was far more complicated, at least for me. At first, the "war of ideas" in which I have been involved since childhood was limited to my own family circle. No matter how sharp the polemics, they schooled us in tolerance. But then I saw the battle take hold of the village, the republic, the country, and finally the world. And now it no longer admitted of tolerance or forbearance. The attack on the Soviet Union became the most persuasive proof that outsiders wanted to destroy us, to annihilate us physically. My choice was determined by the death of friends and relatives, by the grief, suffering, and privations of millions of people.

The Soviet Union emerged from the war a great power, having saved the world from fascism. The victory was identified with the name of Stalin, with the will and might of the Party. Critics of the system accentuate the element of repression and violence, and utterly exclude the vital "embodiment of spirit" summoned up to build, to repel the invasion, and to restore the devastated country. Say what you will, but the much-abused administrative-command system was able to mobilize that mighty reserve for any cause, and it would simply be foolish to claim that this system relied on force alone.

In 1948 I joined the Communist Party. I was attracted to social-political work, since it gave me the opportunity to fulfill my father's commandment to go among people and work for them. Many years later, in speaking about political pluralism, I remarked that the one-party power monopoly had destroyed political life in our country as an arena for the interaction of various political forces. Now I would add that the Young Communist League and the Party, which I joined at the age of twenty, remained the only sphere for political self-expression. Some people were drawn to the Party from an instinct for self-preservation or the realization that there was no other way of finding a place in society worthy of their talents; others, and there were quite a few of them, were prompted by their heart and soul. It would not be truthful for me to claim that in my case only the second motive was at work, without the first. Still, in obeying one of my father's commandments, I ignored another and I was later to regret it more than once. It had to do with choice of profession, which I will describe separately, so that the main choice I made in life can be more clearly understood.

After finishing the eighth grade[2] in Mamati, I entered Tbilisi Medical College at the insistence of my parents. They all wanted me to become a doctor, but not just because it was a prestigious profession. My brother's incurable paralysis, my parents' health, ruined from overwork, the malaria that had once been the scourge of our villages and a nightmare for children and adults, had constantly confronted us with the question of who would help. The local physician was run ragged and couldn't keep up with his numerous patients. Many basic medicines were unavailable. Provid-

---

[2] "Grades" in the Soviet school system are numbered from one *after* completion of a four-year grammar school program.—Trans.

ing hospital beds was a problem no one seemed able to solve. Sound peasant pragmatism prompted people to look for aid and succor in the immediate vicinity. In choosing me, my parents clearly assumed that I would not disappoint their expectations. Sadly, they were mistaken.

When I arrived in Tbilisi, I moved in with my sister in an old house on Pasanaurskaya Street. Life in a semibasement room did not promise much joy, but I remember it as a very happy period. I was at medical school virtually day and night, and if I dropped in at the dark, damp quarters, it was only to share with my sister my overflowing thoughts and feelings. They were boiling up inside me and needed some outlet. My studies were interesting, but finding friends was more important. I wanted to be part of a greater, young and active movement. My classmates treated me well, providing attention and comradely support. But the greatest help to me was an older man, Shota Gordeziani, director of the school. Quite unexpectedly, he became one of my spiritual mentors. He would often invite me to his home. Our talks about studies and extracurricular work—in my first year, I had already been elected Komsomol secretary at the school—inevitably turned into debates. Gordeziani encouraged my boldness and did not try to cut an audacious young man down to size. He listened attentively, commenting briefly now and then on my vehement speeches. As I see now, he held differing views, but he did not impose his opinion on me, merely expressed it tactfully, forcing me to question whether I was right.

There was only one thing he could not persuade me of, and that was the necessity of becoming a doctor. By the time I graduated from the school, I was experiencing serious doubts about the correctness of my choice. A diploma with honors entitled me to enter a medical institute without taking competitive exams. Gordeziani painted a brilliant future for me, rhapsodizing about what he perceived as my inclination for science and my chances for getting into graduate school, and appealing to my patriotic sentiments. "Our people need highly qualified doctors. You can become an excellent physician. You must!"

It was all for nought. I was so absorbed in my political work that I could not think of anything else. When I was called to the district Komsomol committee and offered the job of political instructor, I immediately accepted.

My parents never forgave me for this. Many years later, when I was already Minister of Foreign Affairs in Georgia, shortly before her death, my mother said, "You took to curing social ills. It's a hopeless cause. You would have done better to ease my suffering."

Of course, she was right. How many times, in despair from the realization that it was impossible to fix anything, improve anything, or restore even a tiny speck of health to an ailing society, I would remember my mother's reproach. But it also spurred me to prove that my choice was not in vain.

There was plenty of suffering. I had to pay heavily for my obsession with my work. We labored tirelessly, sitting up at the district committee until three in the morning. An uncomfortable, bare room awaited me for a short, restless sleep. Then I was up again at dawn, off to another day packed with new meetings, tasks, and hopes. I took the ascetic life to be a duty. Many people lived that way. But we believed that someday we would live better. The point was not to spare oneself in overcoming difficulties.

After a year and a half of this hard work, I contracted tuberculosis. Penicillin was worth its weight in gold, and there was none. But I did have friends and the beautiful Georgian countryside, and that's what healed me. I spent several months in the mountain village of Bakhmaro, which was completely unfit for living much less recuperation: a few rough pine cabins, a pathetic first-aid station, and no utilities. But this was more than compensated by the clean mountain air, fresh off the sea—suffused with the scent of alpine grass and pine trees, icy springs and brooks— and marvelous views that lifted the spirits.

All of this helped wipe away my illness. But I was troubled by the sharp contrast between the poverty of everyday life and the richness of nature. Why is that so much of what we possess remains unused? Why do we live so poorly if we are so rich?

I fell back on doctrine to suppress the worm of doubt. More electric power, petroleum, coal, steel, manganese, wheat, tea leaves! Fulfill the plan faster! That was the way to lay the foundation for national prosperity and give people a chance at the good things in life!

When I became First Secretary of the Georgian Communist Party Central Committee and gained an opportunity to act at my own discretion, I remembered my thoughts about using the republic's natural riches and its marvelous resort areas. We created a special administration and began to look for funding. But the project moved at a glacial pace. The system, programmed for centralized redistribution, resisted sensible local initiatives. We managed to accomplish a thing or two, but at what a cost.

I am afraid that I did not fully repay my debt to Bakhmaro, and now I will probably never be able to do so. All hopes rest on the energy unleashed by perestroika, which is alone capable of directing people's intellects, talents, abilities, and resources toward normal, unhindered human enterprise. But that is a matter for the future, and I am still speaking of the past.

In 1951 my sister and I spent our vacation in the mountain resort of Tsagveri. Nestled in the Borzhom Canyon, this resort town is swarming with children in summer and winter. Large factories and institutions maintain Pioneer camps here for the children of their employees and bring in teenagers to work with them. For young people, this is a great opportunity to live out in nature and earn a little money. During their free time, the counselors come to the health resorts and rest homes for concerts, movies, and dances.

That was how I met Nanuli Tsagareyshvili, my future wife.

By that time I had finished Party school with honors and was continuing my studies at the history department of the Pedagogical Institute. I was waiting for assignment to work in the Kutaisi Komsomol Committee. Life seemed to be turning out well. My parents and Yevgraf were still living back home, but now we were able to help them out. I told my parents of my decision to marry Nanuli. They replied that they were happy, were expecting us to visit, and were getting the house ready to receive their future daughter-in-law.

On a summer day, Nanuli and I met in Borzhom Park. The proposal had already been made, and I was awaiting her answer. It completely floored me.

"I can't become your wife," Nanuli told me.

I was not so arrogant that I had counted on a quick yes, but there had been various signs that my proposal would not be rejected. And suddenly this!

"Is it that you can't, or won't?"

"I can't!"

"But why?"

"There is one circumstance that hinders me."

I told her I didn't see any reason why our marriage should be prevented, unless she did not wish it. No other circumstances could stifle this feeling.

"You haven't figured out yet what kind of orphan I am," said Nanuli. "My father was arrested as an enemy of the people. I don't even know if he is still alive. And you have a career ahead of you. Please, while it is not too late, let's part. I won't be hurt, I'll understand."

We did part company, but only to meet again several days later and then never to be separated again. What I had learned from her did not deter me.

During a chat at the Party Central Committee, a high-ranking functionary warned me against marrying Nanuli. "You'll ruin your resumé. Her father, Colonel Razhden Tsagareyshvili, was executed by firing squad as an enemy of the people."

The repressions of the 1930s had crashed upon Georgia with unusual brutality. One might have supposed that Josef Dzhugashvili, a native of Georgia better known to the world as Stalin, would display a greater mercy toward his homeland. This point of view has wide currency, but it is fallacious. The interests and aims of class warfare do not recognize nationalistic feelings. This theory, to which Stalin made an "invaluable contribution," required practical confirmation. Besides, Stalin had his own score to settle with many of his fellow Georgians. He never forgot, for example, the story of the so-called "Georgian question," in which a group of his fellow Party comrades, leaders of Soviet Georgia, resisted his plan for "autonomization," which envisaged the creation of a unitary state and the complete loss of independence for the national republics. The Georgian question grew into a heated controversy about the kind of national state structure the Soviet Union should have. Soon the controversy turned into a settling of scores with the "nationalist-deviationists," as Stalin's opponents were labeled. He also had opponents of another coloration. He knew who they were, and knew that a nucleus of resistance had been preserved in Georgia. While on the whole, for the majority of Georgians, Stalin was their great fellow countryman, the chain reaction of reprisals was not selective. It continued up until the end of the 1940s and the beginning of the 1950s. It is a well-known fact that the Meskhetians, a Turkic ethnic group, were deported from

Georgia. Less known is the fact that several thousand Georgian families were forcibly expelled solely because they had relatives abroad. This was happening in 1951, the same year that I wanted to get married.

Emigrés were also considered "enemies of the people," just as thousands of innocent people, like my father and Nanuli's, were categorized. From "enemies of the people" to "members of traitors' families" the wheel of terror rolled on toward the "enemy nations."

I did marry Nanuli, knowing full well how it could turn out for me. I could be made a pariah, an outcast, with all the consequences that entailed. There were more than enough examples right in front of me.

My case could have been reported under the headline, "When Feelings Prevail over Reason," had it not been far more complicated. I shall not belittle the strength of my feelings; neither do I want to understate the force of my convictions. I will allow myself one admission, however: I was confused by what was happening around me. Hundreds of honest Communists were again being persecuted. Many of them I knew personally; some had helped me in my career. I believed in Stalin, but I could not believe that they were guilty. The only salvation was the thought that Stalin didn't know about it. But there was something else—and perhaps this was paramount—a kind of protest was welling up in me against anyone who claimed the right to decide my fate, against the very idea of subordinating the interests of the individual to the will of the majority. The collectivism that I served with all my might was literally working miracles, transforming barren land, defeating fascism, raising the country from ruins, and therein lay its great authority. But it was also turning into a horrible, lawless force, reducing a person to a cog who could be crushed with impunity. If an individual was only a part in a machine, I asked myself, what will happen to the machine if they keep breaking the parts that are most needed? Many years later, when this machine began to fall apart, I remembered the anxious brooding of my youth. But in 1951 I simply asked: Why must I sacrifice my love to hatred?

∎ ∎ ∎

Stalin died in 1953. Beria was executed the same year. In 1956, Nikita Khrushchev gave his "secret" speech at the Twentieth

Party Congress on the crimes of the "Stalin era." His facts and figures aroused no doubt; they were the life and death of many people I had known. I was shaken, however, by the direct connection between the politics of terror and Stalin's activity. It is agonizingly difficult to acknowledge that you have worshiped the wrong god, that you have been deceived. It shattered my life and my faith.

Criticism of Stalin's cult of personality dealt a painful blow to my national feeling. Not just because he was a Georgian. Deliberately or not, Khrushchev permitted himself to say things that were offensive to Georgian pride. It was not enough for Nikita Sergeyevich to cite facts. He gave free rein to his emotions, like a person humiliated for too long, and descended to degrading attacks on his dead master. He depicted him not only as the tyrant that he was, but as a profoundly ignorant and stupid man. But if he really were so stupid, many asked, how did he build such a powerful state and compel so many millions to follow him? How could he become a worthy adversary and partner with the leading politicians of his era? By scheming, brutality, force, and trickery alone? Impossible!

I now believe that the flashpoint for the explosion of Georgian youth in March 1956 was something far more serious than the humiliation of national pride. It was an unconscious protest against the wrongful methods—elevated into principles—of a struggle to eradicate evil by evil means, the elimination of injustice with injustice. The conqueror was donning the attire of a saint, something he could never be.

Many people questioned Khrushchev's role during the years of mass persecution. After all, he had occupied key posts during the 1930s. To this day, that question has not been sufficiently answered, although a number of sources indicate that he had done his part during the Great Terror.

By March 9, 1956, rallies of thousands of people in Tbilisi swelled into marches and demonstrations, particularly on Rustaveli Avenue. Here, at what was known as the Communications Building, the demonstrators approached with petitions and protest telegrams, but they received a deadly reply: a salvo of machine gun fire. Tanks moved along the banks of the Kura River. On that day, according to the official figures, twenty-two people were killed and dozens were wounded.

It is not true that the first time heavy military vehicles were used against civilians was in Budapest in October 1956. The tank was first deployed as an argument against dissent in Tbilisi in March of that year.

I saw in the East European upheavals of the 1950s and 1960s a reflection of Tbilisi in March 1956. My generation and I acquired a "1956 complex" for the rest of our lives—rejecting force as both a method and a principle of politics.

But tanks and machine guns may only be employed as arguments within the appropriate ideological frame. The use of tons of lethal steel against defenseless human flesh can only be justified by declaring the carriers of foreign ideas to be so dangerous that tanks and bullets might not offer adequate protection. In fact, the executioner has always been preceded by the inquisitor, the axe and block foreshadowed by the dogmas of faith. In that sense the medieval auto-da-fé differs little from the show trials of the 1930s.

The same methods were used to justify the Tbilisi events of 1956. The Marxist theologians came down from Moscow to pronounce the demonstrations and rallies the result of imperialist conspiracies, vestiges of the past in people's minds, and, more specifically, a manifestation of bourgeois nationalism. In other words, the victims themselves, the dead and wounded, were the guilty ones. Either they were enemies themselves, or they were taken in by enemy propaganda and had received their just deserts.

There should have been a confession to match this catechism. But there was none. Times had changed, and different thinking ruled people's behavior. Many people bravely stood up in public to dispute the official version of events. My friends were among them.

At that time I was working in the Kutaisi City Komsomol Organization. Party organizers held meetings all over the republic for the purpose of denouncing "bourgeois nationalism" irrevocably and forever. At a citywide meeting, I dared to disagree with the official interpretation of events in Tbilisi. I said that to label as nationalists the people killed during the dispersal of rallies and demonstrations was not only morally reprehensible, it was politically dangerous. Using force to suppress the manifestation of prevailing attitudes in society would inevitably discourage the most active young people. The new Party leadership had condemned such methods; resorting to them now only discredited statements that a return to the past was impermissible and impossible. The audience supported me.

A few days later, I was elected Secretary of the Central Committee of the Communist Youth Union (Komsomol) of Georgia. I embarked on a new period of my life. I began to travel to Moscow and other cities more frequently. There I met my colleagues, the leaders of republic and province Komsomol organizations. The campaign to develop the country's virgin lands and forests was beginning. Trains packed with young volunteers shuttled to Kazakhstan and the Altai range. I was assigned to lead the Georgian Komsomol brigade. We lived in the Kazakh steppes for several months, tilling the virgin earth, building homes and agricultural complexes. We became acquainted with our peers from other republics. I owe much to this period of my life and retain bright memories of it. Perhaps people of my age are prone to idealize the vanished past, seeing their youth through a haze of nostalgia. But time does not distort the picture of those years or erase the remembered hardship of that life; nor do all my fellow travelers come out looking like heroes. I can clearly recall this grandiose but poorly organized "virgin land" era, the stupid decisions, and the ill-conceived strategies that canceled out many successes. We watched helplessly as equipment brought to the new territories from all over the country began to break down. Thousands of people worked themselves ragged but failed to gather in the gigantic harvest. The crops rotted in the fields, and there was no place to store grain. Billions of rubles and vast amounts of equipment and manpower were squandered.

The virgin lands campaign cost the country a great deal. Now I see that the enormous expenditures of that period could have been effective if we had used another approach to the grain problem. But that alternative was closed to us.

Still, I recall that period as good and glorious, because it gave us what I think youth needs the most: the proof that we are capable of building our lives from scratch when we have nothing, that everything we obtain comes out of our intelligence and strength.

This was also the period when I first met the people who would occupy prominent positions in the Soviet leadership. We felt ourselves to be "people of the virgin lands," tackling untouched fields with nothing but enthusiasm. "Dear Nikita Sergeyevich" promised us life under Communism. The first Soviet cosmonauts were plowing the virgin territory of space. Much of what we had inherited was being subjected to review. I lived with a premonition of great changes ahead and thus kept an especially sharp eye on my contemporaries.

Among my new acquaintances was Mikhail Gorbachev, First Secretary of the Stavropol Territory Komsomol Committee. We had met in Moscow at a Komsomol Central Committee plenary session. Many things had brought us together, and we were eager to get to know each other better. We had the same peasant roots, had worked on the land at a tender age, and had the same knowledge of folk life. He was clearly also a man of learning and erudition. Geographic proximity and common concerns made for a businesslike but informal "neighborliness." It's only a few hours through the Caucasus by car from Tiflis to Stavropol. Georgian shepherds drive their flocks along the way, into the mountain pastures—their shelter and safety was one of my responsibilities, and my good rapport with the regional officials helped me handle problems that were not always simple. In Gorbachev, I had a friend who was always ready to help me out, in word and deed.

But there was something else that made him stand out for me from the others. He was completely devoid of that artificial Komsomol modesty I had always found so annoying; more important, I could see that his thinking went beyond the boundaries of prescribed norms.

We saw each other often, in Moscow, Tbilisi, and in his area, and spoke to each other on the phone regularly. Gradually, unnoticed to ourselves, we opened up to each other, beginning to confide our secret thoughts.

A leap over three decades of friendship brings us to the end of the 1970s and the following scene. In a barren park on the deserted shore near the Black Sea's Cape Pitsunda, the two of us are strolling down a path between the trees. By that time, Mikhail Gorbachev was a Secretary of the CPSU Central Committee and a candidate member of the Politburo, and I was First Secretary of the Georgian CP Central Committee, also a candidate member of the Politburo. This "walk in the woods" was to have far-reaching consequences. We no longer held anything back.

One episode from this period will illustrate the degree and nature of the trust I had in Gorbachev.

At the beginning of the 1970s, an experiment was launched in the Abash District Center to test a new pay system for farm work, which would be tied to cost, quality, and quantity of production. If we decipher the scientific theory behind this, it was very simple: good pay for good work. The Western reader will not understand this: What's so "experimental and innovative" about this? It's an elementary principle of business that a worker has a vested interest in the results of his labor. Any economic activity, to be productive, must take the farmer's interest into account.

The Soviet reader will understand the code words all too well. He knows our whole economy is rigged in such a way that people often find it unprofitable to work. The pay is not equal to the effort and the resulting quality. "You pretend to pay us, and we pretend to work," is the Soviet workers' folk saying, and it describes the real state of affairs.

The problem is not only that the state confiscates too much surplus value and product. It is a fundamental principle that encouraging the worker's "proprietary instincts" threatens the very foundations of the socialist order. If this causes the nation's economy to stagnate, that is a secondary problem. The main priority is to preserve the purity of doctrine.

In Abash District, a corn farmer who worked 400 man-days on a collective farm earned an average of 10–12 rubles a month and 200 kilos of corn a year. As a result, people stopped working, and the collective farms went broke. This occurred not in just one district, or even just in our republic. The very state that set the ideological and economic restrictions upon productive farm labor suffered enormous losses. The system was undermining itself, heading for self-destruction. It was impossible for common sense to reconcile itself to this absurdity. But it also seemed impossible to overcome it.

At this point I should decode the term "experiment." We used it as a cover to ward off accusations that we were undermining the pillars of socialism. We told the ideological prosecutors that we were only experimenting in a limited area, and that our trials and errors would not spread. We just wanted to see how they would turn out.

But by paying the corn growers in kind—10 percent of the grain for fulfilling the plan plus 70 percent of the excess harvest—we were able to triple grain production in the district within two years. By 1980 the average yield per hectare had increased fivefold. About 40 percent of the harvest went into family silos, but the state also began to receive far more than before.

We did not stop there. We reorganized the management of the agricultural processing complex. The peasants began to fatten their livestock with grain they themselves had produced. We abolished the ceiling of one cow per farmstead introduced under Khrushchev, and introduced a contract system whereby the collective farms provided livestock and feed to the peasants, and they fed pigs on their private plots and sold them back to the collective farm. We reduced overhead and raised the volume and quantity of sales. As a result, income rose surprisingly quickly, the population drain subsided, and new homes, roads, public cultural centers, and sports complexes went up, transforming the district.

Overall, our experiment was a successful attempt to change the relations between the peasants and the authorities and to establish new cooperative ties, with the idea of later expanding the Abash experiment through the whole republic.

In charge of agriculture at the time, Gorbachev supported our initiative. Once, having arrived to take a look at the experiment in progress, he asked to see one of the private plots.

"Let's go and see Nadareishvili," I said to Guram Mgeladze, the district Party committee secretary. He blanched. Nadareishvili was a war invalid who had fought at the front. He kept ten dairy cows at his own farmstead. By all Soviet standards, he was a kulak.[3]

"No, come on," I insisted. "Let Mikhail Sergeyevich see how a farmer does when we get rid of excessive regulation."

We went, took a look and had a conversation with Nadareishvili. Later Gorbachev asked me: "What do you think he is, exactly?"

"A farmer," I said. "A good manager. But if you like, we can de-kulakize him. Then there won't be any farm, milk, or livestock."

Gorbachev chuckled.

"We could de-kulakize him, of course, so that your theoreticians won't get angry. But how are we going to improve rural life without this kind of 'kulak'?"

---

[3] The kulaks ("fists") were peasant landowners who were persecuted by starvation and exile during the period of mass collectivization. The euphemistic ideological term used at the time to describe the elimination of this class was "de-kulakization."—Trans.

One of the theoreticians, an executive at the Central Committee, had said to Mgeladze:

"You've got to raise livestock productivity, but don't diverge from Marx."

I told Gorbachev this story, and he laughed. But it was a bitter joke.

We scarcely talked of anything else at our annual winter meetings. People were shackled by numerous nonsensical restrictions that prevented them from laboring with the maximum output and benefit for themselves and society. The economy was weakened at its most crucial point, the worker's standard of living. We spoke about the paradox of our having to import grain, despite the enormous tracts given over to wheat, some of the richest black-earth zones in the world. Despite the huge Soviet lumber industry we suffered constant shortages of building materials, furniture, and paper. We produced more metals and energy than anyone else, but were always on short rations.

We spoke of the many absurdities of our life and came to the conclusion that we just couldn't go on like this.

In December 1979 we learned from the newspapers that Soviet troops had invaded Afghanistan and hastened to meet to discuss it. We agreed it was a fatal error that would cost the country dearly.

In those years we did not project such external questions onto the internal situation in the Soviet Union, although it was clear to both of us that if we did not change our foreign policy by removing the main sources of distrust—the use of force and rigid ideology—we would never create a zone of security around our country. However, at that time those ideas had not crystallized for Gorbachev. The future was covered in clouds, like the evening sky over the chilly winter sea.

Our Pitsunda talks summed-up all of our thoughts. But each of us still had a long way to travel for our ideas to become a reality. By all traditional standards, our path was the path of success. Outwardly, at least, that was true. From the usual viewpoint, that of the man in the street, we had made our careers as successful Komsomol and Party functionaries. But if we go by other standards, this was the path to discovering our political reality, to finding out the reasons for the existing state of affairs, and to an intense search for a way out.

At first my upward path was limited to Georgia. My sphere of action set the boundaries—First Secretary of the Republic Komsomol Central Committee, then First Secretary of the District party committees. At that time the district was the basic link in the republic's territorial-administrative structure, and a district Party committee was the base of the pyramid of the Party–state power hierarchy. But the district Party committee secretary's power appeared unlimited only at first glance. In reality, there were numerous restrictions that bound him hand and foot if he wanted to do something useful. To untangle the red tape, he had to "go upstairs." But there he found that the upper echelons of power were also dependent on even higher authorities.

Thus, however low-level the district committee was, and however narrow the scope of its secretary's activity, he was constantly running up against the system as a whole. Any thinking person could see its flaws, and for anyone who tried to get things done, they were intolerable.

My chief concern and problem was the sovereignty of the district, that is, autonomy for deciding vital issues. Alas, it was insoluble. For me it would grow later into a republic-wide problem. As First Secretary of the republic's Communist Party and a candidate member of the Politburo of the CPSU Central Committee, I often could not resolve the simplest problem without bowing to the dispensers of credits and material benefits at the Center. No matter what the subject was, from allocating electric power to opening a preparatory school for Georgian youth headed for higher military academies, from replenishing the tea industry's stocks to building major public works, we could not take a step without the knowledge and permission of Moscow. And no matter what the critics among my fellow Georgians have said about me, I was constantly dealing with the problem of achieving real sovereignty for the republic—an independent state under the Soviet Constitution.

How I tackled this problem is another story. But to approach it right away, without explaining certain things, would be impossible. Work in the Party committees, first in the rural districts, then in the city boroughs, opened my eyes to many things. I did not immediately see a direct link between the flaws of centralized economic management and bureaucratic corruption. For a long time I thought they were unrelated, and for me corruption took top priority, pushing everything else into the background. The "little man," the ordinary citizen, suffered from it most of all. He could not find relief either from the highest echelons or from the law enforcement agencies, because the mafia had penetrated these structures and was controlling them. Faith in the authorities was undermined, cash on the barrel determined everything, and an atmosphere of despair reigned over society. The processes of rot and disintegration were particularly horrifying when contrasted with the rampant exploitation of Communist and patriotic phraseology. The most cherished concepts were used to camouflage embezzlement. For me, the fight against corruption, against under-the-table deals, against their mastery at the highest levels of public life, became a matter of saving our principal national assets. A nation eaten away by cancerous graft was doomed to degeneration and death.

Vasily Pavlovich Mzhavanadze was head of the republic in those years. Khrushchev had nominated him, an old friend from the war years, for the post of First Secretary of the Georgian Communist Party. A wartime army general, he proved to be exceptionally mild and trusting. He treated me well, and I responded in kind. But I could not close my eyes to certain traits in his character and to the level of his knowledge about the real state of affairs in the republic. Many people exploited this, including those immediately around him. When I had the opportunity to tell him this, I did. As a result, a little while later, I was offered the post of First Deputy Minister of Public Order in Georgia.

I never claimed special status or sought any ranks or posts. I know that many people dispute this. But there are also many who can testify that I turned down the so-called honorific offers whenever I doubted my ability to complete the task competently. I accepted only if I was assured of real support to compensate the lapses in my own preparation.

This was the case with my assignment as Deputy Minister of Public Order and my promotion to Minister of Internal Affairs. I had broad backing in both jobs. It came not only from my colleagues, who were honest professionals concerned about the situation in the law enforcement agencies. A new generation of criminologists, writers, cultural workers, and journalists came forward with proposals they thought would sanitize the public atmosphere.

My main conception of my new job was to rely on these wholesome new forces yearning for change. They had to see convincing evidence that it was possible to save society from the corrosive influence of a few criminal clans who had protectors in high places. Their patrons in the government made them immune to criminal justice. A start had to be made by dealing out deserved penalties to convince people that the law could be enforced. Aggressive measures seemed to be in order.

Society has the right to know of all the vices that endanger it. Official propaganda had hushed them up. Censorship suppressed everything that might in any way attest to the unfortunate state of affairs, for example, reports about the nature and extent of drug addiction. I had to look for ways around this. We came up with the idea of a public opinion institute whose research could receive wide publicity. We established regular meetings with the press to provide greater coverage of information about crime, and although the censors threw up barriers, the news found an outlet to the public.

As a consequence, the Western press began to report on cases of illegality in the law enforcement practice of those years. I will not claim that they did not take place. The penitentiary system in a totalitarian state has its horrifying features, and it is beyond the power of one man to reform it without changing the nature of the state itself. Purges of investigation and prison personnel and the recruitment of people tested in Komsomol and Party work did not help. The inadequacy of the chosen course was obvious to me, but at that point I could not do anything more. In mortal fear of regression to the Beria style, I swept aside anything that could generate a chain reaction of "witch hunts." Even when threats came directly at me, I showed no personal interest and rejected proposals to make the appropriate investigations.

When I was later asked about the genuineness of such cases, I called them mythical. The obvious effort to remove me from the post of Internal Affairs Minister was no myth, however, and this proved to me that our measures had been effective. I took a certain satisfaction in this.

The criminals tried all kinds of tricks. One of them amuses me to this day. At some point our home-grown mafiosi collected a large amount of cash to bribe the then U.S.S.R. Minister of Internal Affairs so that he would appoint me as his deputy. The idea was that I would move from Tbilisi to Moscow and leave them alone. The man chosen as the go-between was a close acquaintance of the Minister, widely known in the art world. I considered him blameless and, chuckling to myself, expected the deal to fall through. And so it did.

This man is still alive and well, and if he should happen to read these lines, he can confirm my story.

I was often mistaken about people, but I never took on faith any report about someone's personal impropriety or professional dishonesty until I could verify it for myself. It is our misfortune that in a closed, unjust society, it costs nothing to slander a person. Not everyone has the opportunity to fend off the abuse. It has happened to many people, and now it has affected me. But I do not want to discuss this now. This book is not a keyhole through which the details of my personal life can be glimpsed, but a key to understanding phenomena of a greater order. That is my intent, at any rate; how well I carry it out is another matter.

What's done is done; I was forced to make unpopular decisions, both in my post as Minister of Internal Affairs and as First Secretary of the Georgian Communist Party. But with whom were they unpopular? Not with the refuseniks, the Georgian Jews who had been prevented from emigrating to Israel, but whom I let go. One of them recently recalled that I had said during those years that "it was time to stop seeing the emigrant as an enemy." Well, if I really did say that, it means my thoughts were headed in the right direction.

I believe I was thinking in the right direction when I sought ways and means to weaken the excessive dictatorship of the central agencies, in other words, to challenge the dominance of the command-administrative system, which was depriving the republic of any autonomy.

There is a saying in our country that initiative is punishable. An initiative that encroaches upon the system's holiest of holies—its right to decide what you do and how you do it, and its right to deal with you however it wishes—is all the more punishable. In politics, where no noble end can be achieved without choosing the right means, one must choose the means appropriate to the actual situation. And the situation was such that a direct and open challenge to the existing order was doomed in advance. As I have said, we had to bring abut innovation under the guise of experiments. Because they were so limited in scope, the guardians of the system were certain to indulge us, and that gave us a chance to develop our project on a larger scale. "Experiment" became a code word, a password for those who wished to change the existing paradox. They all frequented our testing grounds to reassure themselves that the impossible was possible.

For example, it was possible to set up a territorial-branch self-management agency in the city of Poti, because of which the Union-run[4] factories in the areas under its jurisdiction, no longer able to ignore the city's needs, began making their contribution to local development. To their own benefit, I might add.

In the mountainous regions, where large-scale collective farming is impossible and only family farms could subsist, we introduced the so-called family contract.

Anything that was suggested by common sense, we disguised as an experiment. We attracted foreign capital to finance the building of mountain sports and health centers. We organized a chain of private restaurants. We brought computer technology into harvesting. We started mechanized farm teams with more generous labor incentives than on the regular farms, and ultimately boosted productivity.

We rented out vehicles, setting only a few simple conditions for the drivers: efficient operation, adequate garaging, and proper maintenance. How much you earn is none of our business, we said, except for a certain portion of your revenues.

We were already well aware in those years that the financial and monetary system had to be improved. We designed a republic-wide prospectus and set about with energy and determination to implement it. We created a system of state support for the restoration of historic and cultural monuments. A specially created administration concerned itself with not only the restoration and preservation of art masterpieces but the no less important, I would say, use of them in advertising and in familiarizing as many native Georgians and friends of Georgia as possible with our national history.

Local festivals like *Tbilisoba*, a holiday in the capital, served the same purpose by stimulating an interest in preserving the historical and cultural landmarks of the city. I often reflected that

---

[4] "Union" in this case means the Soviet Union, hence the enterprises referred to here reported directly to Moscow.—Trans.

only a nation united around high ideals and capable of working toward their realization has a future. A nation cannot live completely on its past, as many have tried to do. A nation can realize its creative potential only today, and for the sake of today, it must.

I do not know of a capital city that has a monument to its own native language. Except, that is, for Tbilisi. It is not a memorial, but a symbol. More, it is a challenge—to love, preserve, and protect the language, to develop it and improve its study and teaching. Special legislation was passed for this purpose, and a republic-wide program was designed. But simultaneously, the issue was raised of how the teaching of native languages for other nationalities and ethnic groups in Georgia could be improved. Thus modern Greek began to be taught in the Pontius Greek enclaves.

I believe that the first higher school for managers in the Soviet Union was opened in Tbilisi. It has trained top executive personnel to help reform in the republic.

Thus we began our perestroika in Georgia. To be quite accurate, we were the first to start it, never doubting that it was completely sensible if realistic approaches were taken. We undermined stagnation from within, building new structures while at the same time carefully dismantling the old, achieving wonderful results.

Of course, much depended on people, on their bravery. Once you gave them a sign, they would join you. I learned that through my own experience.

When Tenghiz Abuladze was shooting his famous film *Repentance*—also as an "experiment"—and people learned about it in Moscow, a highly placed official said to me:

"Do I hear that you've made an anti-Soviet film?" This was not a question, but a statement with threatening undertones.

"Why anti-Soviet?" I countered. "*Repentance* is a film about what capriciousness and lawlessness lead to. Isn't that very much a current issue for us?"

The director Robert Sturua, whose innovative stagings of Georgian and world classics were always politically edged and courageous, eliciting admiration in some, and grumbling and agitation in others, told his Moscow colleagues: "I'm not familiar with your problems. Back home in Georgia, I put on everything I wish, as I see fit."

At that time in other cities, people in the arts were being

punished with more than just the cancellation of their performances or the banning of their publications. The outstanding film director Sergei Paradzhanov was sentenced in the Ukraine to a labor camp term under articles that had nothing to do with his political views and public positions. He was tried for dissent. When he was freed from imprisonment, he went home to his native city of Tbilisi and once again was subjected to criminal prosecution on different charges.

My Georgian filmmaker friends can confirm how much effort it took to extract him from detention, save him as an artist, and give him the chance to take up his craft once again.

Some of the people at the top perceived this too as an "experiment," whose aim, as with other innovations, was to rock the foundations.

I heard something similar after academician Andrei Sakharov was released from his Gorky exile: "What, has Sakharov really stopped being anti-Soviet?"

My God, is that what we call anti-Soviet?

Everything we did during those years in Georgia could easily have been categorized as anti-Soviet by the prevailing standards of the day and there were plenty of people who wanted to do so. Therefore our initiative, our right to experiment, had to be faithfully defended. In the larger sense, we were defending the right to search for ways to achieve real sovereignty for the republic, even if it was within the framework of the existing system. Reform was by no means an end in itself, nor was it the traditional charade in which, to impress the bosses, people create the illusion of intense activity. Rather, we launched reforms for very specific purposes and they were worth the ruses to which we had to resort. Given the "feudal" vertical system, I had no other choice than to play by the rules. That meant obtaining the suzerain's support.

I did receive it, but it would be unjust to claim, as my opponents do, that I received it only by glorifying Brezhnev. He had plenty of flatterers without me. He and I met and conversed several times. I confided my plans to him, and that impressed him. The well-known facts about the misbehavior of his relatives were concealed from him. One of them was particularly active in Georgian affairs. I told Brezhnev about this. He was outraged and told me that I should act as I saw fit.

On the day of my resignation, leaflets containing my positive statements about Brezhnev were passed out in the halls at the Congress of People's Deputies. They could have printed other speeches in which I said things that were altogether unflattering to him, something that no one else did. Someday, I'll publish those speeches.

At the Twenty-seventh Party Congress I was asked how I could reconcile my former praise of Brezhnev with my current position. I replied that the General Secretary not only did not hinder our efforts (and of course he could have done so because of their "heretical" nature), but even supported them. There was no stagnation for me from that quarter. So am I supposed to sacrifice fairness, decency, and good memory to the attitudes of the day? How would I look to myself?

The acts and words of a politician should not be torn from the context of the job he is doing, with no regard for its overall direction. After all, there was a great deal of risk in what our sociologists called a revolution in values. Our experiments, which ran counter to sacred dogmas, did not just irritate the highly placed guardians of orthodoxy, they drew fire and a thirst for revenge. I wish I had been the only one threatened!

I will never forget the dramatic passage of the new Georgian Constitution at the April 1978 session of the republic's supreme Soviet. The majority demanded the retention of the article that made Georgian the republic's official language. This official status was contained in the first Fundamental Law of Soviet Georgia passed under Lenin and had remained in the Constitution of 1938. But the status had been omitted from the new draft at the behest of government legal experts in Moscow, who claimed that the "article contradicts Marxism-Leninism."

I expressed my concern about this to Brezhnev. He advised me to speak with Suslov and Chernenko, "and if it is especially difficult, let me know."

It was not easy to convince them that it was unwise to remove the article on the official language. For me the "1956 disturbance" remained as vivid as ever. It was already known that a powerful student demonstration in defense of the native language was in the works. I knew where it all could lead. On the day of the Supreme Soviet session, several hours before it opened, I had a telephone conversation with Suslov at dawn. I asked him to report to Brezhnev, reminded him of 1956, tried to persuade him, and finally said that I would act at my own discretion.

People can talk about "maneuvering" and "playing games with Moscow" as much as they like. We prevented a great tragedy and adopted a Constitution in conformity with the will of the people—that's the main thing for me. True, I had to take some risks, but I knew why I was doing it, even in those instances when there was a threat to my personal safety.

The real risk is to take no risks at all. When you timidly protect yourself, you risk everything: trust, respect, the people's support, and the right to be a leader. As one of my very old friends once said, the nation must be ruled not only by the wise, but by the brave.

Perestroika is accused of inflaming national and ethnic passions. That is not true. A backlash of discontent and outrage can always be expected from the anomalies in nationalities policy, from simplistic and vulgar exploitation of the thesis of the assimilation and blending of nations, crudely translated into the practical realm. Sparks smoldered under the ashes of bygone defeats, and the memory of them was never extinguished. At any minute, they could be stamped out by the boot of an accusation of nationalism. Perestroika removed the boot, and the sparks flared up, now labeled separatism and extremism. Does this mean we should regret the missing boot and summon it again? If we must regret anything, it should be that perestroika did not at the outset elaborate a nationalities policy suitable for its purposes and projects. At the very beginning, after all, in 1986 and particularly in 1988, the symptoms of deep-seated ailments were all too evident, requiring radical reform of the country's nation-state system.

That is the first "charge" in the bill of indictment I present to myself. As a member of the leadership who had thoroughly analyzed all the subtleties of life in the national republics, knowing firsthand how serious and complex were the problems troubling their populations, I could have more actively promoted the right decisions. After all, I had been through a very tough school. Inter-ethnic friction had broken out in virtually all the regions of Georgia. The end of the 1970s and the beginning of the 1980s were particularly difficult. My comrades and I had to enter into tense communication with tens of thousands of people, who were reviling us with anger and hatred. But we established a dialog, an effort to reach hearts and minds and, in turn, to listen and understand.

Once, a rally of 20,000 people in Sukhumi refused to listen to us. We had two choices: to get out and leave everything as it was, or to try to engage people in conversation. We chose the second course. We conferred all night, and in the morning people went off to their villages, cities, and work collectives. It was incredibly difficult to find a common language. This tense conversation, acutely painful to our pride, went on for months. But it was a conversation between equals, without shouts or threats, flattery or cajolery—a real dialog. We escaped the worst outcome, ethnic bloodshed, and prevented the sparks from bursting into flame.

It is very important to understand national sentiments, which means understanding a people. One must find out what causes it alarm, why it is taking offense at neighbors and former friends. To our misfortune, not everyone has proved capable of doing that. Few even give the matter much thought. A condescending, master–pupil tone prevails. Even some Politburo members, and even during the perestroika years, were guilty of this. They came to the republics and held forth in such a manner that the audience flew into a rage. Perhaps those trips and speeches were the very thing that provoked what would later be called nationalist extremism.

Authority that lacks even elementary sensitivity will inevitably suffer defeat. Some will say that power and sensitivity are incompatible. Well and good, but if there is no sensitivity, at least there can be sense—although I prefer the word "sensitivity," since it is more precise—but even sense, or intuition, is something that now and then we woefully lack.

I would like to speak sincerely and openly about my attitude toward the dissident movement. Much criticism has been directed at me on this score in the Western media and in the current Georgian press. Without disputing them, I would like to say simply, yes, there were problems. But that is not enough for me now.

The battle with dissent was waged throughout the whole country under the flag of the war against anti-Sovietism and nationalism. Of course, this was a nationwide policy, making extensive use of a repressive and propagandistic bureaucracy. Could I have prevented this or stopped it? Of course not. But I was obligated to protest. At the time, however, in the 1970s, I was not prepared to do so, either inwardly—psychologically—or politically.

I knew many of the people in the dissident movement in Georgia quite well. I spoke with them a number of times. The word "dissident" is the kind of label that conceals the real motivations of an individual. These were not dissidents, they were ordinary, normal people who were angry at the existing order of things. I believe we conversed without using labels, and I was largely in agreement with my interlocutors. I agreed, for example, that the tank and artillery practice range had to be moved farther away from the Udabno Monastery, which was crumbling from the vibrations, and I agreed with demands to improve the procedures for preserving priceless ancient manuscripts. These matters and many others that I discussed with those people were my concerns as well, but they turned out to be beyond my power. I never succeeded in persuading the central ministries to move the practice range to another area or to allocate the funding to build a modern repository for manuscripts.

It was also not within my power to protect the angry men and women who went far beyond words to expose the system's faults and took steps that failed to conform to the Criminal Code.

But there were hundreds of young people—students, scientists, and writers—whom I did manage to keep out of harm's way. We held open debates. Each of them fell under certain articles of the Criminal Code, which, however, were not invoked.

My position on each individual was only formulated after a difficult internal struggle. Perhaps it is this inner conflict that has made me an active proponent of perestroika. This struggle, along with my knowledge of the true state of affairs in our country, has led me to conclude that the root of existing evils is not in the individual people, but in the system. And if some people seethe with hatred for the system, that is only because the system is ruthless toward the individual. Under conditions of totalitarianism, it is impossible to guarantee observance of human rights and freedoms, and that means it is impossible to guarantee the normal development of the country.

"Everything's rotten. It has to be changed." I really did say that to Gorbachev on a winter evening in 1984 at Pitsunda, and I will not recant those words today.

But before my story reaches the present day, I ought to recall the day in mid-June of 1985 when the phone rang in my Tbilisi office and I heard Gorbachev's voice on the line.

"I have some very serious intentions with regard to you. Two proposals, but I cannot be more specific yet. Both of them involve your moving to Moscow to work."

I reacted somewhat cautiously. I said that my current work in Georgia needed support, and I hoped I would get it. I didn't need anything else.

"Take your time to decide," said Gorbachev. "This is a very important offer."

On June 30, he phoned again.

"I want to continue our conversation. We have made a final determination and we are offering you the post of Minister of Foreign Affairs. We'll expect you tomorrow morning in Moscow."

To say I was surprised would be a massive understatement. Although I repeatedly told various people that this was the greatest surprise of my life, I was not expressing one thousandth of the feelings that overwhelmed me. Try to describe the feelings of a man who was completely engrossed in the affairs of his little homeland and suddenly, in an instant, was pulled away from them with a single jerk.

I had a relief map of Georgia in my office; I knew every inch of it by touch. I had never kept any other maps around. I had traveled some, but not extensively—I had visited nine countries. I had hosted foreign delegations in Tbilisi many times, sometimes of very high rank, but they were only guests, and I was only a gracious host. If I had to resort to diplomacy, it had been only in the circle of my fellow Georgians, sharp of wit and tongue, and in contacts with the Moscow hierarchs, from whom I was trying to extract something. I did not know any foreign languages, only my native Georgian and Russian, which I spoke with an ineradicable accent. I lacked experience, special knowledge— But wait a minute, was I hearing things?

No, I wasn't hearing things.

"Well, I would have expected anything but that. What about Gromyko?"

"Gromyko supports your candidacy. Come here and we'll talk."

I flew up to Moscow early the next morning. My conversation with Gorbachev lasted about forty minutes. I took up most of the time with arguments against my appointment. Minister of Foreign Affairs is not a position, it's a profession, I said. Diplomacy is a complicated professional world, hard to break into and obtain recognition. For me it would be all the harder. My nationality was by no means a side issue. Historically, this post had always been held by either a Russian or a student of Russian culture with roots in Russia. My appointment would be met with ambivalence in Russia and the other republics. Some hard questions would inevitably be raised abroad as well.

"The issue is already decided," Gorbachev said. "It has been endorsed by the Central Committee secretaries. And as I already told you, Gromyko supports your candidacy. As for your nationality, yes, you are a Georgian, but you're a Soviet man, after all! No experience? Well, perhaps that's a good thing. Our foreign policy needs a fresh eye, courage, dynamism, innovative approaches. I have no doubt that my choice is right."

Immediately after this conversation, a meeting of the Politburo was convened. Gorbachev informed his colleagues and outlined all the reasons he had given me. The floor was given to Gromyko. Andrei Andreyevich spoke about the kind of foreign policy he thought the country should have at this stage of perestroika, and how he envisioned the work of the new Minister of Foreign Affairs. He made a number of kind remarks about me and generously pledged his support for the diplomatic corps. In reply, I once again expressed my doubts. I am afraid that I was unable to conceal my agitation. The transition from one condition to another, from the measurable dimensions of my accustomed life to an absolutely immeasurable scale was a powerful shock to me.

Why did I not refuse? If I were to say that refusal was just not done, that it would go against tradition, I would be less than straightforward. I had broken the rules and violated tradition too often before to behave differently now. True, I was not schooled in the fine points of professional diplomacy, but I knew myself to be capable of plunging into a job so that no one would consider me a dilettante. It was a challenge I could not refuse. I had always sought strong opponents and partners; that had helped me to mobilize all my internal resources. But the main point was that it was Gorbachev's choice, which for me was the choice of a comrade. I knew what he wanted, and knew that I wanted the same thing.

A Central Committee plenary session met on July 2 and elected me a member of the Politburo.

Several days later, before the final transfer to Moscow, I spent several hours in Mamati. I was met with the smiles of relatives and fellow villagers at my parents' home. A modest dinner was held to remember those who had passed away. Then I went to the cemetery and stood for a little while at the graves. I will refrain from describing the feelings that overwhelmed me.

From the balcony of our house the whole village unfolded before us. The silvery Supsa River snaked through the valley. Somewhere far away, it flowed into the Black Sea. My gaze could not see any farther; as before, it was difficult to imagine myself standing "in the eyes of the world."

CHAPTER TWO

My Introductory Course in the New Thinking

It is only a few minutes' drive from the Kremlin to Smolensk Square, where the Soviet Ministry of Foreign Affairs is housed. On my way to my first meeting with my colleagues, my thoughts traveled a much longer route. On July 2, 1985, at the close of the Central Committee plenary session, Gorbachev had proposed that I get down to business immediately. It was easy to say "immediately," but where was I to start?

The head of the Secretariat waited for me at the entrance. We took the elevator to the seventh floor and went into the Minister's office. From July 2, 1985 until January 16, 1991, I spent five years, six and a half months in this office. Believe me, I do not remember each and every one of those days, but the very first day is etched in my memory down to the tiniest detail.

Anyone who visited this office with the number 706 over the door can confirm that nothing was changed in its interior design. Everything remained as it had been with the previous occupant. But from that very day, foreign policy had to be changed, and although I knew that, I did not know where to start.

I asked that the deputy ministers be invited in. I was acquainted with some of them, but it was one thing to meet at Central Committee meetings and quite another to take a new position that would place my good acquaintances under me. Even for the most kindly disposed, I was an outsider and a dilettante.

Suppressing my excitement with difficulty, I suggested that they bring me up to date, tell me who was in charge of which section, and acquaint me with the most urgent issues. After hearing my colleagues out, I said:

"I am completely in your hands, and my situation is as bad as you can imagine. I cannot impress you with my knowledge of foreign policy. I can only promise that I will work in such a way that I won't be ashamed of myself, and you won't be embarrassed by me. But I'm still not sure it'll work out. It's especially hard in view of Andrei Andreyevich Gromyko's authority and the legacy he has bestowed. Who am I compared to Gromyko, the battleship of world foreign policy? I'm just a rowboat. But with a motor."

My colleagues' friendly chuckles dispelled the tension. Getting a little ahead of myself, I'll say that my "motor" got a great kick-start from their good will and sympathy, their readiness to help, to enlighten, and to draw me into their affairs without rubbing in their own professionalism and the gaps in my knowledge so as to spare my pride. Naturally, I felt grateful, but it was more than that. I was an object of intense scrutiny in the Ministry and beyond. My prediction that my appointment as Minister of Foreign Affairs would produce mixed reactions came true. Surprise was mingled with puzzlement and even indignation. I tried to extricate myself as quickly as possible from the humiliating position of a student appointed as leader over his masters. But I took my time. This was not at all a paradox. I had a formula: maximum concentration on the business at hand, minimum external pretensions to a formal supremacy not backed by real authority. That helped me to handle the job rapidly, but not hastily.

Nevertheless, the greatest surprise of my life was to become the greatest, most difficult test, both in my personal experience and in my entrance to the intricate world of diplomacy at such a difficult time for our country and the world.

It was a trial that strained to the limit my own strength of will and my usual ability to grow with a job. My knowledge and perception of my country's domestic affairs and foreign policy, of its place in the world, what it really was, and what it should and could become, were put to a test. Everything that was to torment me for years to come, that had demanded but had never received an answer, flooded over me in those first days, weeks, and months in the office of the Minister on the seventh floor of the tall building on Smolensk Square in Moscow.

My overriding concern was for my colleagues' welfare. While subjected to such a strenuous ordeal, I was duty bound to protect them from the upheavals resulting from the change of course. The turn had to be executed smoothly and naturally.

Before proposing a clear, precise program of action, I had to decide what I considered the key priorities for the head of the Soviet diplomatic corps. I had deeply respected my predecessor, admiring his enormous experience, competence, and erudition and knowing the authority he commanded among Soviet and foreign diplomats as well as among ordinary people. I feared that I would inadvertently present a contrast to him by taking on the role of the "new broom," furiously sweeping everything away, but raising a cloud of dust and dirt in the process.

To repeat, I took my time, watching people carefully, observing, accumulating information about the Ministry, listening more than speaking, studying rather than lecturing, taking on as much as I could and giving out only encouraging interest and attention to the potentially strong sides of my colleagues. Meanwhile, I clearly realized that perestroika could not wait. It was not going to bypass our ministry, which needed new guidelines in keeping with the new realities of the day. At the time, it seemed a difficult dilemma to resolve, but I saw three interrelated tasks ahead.

The first was to define and establish myself as Minister, that is, as head of a ministry and as a diplomat recognized by my colleagues, and not just formally, by virtue of my high appointment.

The second was the restructuring of the Ministry's work in keeping with the strategic aims of the new foreign policy declared by Gorbachev at the April 1985 Communist Party Central Committee plenary session.

The third was the most important and the most difficult: our participation in the practical realization of the new foreign policy strategy, closely linked with the efforts of perestroika and democratization of society and the whole country. Soviet diplomacy had to make a direct, effective contribution to the new conceptual approach in the conduct of international affairs.

I have already indicated, here and earlier, how I tackled the first job. I worked without sparing myself. I learned from those who had something to teach me. I looked for and found support among knowledgeable people. I encouraged them to blossom, awakening a sense of professional worth that had been largely stifled in the past. I did not claim a monopoly on ideas and was open to the most diverse opinions. I may have been mistaken and unfair at times, but on the whole I was able to uphold the standards of normal office relations. On the personal level I missed a number of opportunities. Dissatisfaction with oneself is the normal state of a normal person. Again, no matter how many sleepless nights I spent trying to master my new job, my diligence would not have produced any noticeable results without the concentrated, purposeful support of my colleagues, advisers, and aides. Nor without the good will of my foreign colleagues, who gave me their sympathetic and interested attention or, to be more precise, gave it to the course of perestroika, which I represented and was bringing to fruition in foreign relations to the best of my ability.

The second task is also far from finished. It cannot be completed. In today's world the foreign policy office must be like a flexible production line, capable of switching to the product needed at the moment, with an eye to its short-term and long-term prospects, its competitiveness, and so on.

In keeping with the new foreign policy aim to curb the arms race and resolve security issues through peaceful means, a new subdivision was created within the Foreign Ministry: the Department of Arms Limitation and Disarmament. New approaches to human rights and the proclaimed principle of the rule of law warranted forming two special offices: the Administration for International Humanitarian Cooperation and Human Rights and the International Law Administration.

In time, amendments to the program for internal perestroika prompted us to deal more extensively with questions of international cooperation in science, technology, economics, and environmental problems, and we reacted to the emergence of new priorities with rapid innovations in our internal structure.

The principles of glasnost and candor motivated us to improve our contacts with the public and press. A Department of Information was created and began holding regular briefings and press conferences with the Minister, his deputies, and ambassadors.

The most indicative example of change was the perestroika and renewal of several European desks within the Ministry. In the past, the division of these offices was an obvious reflection of the ideological divisions of the continent. Now they are one powerful "tree," with strong structural branches, which I defined for myself as an intellectual and political center dealing with the problems of creating a united Europe. Major reorganization was also made of the desks responsible for the United States, Africa, Latin America, and the Asian Pacific.

What will happen tomorrow? I will not venture to advise my successor in the post of Minister; he must decide for himself. But the correct answer will probably involve responding adequately to the challenges of the day.

And now I come to the third and most important of our tasks, the profound changes and improvements in Soviet foreign policy predicated on the policy of perestroika. This is the practical politics of the new thinking.

Shortly before my appointment to the Foreign Ministry, I read in a topical book the complaint that the new thinking had not become the dominant tendency in international relations. After resigning, I was to learn of another opinion: The concept of new political thinking allegedly clashed with the processes of real life. Yet another thesis has recently made an appearance: The new thinking sufficed for destroying the old world order but is not capable of creating the new one, so now something else is needed.

The evolution of international relations and their current state disprove the first point. As for the second and third, I intend to dispute them later.

Meanwhile, I would like to discourse a bit on an old, well-known subject, keeping in mind that some eternal truths only improve with repetition, especially in times when many people have forgotten or refuse to remember them. Born in great minds, great ideas long await their hour. Sometimes the wait goes on for centuries. But the hour chimes sooner or later.

"The plan was not good enough for Europe, because Europe was not good enough for it," Jean-Jacques Rousseau said regarding one of the countless schemes for unifying the countries of the Old World. His meaning is clear: Europe at that time did not have the right conditions for realizing the plan. The idea ripened too early, but now it is not too late for us, the inheritors of those great thinkers who foresaw the time when European countries and peoples would be unified.

Now that this time has arrived, and for the first time since antiquity the European idea has a chance to be put into practice, its proponents share the copyright equally with their great predecessors. Along with the copyright, they bear an enormous responsibility that knows no analog, since this time they must translate the project into reality, that is, into the daily lives of millions of people.

The parallels with the new thinking are quite obvious. The idea was first advanced at a time when thinking in categories of power and confrontation predominated in international relations, and force was considered the main instrument of national policy. The opposing polarities of the world seemed irreconcilable, and really were, and people attempted to minimize the risk of a clash, which would be fatal for all of humanity. The building up of forces on both sides only increased the risk many times over.

It seemed that nothing could break this vicious circle, nothing could shed light in the gloom of a feverish arms race. The nightmare existence under the Damoclean sword of mutual nuclear annihilation became a daily reality for humanity. Nor did the scales fall from our eyes when these words resounded: "We need a new way of human thinking, so that humanity will survive and develop further. . . . People find themselves in a new situation, to which they must accommodate their thinking."

The Russell–Einstein Manifesto offered politicians the key to the most troublesome and complex riddles of the age. The atom bomb had so changed the world that to continue thinking in the old categories meant running headlong into the abyss.

Politicians, however, did not wish or, more likely, were unable to make use of that key at the time. Centuries of defensive practice were so firmly ingrained that human intelligence could not force a life-saving breach through it. So fragile and defenseless, and yet so omnipotent, intelligence often manifests its strength in a fierce aversion to the new.

The tenacious age-old notions of the right to use force fed upon considerations of clinging to power, which no one has ever voluntarily relinquished. The new thinking—a global revolution of the mind—must await the hour when recognition of the impending dangers inherent in the inevitability of the historical process convinces politicians of the necessity to think anew.

There had to be someone in the world who would find the courage to correlate the new realities of the day with a new idea.

On February 25, 1986, in Moscow, in the Kremlin Palace of Congresses, I and the other delegates to the Twenty-seventh Party Congress heard Mikhail S. Gorbachev read the Political Report to the Central Committee.

I knew what kind of document would be offered to the Party and the country, how it had been drafted, and what kind of opposition various provisions had encountered. The preparation of the report, a program for a new leadership of the country, reflected the widest and most contentious spectrum of opinions. It looked to me at the time like a simple debate among people with different ideas. Now I would venture to say that it was a clash of the interests and positions of the various forces represented in the Politburo, which was far from the "monolithic unit" it claimed to be.

By long-standing tradition, Politburo members receive drafts of all the most important documents and submit their comments. The draft of the Political Report to the Twenty-seventh Congress had been reworked many times, and comments were coming in almost constantly. A day before the opening of the Congress, I received a final draft of the report and discovered that it contained no mention of the need to withdraw our forces from Afghanistan. This clause, crucial in our view, had been in the earliest drafts of the speech. Why had it disappeared? At whose insistence?

I phoned Gorbachev and told him that not a soul in the U.S.S.R. or the outside world would understand us, if this sentence were omitted.

Getting a little ahead of myself, I want to make the point that after the settlement whereby Soviet troops were withdrawn from Afghanistan, the civilized world began to trust us. That opened up great prospects for putting into practice the principles of the new thinking. Perhaps it was the experience of the Afghan epic that prompted us to think of the possibility of partnership and cooperation with the West.

But back then our concern was the philosophy of foreign policy. As I met with Gorbachev almost every day, I detected his thoughts moving in a completely uncharted and, frankly, dangerous direction. It was dangerous from the viewpoint of the exponents and defenders of those dogmas that had prevailed for decades. The iconoclast of centuries-old doctrines always takes a risk, because orthodoxy, which cannot forgive an encroachment upon its holy of holies, will automatically transform itself into an inquisition and will hasten to punish the "heretic." Sadly, the drama of ideas is always fraught with personal tragedy for their author and defender. Nevertheless, when I reflected on the report's ideas, I was all the more convinced: This is it, the *sine qua non* of an escape from our current plight.

The theory of peaceful coexistence advanced back in 1917 does not and cannot remove the cornerstone of confrontation: the original premise that the victory of one sociopolitical system over the other is inevitable. Neither can it eliminate the underlying premises of Marxist theory. From the practical standpoint, the premise is static and passive, although overactive advocates of class warfare have translated it into the sphere of intergovernmental relations. In order to justify this and reconcile the irreconcilable, they declared the peaceful coexistence of states with various social systems "a specific form of class warfare." At the Twenty-seventh Congress that definition was destined to be scrapped, and peaceful coexistence would be redefined as a universal formula for intergovernment relations.

This was not merely a scholastic definition. The "form of class warfare" inevitably entailed a view of the world as a field of permanent struggle between systems, camps, and blocs, and the "image of the enemy" captured the minds of millions of people all over the world.

The eradication of that image is a primary goal, at a point in world development where the real enemies of humanity are emerging in their full magnitude and threatening our destruction: thermonuclear war, environmental catastrophe, and the collapse of the world economy. We had to remove the stone of enmity and mistrust, so that the world can look through the opening it leaves and see the signposts to consolidation.

By this time the basis of the new thinking had already been articulated and even implemented in a practical way. At a Soviet–French summit in Paris, Gorbachev had declared his idea of a common European home. At the Geneva summit, the Soviet leader and President Reagan had stated that nuclear war was unacceptable. Gorbachev had announced on January 15, 1986, that he was prepared to make a gradual elimination of all nuclear weapons stockpiles by the year 2000. The Soviet Union had discontinued nuclear tests and had called upon the United States to follow suit.

And that brings us to February 25, 1986, and the Twenty-seventh Party Congress.

In rereading the Political Report today, I see the drama of an individual standing at the frontier between old and new. He can see that the path to the new is open, but invisible to those who live by the old propositions. In the Middle Ages that would have led to an auto-da-fé. What about today? Must a progressive politician be burned at the stake? To instill new ideas, he is compelled to diverge from what is accessible, familiar, and understandable to others. A new idea by itself, after all, is nothing but words if it does not capture the minds of the majority and at the same time provide motivation for practical behavior.

When it has been drilled into you for decades that the peaceful coexistence of countries with different social systems is a "specific form of class warfare," and you have come to believe it, it is incredibly difficult to accept something different immediately, in a flash.

When you have been taught that international relations are subject to the interests and laws of class warfare, it is impossible to assimilate all at once the idea—even if it does go back to Lenin—that universal human values have priority over all others.

In an atmosphere where the world is divided into blocs by the type of their socio-political systems, how can we recognize the world as it is, interconnected and integral, where the sheer necessity for human survival breaks down the walls of ideological hostility?

Before the fundamental principles of the new thinking could be formulated, we needed a thorough analysis of the basic trends and contradictions of the modern world as they directly related to the condition of our country. This task was no less difficult than the proclamation of new goals, and it could not be achieved without the tools of the new thinking. But it was accomplished beautifully.

All of the points in Gorbachev's Political Report resounded with a categorical "no" to the system of prevailing views: The key idea of a contradictory, interdependent, and essentially integral world; the thesis that human life is the highest aim of social development, which later evolved into the imperative of the priority of universal human values; the principle of freedom of choice, which can be realized only in a world without arms and violence; the guaranteeing of security and the resolution of all conflicts exclusively by political means, that is, a declaration of the primacy of the force of politics over the politics of force.

Extremely important from both a theoretical and a practical standpoint is the conclusion that security is indivisible: In bilateral relations, both sides had to have equal security, and in international relations, global security had to be paramount. In our century, security is gained not by the highest possible level of strategic parity, but the lowest possible level, and nuclear and other weapons of mass destruction must be removed from the equation.

Another premise is simple and appears to be devoid of any traps, but actually rejects the factor of ideologization: We should conduct ourselves with restraint on the international scene, according to the standards of civilized communication, guided by the criteria of universal morality.

The foreign policy section of Gorbachev's report was applauded. The applause reflected, to use the Soviet parlance, unanimous support and approval.

Today, when these principles and proposals are being questioned, when there are demands to admit they were mistaken, I cannot help thinking about that mass expression of agreement and enthusiasm. What was the applause about then, a display of discipline by those accustomed to clapping for the head of the Party? Was it a tribute to ritual, "approving" and "supporting" by tradition, while assuming that words would remain no more than words? Did they really not understand that the report's ideas meant the dismantling of the system? The most likely conclusion, I think, is that people were clapping because many of them wanted change but were unaware that these changes would affect their position.

But at the time, I saw this expression of agreement as proof of the universal support of new standards for our foreign policy, the principles of the new thinking.

Unshakable dogmas, which had always prevailed over the common sense of even the most intelligent and sober people, because the threat of ostracism for heresy always loomed, were finally being shaken. I recalled in this connection my own past difficulties, when any effort to introduce something new, sensible, and effective would run up against the fierce resistance of the supreme guardians of orthodoxy, which they themselves were perverting. I knew that our country had enormous reserves of intellect and will, but was hopelessly straitjacketed by despotic dogmatism. If we could not free ourselves, the country would not move forward. Now it was finally happening.

As Minister of Foreign Affairs, I had my own reasons for rejoicing. With Gorbachev's speech, my colleagues and I had received a working program extremely close to our own aspirations.

Our guidelines were precise: to stop the preparation for nuclear war; to move Soviet–American relations onto a track of normal, civilized dialog; to reject the dead, brutally rigid positions in favor of intelligent, mutually acceptable compromises; to move our affairs toward a balance of interests; to strive for the confinement of military capabilities to the level of reasonable sufficiency; to confirm the principle of comprehensive control and verification; to seek ways to end nuclear tests and dismantle the American and Soviet intermediate range missiles in Europe; to bring Soviet troops out of Afghanistan; to create a security system in Europe on the basis of the Helsinki process, radically cutting nuclear and conventional arms; to defuse regional conflicts; to normalize relations with China; to build relations with our neighbors on a basis of respect of their interests and the principles of noninterference in their internal affairs; to concern ourselves with global problems.

All this had to be embodied in a practical policy. I shall leave aside the understandable worries of a man pondering the best use of a road map, and shall say only that, for all the buoyancy I felt from Gorbachev's speech, I remained apprehensive.

I don't recall which of the German thinkers wrote that Calvary is always in the place where great thoughts are articulated. The initiators of perestroika would have to carry an incredibly heavy cross, and of course the climb did not look easy. It turned out, however, to be far more difficult than we had expected.

It is said that the most enjoyable journey is the journey of a searching mind. But even when it extends over the whole world, it does not attract everyone. Quite a few people try to block progress.

My present quarrel with them is free from any personal motives. Whatever the twists of fate, I do not consider my lot unenviable. My wish to defend the philosophy and politics of the new thinking was dictated by the interests of the country, closely linked with the interests of *mir*.[1] I mean the desired state of humanity, peace, and the community of the family of nations which make up the world. I am not so self-confident as to underestimate the immense scale involved here, but it is dictated by the scale of our perestroika, and its role and significance in the fate of the country and the world.

I have called this chapter "My Introductory Course in the New Thinking." I ask the reader not to see any pretentions to scholarliness in this title. I simply want to tell how my personal introduction to this new course of Soviet foreign policy proceeded. It was not easy or untroubled.

Everyone, including those in the leadership, may possess, express, and defend their own opinions. At the stage when decisions are being worked out, this is essential. But after a decision is already made and formulated as a strategic course, for a member of the leadership to oppose it is to undermine faith in the course itself and its designers, and to work against the implementation of consensus politics for which that leader had voted.

I recall July 1988. The Nineteenth All-Union Party Conference had just ended, having reaffirmed the main priority for us: to secure by political means the favorable external conditions needed to bring about change inside the country. Three years of perestroika had been reviewed, and the reasons for delay, even then quite noticeable and severe, had been analyzed. The blueprint for political reform proposed at the conference required clear notions of how foreign policy should look in the new superstructure, and of how it would operate under the new institutions empowered by the Constitution. We had managed to achieve something in the Ministry by that time, but much remained on the drawing board. Many ideas could not be implemented because the philosophical and conceptual "field" was constricted. The principle of class warfare, extended to international contacts, had canceled out the obvious working advantages of the formula of peaceful coexistence as a universal principle of international relations. A relic of the old thinking, "peaceful co-existence as a specific form of class warfare" prevented the latter formula from operating fruitfully.

I had long reflected on this. I wanted to float some of my ideas

---

[1] The author takes advantage here of the double meaning of *mir*, which translates as both "peace" and "world."—Trans.

among a wide circle of professionals, to invite the judgments of scholars, consultants, and partners in the foreign policy process. That is how the idea of the conference of scholars and practitioners arose. In preparation for it, we conducted a survey in the Foreign Ministry. The results exceeded all expectations. We received numerous pointed, original proposals, which enabled us to see our job in a new light. Moreover, the survey results proved that people were finally believing that their ideas could be used. Much of what they said coincided with my own thinking.

At the conference, I said in my report that I was submitting our collective labor for discussion.

Much of the report was taken up with the issue of peaceful coexistence. The new thinking looks at it in the context of the realities of the nuclear age. We are on firm ground in rejecting it as a special form of class struggle. Coexistence based on such premises as non-aggression, respect of sovereignty, noninterference in internal affairs, and so on is incompatible with class struggle. This illogical symbiosis leads us nowhere. Equating intergovernmental relations with class struggle places an insurmountable barrier in the way of mutual cooperation between countries with different sociopolitical systems.

An even higher and more massive barrier was the "theological" tenet, said to be the leading trend of the modern era, about the antagonism between the two systems. If humanity was capable of surviving only in conditions of peaceful coexistence (and it had no future under permanent confrontation) then the antagonism of the two systems must not be the leading trend.

Now at the forefront was a growing tendency, dictated by the realities of an increasingly interdependent world, for states to cooperate in the global community.

Everything that we were to achieve—the new quality of Soviet–American relations; dialog displacing confrontation; a shift of emphasis from forceful confrontation to political means for solving international problems—was the consequence of practical implementation of these ideas.

They were broadly supported in the country, but also attacked by highly influential people. Yegor Ligachev declared that by "planting" these ideas, we were confusing the Soviet people and our friends abroad. Now perestroika is held to be a Pandora's box. Critics blame it for everything, even the weakening of national

security. It is said that idealists and political romanticists, who
have traded the principle of proletarian internationalism for the
priority of universal human values, have left no room in their
concept of the new thinking for such categories as "national security" and "national interests."

That is not true. Perestroika was brought to life by the objective need to overcome the crisis endangering national security
and interests.

In May 1986, at a meeting at the Foreign Ministry, we emphasized that some strategists' deep-seated belief that the Soviet
Union must be as strong as any possible coalition of countries
opposing it was absolutely fallacious. Pursuing it would mean to go
against national interests.

We became a superpower largely because of our military
might. But the bloated size and unrestrained escalation of this
military might was reducing us to the level of a third-rate country,
unleashing processes that pushed us to the brink of catastrophe.
Our military expenditures as a percentage of gross national product were two and a half times greater than those of the United
States. Although we take pride in achieving military parity with
the Americans, we could not even dream of equaling them in the
manufacture of disposable syringes, food products, and basic ne-
cessities. The catastrophic shortages of these goods hardly
strengthen our security or serve our national interest. We have
captured first place in the world weapons trade (28 percent of the
entire sales total), and have made the Kalashnikov submachine
gun the hallmark of our advanced technology. But we occupy about
sixtieth place in standard of living, thirty-second place in average
life expectancy, and fiftieth in infant mortality.

What kind of national security is this? It is not just immoral
but politically dangerous to equate national security with tanks
and nuclear warheads, while leaving out such "trivia" as human life
and welfare.

It is not true that issues of national security and protection of
national interests have been overlooked by Soviet diplomacy, the
foreign policy establishment, or the Foreign Minister. At the outset, we questioned why the security of such a powerful military
state had become so vulnerable in terms of economy, scientific-
technological potential, the government of the republics, and the
citizen, and his spiritual and material welfare. Why had all these

factors been relegated to an auxiliary role, pressed into the service of military power?

Traditional, centuries-old notions of national security as the defense of the country from external military threat have been shaken by profound structural and qualitative shifts in human civilization, the result of the growing role of science and technology and the increasing political, economic, social, and informational interdependence of the world. States that rely mostly on military means of protection cannot consider themselves safe. They are in a no-win position, for the source of political influence in the world and the protection of national interest increasingly depend on economic, technological, and financial factors, whereas enormous arsenals of weapons cannot provide rational answers to the challenges of the day. These weapons cannot be used without risking the destruction of one's own country, its neighbors, and half the world.

In trying to trace how, when, and why the Soviet Union was compelled to stockpile nuclear arms, one must conclude that we were always trying to catch up to the Americans. Of course, given the conditions at the end of the 1940s and beginning of the 1950s, the Soviet Union was compelled to develop its own nuclear potential. But in allowing ourselves to be dragged into the arms race—both nuclear and conventional—and infatuated with volume and quantity, we responded with excessive zeal, when it would have been possible to give asymmetrical, quantitatively less, but qualitatively better "answers."

Along with their losses and wounds, our long-suffering Soviet people emerged from World War II with a sense of pride in themselves and their country for having saved the world from fascism. Later they were willing to sacrifice everything for the sake of strengthening the country's defense. And their sacrifices were accepted without the slightest thought given to the fact that a country of socially and politically humiliated people cannot gain security. In such a country, a human being is only the means for obtaining security (we might ask: whose?), not the object of that security.

In overcoming the inertia of customary notions, we discovered that the possession of a bloated nuclear arsenal undermined rather than augmented national defense, draining resources from the effort to ensure a high technical level of peaceful production, education, and health, and maximum satisfaction of the population's needs. It became abundantly clear to us that any foreign policy programs, plans, and actions, including methods of achieving national security, must be strictly measured against real national priorities, with the long-range interests of the citizen in mind.

There is no question that over the decades the U.S.S.R. has created an enormous technological, intellectual, and economic potential. But how is it being used? How do factors of "national might" like size of territory, natural resources, intellectual potential, and state and national institutes of learning work—if they are working at all?

Vast expanses have been turned into ecological disaster areas under pressure from irrational centralism. What about natural resources? Avaricious exploitation—"fulfilling the plan at any price"—has exhausted national resources and has not even compensated with a qualitative growth in the economy. Having earned a "quick and easy" 180 billion dollars on oil, the Soviet Union derived no economic benefit at all, nor any improvement in the material status of its citizens. The morale of the society and the stability of national and state institutions were maintained by a mendacious "propaganda of success," the suppression of dissent, and the encouragement to fear internal and external enemies, with threats of punishment and revenge for wrong behavior.

Today's critics accuse the political leadership of weakening the country's security by exaggerating factors in the international situation and understating national might as the chief guarantor of the success of perestroika. I would be prepared to agree—I have already admitted that domestic policy lags behind foreign policy—if I did not know that internal reforms were slowed by the system's desperate resistance. For decades, the system itself undermined national might by concentrating its efforts only on the military means of ensuring national security. And this was the very system that today, in the words of its most zealous guardians, is passing sentence on the policy of new thinking: "By counterposing universal and class interests and giving priority to universal values, we have done a disservice to the socialist ideal. . . . The dialectical unity of the class and the universal has been disrupted. We all know very well that no one has ever expressed universal human values better than the working class."[2]

---

[2] Materials from the Joint Plenary Session of the Central Committee and the Central Control Commission of the CPSU, *Pravda*, February 4, 1991.

It is hard to argue with a statement like that. It is hard to even discuss it, when the topic of discussion is being deliberately destroyed by dogmatic bludgeoning. How can we object to the statement that the best embodiment of universal human values is a working class that for decades has been deprived of the elementary conditions for human existence? How can we contest the claim that damage has been done to the socialist idea, when the greatest harm has been caused by its criminally false distortion and its embodiment in inhumane forms absolutely contrary to its original purposes?

There is something painfully familiar about the passages on de-ideologizing, which now "can only mean the sacrifice of socialist interests, goals, and values to bourgeois ones. Can democracy, freedom, and justice exist outside of any kind of social order? In the modern world, there are no social systems besides socialism and capitalism."[3]

How does one join such an argument which smacks of medieval scholasticism? One might fight dogma with dogma, and thus lower oneself to this level of thinking. One can appeal to impartial statistics and establish that the indicators of living standards for each of the two systems are clearly not in our favor, hence it is pointless to speak of any values to be sacrificed, since we have already rendered them worthless. One can say: "Yes, democracy, freedom, and justice cannot exist outside of any kind of social system, but we would have to ignore reality altogether to assert that the 'socialist model' we have constructed here contains any semblance of those qualities." Or one can simply go out on the street and see people's faces, how they are dressed, what kind of apartments they live in, what their working conditions are, and how little it all resembles a life worthy of a human being, how hopelessly far it is from the socialist idea.

This alone would quell any desire to lower myself to a discussion about the relationship between the class and the universal, if I did not detect a very definite practical aim behind the outwardly scholastic construct of the opponents of the new thinking.

Renouncing the principle of the supremacy of universal human values and returning to the absolute of class origin means to resurrect the "image of the enemy," internal or external, and thus

[3] *Pravda*, February 4, 1991.

justifies repressions inside and outside the country. Presupposing a totally hostile encirclement means cultivating a siege mentality, preparing for war, and engaging in confrontations and conflicts without respite. That would mean a return to the cold war, so draining for the country, a return to the arms race, and the support of regimes based on their "solidarity" with us.

A relapse into this type of imperial logic was apparent in the recent vociferous support for the regime of Saddam Hussein, in other words, support for the rule of lawlessness and arrogance, inspired by the false idol of "true friendship." The "image of the enemy," which we had so much difficulty overcoming, was fashioned to contrast with the true character of the Soviet people, but it was alien to their friendliness, bravery, wisdom, and self-sacrifice. Belief in the Soviet people's creative, peace-loving nature was undermined by reprisals against "dissidents," statements like "we'll bury you," wrongful actions (to put it mildly) with regard to our friends, and the preaching of peaceful coexistence as a specific form of class struggle.

Foreign policy was made in the name of the people—behind their backs. It had always claimed to be in the national interest. But was it really? Did the paranoid obsession with military security, which led to the massive deployment of RSD-10 (SS20) missiles, benefit the people? Did the habit of "slamming the door," formed in the 1950s, which became a stereotype of behavior in the early 1980s, when we walked out of the Geneva talks and thus accelerated the creation of a hostile second strategic front in Europe? Did the self-defeating policy of pseudo-support for developing nations, mainly through guns and armaments? Was the sending of our troops to Afghanistan for the welfare of the people? Alas, questions of this type could be continued at length.

I well recall the storm of applause that greeted the words of a politician I very much respect, who said that not a single question in the world can be decided without the participation of the Soviet Union, especially if contrary to its interests. That is truly the case. But the question is *how* it is decided, and at what cost to the Soviet Union itself. The war in Afghanistan cost us 60 billion rubles. By the most modest calculations, the confrontation with China cost us 200 billion rubles. Over about three decades we have built a colossal military infrastructure along the 7,500–kilometer border. Who can tell us the cost of the long presence of our troops in Czechoslovakia, Hungary, and Poland? Or the cost of the escalating production of chemical weapons, while the Americans discontinued their production in 1969?

Let us have a look at the political and economic cost of the cold war. The last two decades of ideological confrontation with the West, by some estimates, added 700 billion rubles to the cost of military defense, in excess of what it cost to achieve military parity with the United States and the West.

By worshipping the idols of pseudo-ideology, we impoverished our whole country. Unrealistic, essentially confrontational doctrines and an entrenched bureaucratic-command system for making the most important foreign policy decisions have proved to be unbearably costly. Now we are being called to account supposedly because the philosophy of the new thinking has come into clear conflict with the interests of national security. I am prepared to accept this argument, but with one slight amendment: It is in clear conflict with the superpower philosophy and psychology.

We could, of course, eliminate the conflict by sacrificing the new thinking, but then we would doom the country to a final break with world civilization, with all the attendant consequences.

I want the critics of the new thinking to name the price they are willing to pay for this "back-tracking" in terms of the only possible standard, the one we scorned in the past and, by doing so, turned ourselves from victors into losers. I mean the standard of human life.

CHAPTER THREE

Finding the Human Dimension

Confessions of an "Idealist"

In July 1985 the "eyes of the world" my father had told me about finally became visible. The foreign ministers of thirty-five nations of Europe, the United States, and Canada gathered in the capital of Finland to mark the tenth anniversary of the Helsinki Final Act and to discuss the future of the European process. I was a novice among them, and the conference turned into a "coming out party" for the new Soviet Foreign Minister. Lively human interest showed through the expressions of official courtesy. I sensed sincere good will coming from my colleagues, along with an unconcealed desire to find out what kind of man had joined their circle so unexpectedly. I cannot say that I felt right at home under this scrutiny, but I was taking their measure too. I looked carefully into each face attempting to discern the human being. I tried to remove from my own eyes the ideological lenses that would make any representative of the West look like a crafty enemy. The canonized ideology of antagonism warned me to keep my ears open: "Watch out that they don't fool you or wrap you around their little finger." I was embarrassed by the long-entrenched stereotype of diplomacy, holding that any means, even deceit and fraud, may be used to achieve the necessary end. The mores of the era of the Talleyrands and the Metternichs, even in their modern-day dress, did not square at all with the standards I wanted to uphold. I wanted my partners to trust me as I wanted to trust them. Much of what I am saying has to do with the philosophy I eventually adopted, but much came as well from an impression of specific individuals, and a desire to understand their motives. The one cannot be separated from the other, incidentally. Still, I would like to touch upon the philosophy.

At the negotiation table, I always tried to be seen primarily as a person, and not the personification of a hostile idea. I wanted my partner at least not to feel that some idea stood between us—otherwise, we would not be doing business. I did not back down from my convictions, but at the same time I didn't hold the negotiation hostage to them. Naturally, I had my country's interests uppermost in mind, but I also respected my partner's interests. And I expected the same of him. I was always aware of what divided us, but I tried to discover what united us. Common interests and values would come to the forefront, sweeping aside everything else.

By making universal human values a priority, we obtained a fresh outlook on the world. In this connection the philosophy of peaceful coexistence as a universal principle of international relations took on a different meaning.

Not every reader will understand why the word "universal" carries such weight with me. I should explain that until 1986 the principle of peaceful coexistence was applied only to our relations with potential adversaries. Another principle existed for the relations with our friends and allies: proletarian internationalism, which gave us the right to interfere, even with armed force, in the affairs of our Warsaw Pact allies, for example.

Today the principle operates differently. Since the antagonism between West and East has receded into the past, the building of a new Europe has begun, and the world community has coped with the Persian Gulf crisis, the very term "peaceful coexistence" is insufficient. Now the universal principle of partnership, cooperation, mutual understanding, and joint action comes to the fore. This principle harbors enormous potential for preserving and rebuilding the world while eliminating any differences, whether of class, nationality or religion. As it is incorporated into the living practice of international relations, perhaps this principle will allow us to instill in the new world order a synthesis of all that is best in humanity.

At the Twenty-seventh Party Congress, one of the delegates asked what I saw as the main difference between the interests of the working class and universal human values. I replied that I did not consider the phrasing of the question legitimate. I have never counterpoised class interests to universal human values; I had spoken only of their interrelationship. There are no contradictions between them. The relationship is one of a part to the whole. The priority of universal human interests means that all normal people, regardless of their differences, have an equal stake in peace, prosperity, progress, the health of society and the individual, the deliverance of civilization from nuclear and ecological danger, and a solution to problems of development.

In order to evaluate our national interests correctly and ensure their protection, we must be cognizant of the leading trends and understand the general direction in which humanity is headed. We must realize that each social group, class, nationality, people, and country can realize its aspirations only by relating them to the common good.

If peace and security set the general design for the panorama of the new world order, then the harmony of universal and national interests makes an ideal composition. As each of us brings his national fragment to this fresco, he must see its organic, indissoluble unity with the others. And although, unfortunately, disruptions still occur here and there, they do not imply that the philosophy of the new thinking is bankrupt. In the modern world, such disruptions are the exception, not the rule, and like any pathology they require specific treatment. The most obvious example is the aggression of Iraq against Kuwait, but even here the world community affirmed universal human values, and only after exhausting all political means was compelled to resort to force. We must see the difference between how force used to be applied and how it is used today. This is essentially the difference between lawlessness and law.

The new thinking logically led us to reject antagonism as the basis for foreign policy, to discard ideological clichés, and to deideologize international relations. We did this so that governments could learn to cooperate with each other and respect each other's interests despite differences in ideology, and to look for points in common instead of subjecting their foreign policies to ideological tenets which are often at odds, and are the product of only some part of humanity, be it small or large. Naturally, this understanding of foreign relations does not negate our own world views, but neither does it give us the right to demand this of others.

In reality, any country's policy is based on ideology. The only question is, what kind? A policy can be successful only if the ideology behind it rests upon the principles of goodness, justice, humanism, and spirituality. The preaching of ideological sectarianism and intolerance has never produced anything good, nor will it today.

Pardon a slight digression here. I have always felt discomfort at attempts to link ideology with human rights. In some societies, ideology is like a religion. Every person must be allowed to choose his faith, at least every adult.

It is said that the Soviet people made their choice in October 1917. Yes, it's true that our grandfathers made the revolution. But does that mean they chose what came afterward, even the distortion and misuse of the idea, and outright criminal acts? And is their choice or ours obligatory for our children and grandchildren?

By closing our borders to our own citizens, and screening those allowed to make trips abroad almost like cosmonauts going to the moon, we left people no choice. One choice was considered legitimate: socialism. But if we believe that our ideology is true and is the most advanced, then why did we so fear contacts with representatives of another faith, so to speak? Why did we ban books, jam radio broadcasts, and punish people for looking at the wrong films, listening to the wrong music, and dancing the wrong dances? It was wrong to lock people in the church, never to let them out of the country, claiming that beyond our borders reigned sin and corruption. A person should have the freedom to make and follow his own choice.

To me, de-ideologizing international relations has always meant liberating them from the heavy accumulation of twisted, falsely interpreted ideology, from the elements of ideological extremism and petrified fundamentalism. In general, we need to eliminate the myths that have encumbered them. We must learn to see the world around us as it really is and not as we have been told to see it.

From ancient times, morality and politics have been regarded

as antithetical. Many prominent authorities maintain that "there is
no morality in politics, there are only interests." Many politicians
publicly repudiate Machiavelli but follow his advice in their affairs.
Political "morality" justifies everything that leads to success. But
at the end of the twentieth century, many things cannot be justified, because the former differences over purposes are now increasingly giving way to common goals. True, force has not yet
fallen into disuse, but more and more it is seen as pointless and
immoral. The new thinking has given an impetus to the political
idea that moral criteria take precedence over narrow, selfish considerations of political advantage.

Life itself has taught us this. Now, not a single political decision or diplomatic action can be considered to be in the interests of
the people and the government if it is immoral. Of course, this
general rule does not fit all circumstances. The Persian Gulf crisis
attests to the fairly broad support within Iraq itself for the obviously immoral actions of its leader. One would not have to look far
for an example in our own country of the excesses of immorality
under a banner of the "national idea," raised up by many hands.
But this is an anomaly, an illness, and unless it is cured, a nation
will have no happiness, freedom, or independence. Untreated, it
can be fatal. The new thinking can prevent that.

Here I would again want to digress on a subject unrelated to
politics.

In the 1860s, modern art was born and the Impressionists
appeared on the scene. Their manner of painting was based on new
conceptions of the nature of light. The growth of knowledge and
the understanding that human life would change decisively under
the impact of scientific discoveries gave impetus to a new style, a
different choice of subject, and a different presentation. The Impressionists seemed to be depicting the same old world, but their
canvases conveyed the truth about the new world, a world that
could not remain the same after the invention of new technologies,
spawning a new way of life.

It is interesting to recall how the new artistic thinking was
received by the academicians—of course, without enthusiasm. One
art critic accurately summarized this aesthetic revolution: "When
art is renewed, we are renewed along with it." The same can
perhaps be said of politics.

The old masters will always be with us, because, as W. H.

Auden wrote, "About suffering they were never wrong." But people do not live by fears alone; they need the joy of life as well.

Accepting the new thinking is not easy, just as it is not easy to conquer the inertia of the old within oneself. You come to the new thinking having lived through and absorbed with your mind and heart the experience and lessons of the past. In foreign policy, the new thinking also involves a rejection of the outdated and a reassessment of what had seemed correct for many decades.

First and foremost were the stereotypes of the existence of "the enemy." Confirmed by centuries of war and partitioning of the world, they reflected historical reality. But often the notion of the enemy was artificially cultivated in the interests of ruling regimes and monarchs, passed off as the interests of the nation and the people as a whole. Crooked ideological mirrors distorted the real face of "the enemy" to the point of absurdity, instilling in people fear, hatred, and a readiness to accept the existing order of things as something natural and necessary. When you present your own people with an "enemy," you can force them to bear any privation, make any sacrifice. The moment comes, however, when their reserves of patience are exhausted. Worse than that, the human element is denigrated, the country and the people run the risk of exclusion from the universal civilizing process. That is when the real threat to security arises.

"Whatever is real is rational; whatever is rational is real," Hegel wrote. But if we paraphrase this, does it mean that "whatever is irrational is doomed"? Has the time not come to realize how much irrationality continues to poison our life? And is it not time to oppose it with new, rational ideas that pass the test of universal human morality?

Yes, the modern world exists in a state of complex and subtle balance, among contending interests, centripetal and centrifugal movements. It is variegated and multifaceted, yet single and indivisible from the standpoint of security, which has many aspects today: military-political, economic, humanitarian, cultural, and ecological.

While nuclear weapons exist, national security is a fiction, regardless of the level of armaments.

While effective environmental cooperation is still not established on a global scale, every state is in danger of ruining the physical conditions for its existence. While governments are burdened with crippling debts, and in the absence of a just economic order to guarantee everyone the high standard of living made possible by the present level of technological development, international security is shaky and unreliable. As long as nations do not accept a single standard of respect for the rights of the individual, none of the problems confronting the world community can be successfully resolved, nor can common security be safeguarded.

The logical interconnection of all these links today is such that if one falls out, the whole chain is in danger of collapsing. This must always be remembered, so that centuries-old habits and traditions do not cause humanity to capsize from an overload of narrow and selfishly interpreted national interests.

Someone once said that reason is "terrible, if it does not serve man." But only at the close of this century has it appeared absolutely necessary to organize human life rationally on a global scale, to free it from inherent self-destructive vices. When humanity looks at itself through palisades of nuclear missiles, through holes in the ozone layer, and through the prism of actions by latter-day führers, it recognizes—it must recognize!—that it is a single whole, despite the differences, which calls upon us to preserve what we have in common and what unites us.

Even with all the upheavals of our time, the prevailing drive is still toward the renaissance of humanist ideas, toward the return to the individual and the human scale. The new thinking is a view of the world through man and his interests. "Man is the measure of all things." In that sense, the new thinking is new only in the sense that an orientation toward human welfare has become a greater political imperative. Is this idealism? Perhaps. But if we reject it, we must acknowledge that the only correct policy is one that excludes from its main guidelines the individual, his safety and his welfare, one that sacrifices him to a false and self-serving interpretation of national interests.

That is what happened with the war in Afghanistan. With the endless arms race. With the reallocation of a large portion of the budget to military production. With the imposition on Europe of the psychology of division and other inhumanities with which defenseless humanity has been threatened.

Architects coined the term "human scale." This term does not completely coincide with the term "human dimension" now current among politicians. "Human dimension" presupposes a proportionality between a person and his dwelling, between the environment and its inhabitants. The disruption of this proportion results in discomfort and severe psychological, physical, and social consequences.

The architects of politics often think in categories that leave no room for the human being: "the people," "the country," and "national security," that is, the sum of sublime values, ignore the most important detail, human life. It appears to be taken for granted that a collective approach will guarantee the welfare of each individual. But even in the most prosperous, most intelligently planned, and most beautifully constructed city, many citizens live miserably. Politics should be human-sized. At least they should be comfortable for the individual and should not demand brutally hard adaptation to unbearable conditions, dictated by the requirements of "higher interests."

I realize that this reasoning also sounds idealistic, but what is an ideal if not a goal for which to strive? Unlike the many devastated utopias of our day, this goal is grounded, sensible, and rational, nor does it contravene the traditions of the major belief systems. The more the individual gains from a rational state policy, the more the nation, society, country, and national security stand to gain. If politics is the art of the possible, then it must be inspired by the idea of the impossible in order to transcend the bounds of the ordinary. I am afraid, however, that the architects of policy find it uncomfortable to live in their own buildings, which will never be finished or perfected. The lowest galley slave could not envy the lot of say, James Baker or Hans-Dietrich Genscher, who are so heavily burdened and subjected to such great pressure. But this is the lot of any man who takes upon himself the burden of responsibility. I touch upon this fairly banal topic so as to come nearer to the subject of my narrative, which is the people with whom I had dealings and for whose sake I worked.

On the day I announced my resignation, one of my opponents accused me of withdrawing Soviet troops from Eastern Europe too hastily. As a result, families of servicemen were left in tents pitched right in the snow. The speaker expressed doubt as to whether I could look these people in the eye. But I can. Just as in Afghanistan, I looked in the eyes of many a twenty-year-old boy in army uniform, recoiling inside from what I saw. Just as I looked in the eyes of mothers, filled with pain and tears, whose sons had died or were missing in action in Afghanistan. Perhaps it was the expressions in these human eyes, and not the annual U.N. vote against our military presence in Afghanistan, that strengthened my resolve to do everything in my power to stop the heartless machine of war from crushing the lives of our boys and their parents and, of course, the Afghan people themselves. I cannot forget the look in their eyes, either.

People can go on accusing me of neglecting the "macro-scale," great-power politics, requiring the manipulation of large blocks of state interests. I have always proceeded from the premise that these interests cannot be secured if the "micro-scale," the individual, is constantly ignored.

The story of people living in tents in the snow is a case in point. I am prepared to go live with them in those tents, because I could not stop the war machine in time. This book is an attempt to describe how and why that happened, and to provide an answer to the difficult questions I am asked. I shall return to them at a later point, when I can demonstrate that our foreign policy made human life its cornerstone, and that we deemed it immoral to divide it into "ours" and "theirs."

The figures of our casualties in Afghanistan are widely known. People often refer to them, but are silent for some reason about another horrifying figure: one and a half million Afghans killed. The "human dimension" is single and universal; it is difficult for me to tolerate attempts to use it selectively.

On my assignment, a leader of the intransigent Afghan opposition was asked to facilitate the return of Soviet prisoners of war to their homeland, and he consented. "But just help me learn the fate of my relatives left behind in Kabul," he added. "I haven't had any word of them."

In my view, politicians who forget that people are first of all people, and only afterward the exponents of certain views, have no business in politics.

On the day the Geneva accords on Afghanistan were signed, I must admit that my feelings were mixed and far from joyful. It would seem that I should have been happy. The goal announced at the Twenty-seventh Party Congress had been reached, and the principled political decision made in December 1985 was now realized. It had been an incredibly difficult problem, and if it had not been resolved, perestroika would have lost heavily. Our involvement in the fratricidal Afghan war was perceived by the majority of countries of the world as an effort to exploit regional conflicts to expand our sphere of influence. The presence of our troops in Afghanistan not only hindered relations with many countries but also sowed doubt as to the sincerity of our desire to conduct international affairs in a new way.

Now this was all brought to a close. The coffins of boys who died in the war would stop flowing into the country. In a few months, all our officers and soldiers would come home. There was much cause for rejoicing. But I felt no joy. Outside my airplane window, a range of the Alps faded into the twilight. The stewardess brought wine. One of my aides poured it into glasses. "To today's success!" I could not even take a sip. My heart was heavy. I saw the faces of my friends in Kabul. Now they had no one to rely on except themselves. Could they last after the withdrawal of our forces? How could they be helped to achieve national reconciliation, stop the bloodshed, and restore peace to Afghanistan? Thoughts about the people who had trusted us and who were now left all alone with their bitter enemies would give me no peace. I knew that we would not lessen our political efforts for a peaceful settlement in Afghanistan, but still I could not rid myself of a sense of personal guilt toward my friends.

I suppose I now have the right to make public one particular fact. After our last soldier crossed the Soviet–Afghan border, V. A. Kryuchkov and I once again flew to Kabul. That evening, we were guests of the Nadjibullah family. The city was the target of missile launches, and heavy fighting was under way in a number of key provinces. The echoes seemed to resound in the room, where we guests sat at the table with its modest fare, along with our host, his wife, and their children.

"Perhaps," I began cautiously, "your family would be better off leaving the country? We could help you move to Moscow."

Our hostess answered politely but firmly:

"We would prefer to be killed on the doorsteps of this house rather then die in the eyes of our people by choosing the path of flight from their misfortune. We will all stay with them here to the end, whether it be happy or bitter."

It occurred to me then that ideas and ideals are worth something only if they are imbued with real humanity. I try to avoid injecting special political terms into a discussion of ideals. But I will say that everything we did and are doing now for an Afghan settlement is for the sake of each Afghan, regardless of what camp he is in. That is why we supported Nadjibullah's compromise peace plan for an end to the fratricidal war, the establishment of intra-Afghan dialogue, the holding of free elections, and the creation of a broad-based government. For this reason, we are reactivating trade, renewing cooperation on facilities we had helped to build, bringing back specialists despite the continuing hostilities, establishing direct ties between Afghan provinces and Soviet republics, and participating in the U.N. program to provide humanitarian and economic aid to Afghanistan. For this reason, we are trying to bring together Soviet and American positions on Afghanistan, which has been made possible by the qualitatively new nature and level of relations between the United States and the U.S.S.R. since the end of the cold war, just as it was possible before it began.

On that long-ago day in July 1985 when I first met my foreign colleagues in Helsinki, I passionately wanted each one of them to accept my chosen criteria. I wanted us to talk among ourselves as people with common concerns: peace for our families, the future of our children and grandchildren, and the welfare of our fellow citizens. I did not want the walls of mistrust and fear to divide us.

My wish was destined to come true. With almost all of my colleagues, I was able to establish personal contacts that greatly enabled me at least to understand them, if not to improve the relations between our countries. I am grateful to each of them for that. I would like very much to mention each one by name. But how can I do that, if each one deserves not just kind words but a conscientious account of the problems we tackled in difficult, but always honest, cooperation?

I suppose I should say something anyway, and I'll begin with George Shultz. I don't know if he is aware of the colorful yarns spun in my homeland about our first meeting. I have always been blessed with fellow Georgian myth-makers to weave intriguing legends and folk-tales about my life. Some are good and others evil. Some I like, and others, not so much. But there is one charming little story about George and me that is very close to my heart, because it reflects human expectations and the people's dreams.

Once upon a time in Helsinki, so this story goes, I placed my

Georgian *kinzhal* (sword) on the table in front of the U.S. Secretary of State and said:

"I have disarmed. Now it's your turn."

Alas, this was not a true story, but something that did happen is as good as any legend. At our second meeting, which took place in New York in September 1985, I said to Shultz:

"Much in the world depends on the state of Soviet–American relations. And they in turn depend on the relations that you and I have. I intend to do business as your honest and reliable partner, and if you wish, to be your friend."

Shultz suddenly stood up from the table and extended his palm:

"Here is my hand. Give me yours!"

Ever since, I always felt his firm handshake. Sometimes it weakened for reasons that did not depend on us, circumstances related to the serious differences in our countries' positions, unforeseen situations that arose in spite of us to bring elements of frustration and irritation into our meetings. But the obstacles were never stronger than our mutual desire to listen to and understand each other and to achieve a mutually acceptable outcome. That was how it was at the most dramatic moments: after Reykjavik, at the final stages of the drafting of the treaty on IRBMs, and before the signing of the Geneva accords on Afghanistan. Even at those moments, we always found a way to communicate our positions like human beings and to search for ways out of whatever situation had developed.

Gradually, our contacts moved out of the official framework. Perhaps for the first time in the history of relations between our two countries, the foreign ministers of the U.S.S.R. and the United States visited each other's homes and met each other's children and grandchildren. Never at a loss for ideas, George organized family boat trips on the Potomac; arranged a purely American-style party with banjo playing, one of the tunes being "Oh, Georgia, Georgia";[1] and surprised me at the State Department with the magnificent Yale Russian Chorus, which sang the Georgian folk song "Mravalzhamier." I made every effort to repay him. When we sat at the negotiation table—either surrounded by colleagues or one on one—nothing prevented us from remaining

[1] Possibly "Georgia on My Mind."—Trans.

ourselves in outlining our positions and trying to bring them closer. If one of us said "I can't go any farther than that," the other understood: "That's how it really is. He isn't bluffing."

Shultz's successor was worthy in all respects. Although a man of an entirely different make-up, James Baker missed no opportunity to place his contacts with Soviet colleagues on a footing of maximum mutual trust. We first met in Vienna, if memory serves, at the opening of the talks on conventional arms limitation. It was his debut, and he performed magnificently. He gave an intelligent speech, but somewhat tough in comparison with Shultz's manner. Yet afterward he came up to our delegation with his wife, Susan, and said that he was looking forward to a fruitful collaboration. I think his hope was justified.

Thanks to Jim, both the geography and the content of our meetings were expanded. We began to open up our countries to each other, to show how people live and what matters to them. In Jackson Hole, Wyoming, we came to the conclusion that the U.S.S.R. and the United States were shifting from confrontation to cooperation. And so it was in the ancient city of Zagorsk outside of Moscow; in Irkutsk, on Lake Baikal; and finally in Baker's native state of Texas. That was to be the last meeting before my resignation, and he invited my wife and me to the home of his elderly mother. Of course, I was very touched by the gesture.

After my resignation, my wife received a letter from Susan Baker. "We are crying and praying for you," she wrote. I had no reason to doubt the sincerity of Jim's and Susan's feeling toward us. If anything, Jim could have had some doubts about my honesty, in connection with an unpleasant story I do not intend to tell here. Since I was not to blame for it, however I preferred not to undermine our business alliance with mistrust. If things had continued as they were going, I would not have been able to look my partner in the eye. If you like, this is also one of the reasons for my resignation.

Lying is always unproductive. It is more profitable to be honest. I was guided by this principle in my relations with all my partners. I trust they paid me in the same coin. Otherwise, we would not have achieved what we did, laying the groundwork for a new security structure and collectively resisting aggression in the Persian Gulf.

All these years, I met with my colleagues so frequently because it was necessary. For example, Hans-Dietrich Genscher and I met more than a dozen times just during the period when an agreement on German unification was being prepared. The geography of our meetings extended from Brest to Windhoek, Namibia. They contained tense negotiations, sometimes punctuated by head-on collisions, over the future of Germany and Europe and the interconnected issue of Soviet security.

I have every reason to have the highest regard for the high level of professionalism and the purely human qualities of Genscher and Dumas, Hurd and Andreotti (the Italian Foreign Minister at the early stage of my work); Qian Qichen, Gianni De Michelis, Joseph Clark, Francisco Ordoñez, Nakayama, and others. In recent years I have had the good fortune to speak with the greatest political and state figures. Each one merits a separate description, and I hope I can do them justice in the future. For now, I would like to reiterate that despite all the differences in our positions, we strove for a common denominator; without which the best ways to secure our own interests could not be found.

We argued, of course, but never so that the debate turned into a confrontation. If a country wishes to renounce antagonism and move toward cooperation, then the people who represent that country in international affairs must be the first to do so. Without professional and personal refinement, a broad view of the state of affairs, and impartiality in assessing facts and events, this will not come about.

I believe it was Bertholt Brecht who said that thought is capable of providing an almost sensual pleasure. No matter how difficult our official meetings, I gained pleasure from conversing with my partners, so uncommon were the form and content of their self-expression.

One more precious gift I value highly, and which is not granted to everyone, is a sense of humor. In my observation, a sense of humor is an indispensable feature of a vivid individuality, the truest indicator of an internal sense of freedom. When I am asked about the purpose of a joke in a serious discussion—is humor a person's inborn trait or a professional "diplomatic tool"?—I reply that I like it when a person does business with a smile and gets the point of a witty remark. We are, after all, just people, looking for ways to get to each other's hearts and minds, and diplomats are people who are doubly sensitive. We achieve little with dour solemnity and immobile facial muscles.

True, there are times when you are just not up to joking and smiling. I don't think I smiled once during my last meeting with my Iraqi colleague, Tarik Aziz, when I told him the possible consequences if Iraq did not get out of Kuwait. And Aziz looked grim himself, not at all as he had at our earlier meetings in Baghdad, Basra, and Moscow.

A smile is evidence of harmony, an indicator of a normal situation. If you want to smile, then you have no choice but to find agreement with your partners. And for that you must get to know them better. Yes, Mr. Genscher and I spent dozens of hours at the negotiation table, and I think we got to know each other fairly well. But he revealed very unexpected sides to me in Brest, at the memorial stone with the name of my brother killed in the war, and in Halle, in the house where he was born and spent his childhood.

The same was true of M. Roland Dumas. Our talks covered the most varied subjects, from the new quality of Soviet–French relations to the art of Henri Rousseau and Niko Pirosmani. I was impressed with his great knowledge, his modest refinement, and the nobility that shone through his every movement. Yet the entire subtlety and breadth of his heart was revealed to me only after my resignation, when he made an unusually thoughtful gesture addressed to me personally.

It is sad, of course, to realize that I am not likely to meet my former colleagues as often as before. But still, I have been fortunate. Our relationships were beneficial to the world and to our peoples.

The human scale I proclaim requires honesty. People are worse off because of perestroika, our hawks contend, and they cite facts that are difficult to dispute. Bitter conflicts between nationalities; bloody clashes on ethnic grounds, threatening to turn the Soviet Union into another Lebanon; the danger of destabilization; the impoverished lot of Soviet citizens, exacerbated by economic stagnation; and the environmental crisis—all these are the sad reality of our time. But how much is the new thinking to blame? And how legitimate is it to blame our internal ailments on foreign policy?

I submit that while this cannot be taken seriously, it is not harmless. Here is something both serious and dangerous: It is not the new thinking that is to blame for our internal cataclysms, but an inability or a refusal to follow the new principles in our domestic affairs. Today the compulsion to act in contravention of them by using the old, mostly violent methods, the renunciation of which abroad has been one of the main foreign policy achievements of perestroika, is all too obvious.

If foreign policy is "guilty" of anything, it is overcoming the country's isolation from the rest of the world and providing our citizens with the chance to see for themselves that it is better off, more tolerant, and more humane than the champions of ideological messianism have painted it. Foreign policy freed Soviet man of his innate xenophobia, just as it freed society of the image of an external enemy and turned the "opponent" into a "partner." It showed him that abroad, where supposedly "man is a wolf to man," people want to live and do live by normal human laws. It showed him that material sufficiency and life's blessings, attained through judicious enterprise founded on a sense of personal freedom and the ability to work productively, did not at all strip those people of their humanity or ability to empathize with others' troubles.

What about the brain drain and the flight of labor, the long lines of people wishing to travel abroad standing outside foreign consulates? We should not confuse cause and effect. If a "citizen" (a classic example of a distorted concept) has too long been deprived of the status of a human being, the only thing that could keep him in his homeland is the granting of that status. But the system could not or would not give it to him, just as it could not or would not give him many other things. Now, when people refuse to go on living in the old way, the system blames everything but itself for the brain drain. It is most interesting that the system's experts are not proposing any sensible alternatives to the new thinking, unless we regard as alternatives the fist and nostalgic appeals to the class approach. Accustomed to crushing the "human dimension" with impunity, the system is not capable of reversing itself for the benefit of its renewal.

I recall the tragic days of the Armenian earthquake, when the people all over the world showed their sympathy. We—the foreign policy community included—did not conceal from the world the wounds and ruins of Armenia and allowed international aid to flood into the republic. Aside from everything else, we showed that our enunciation of universal human values was not just empty propaganda. We are a country of people, and not an empire of monsters.

So who should be blamed for what? Foreign policy, for mobilizing a huge international effort to help suffering Armenia? Or the system, which was incapable of rationally and effectively distributing the aid to help the victims?

It is unreasonable to blame foreign policy for the instability inside the country and the raging ethnic conflicts. Perestroika activated the human factor; opposition to it deprived the human factor of its proper political course. The transition from the universities of totalitarianism to the academy of democracy, which was too fast and disregarded people's actual state of mind and the level of political culture, was fraught with painful excesses and costs. Democratic institutions were used to make an overt grab for power, and the entire arsenal of totalitarian expedients and means was shamelessly exploited: the persecution of dissenters, the labeling of "enemies," the brandishing of ideological clichés, the application of brutal, uncompromising force. The internal consolidation did not take place, even as the outer consolidation was showing noticeable movement. Against the background of such an obvious discrepancy, foreign policy was an easy target for domestic sharpshooters pursuing an internal political agenda. I fear, however, that they know now what they do: Such indiscriminate sniping can undermine the international position of the country and, more important for me, hinder the movement toward a new hierarchy of values, crowned by human life.

These thoughts would be unbearable if I were not persuaded that "the human dimension"—the "golden mean" of politics, the "gold reserve" of every nation—is still preserved intact in our country. The imperious subjugation of the individual to the system, the harsh repressions, the replacement of moral principles with the imperatives of "revolutionary expediency"—none of these have been able to undermine it. And while it still exists and continues to manifest itself vigorously, my hope is still alive.

Policy is made by people. At least, those who make policy ought to be people. But that is only one side of the coin. The other side is that policy is made for people. "We weep and pray for you," an American woman wrote me. I would regard these lines as a unique manifestation of humanity, had I not received thousands of others like them. This flood of mail astounded me. The living human soul radiated through them, yearning for truth and justice, expressing itself in words more appropriate for prayers or confessions. I was shaken as people appealed to my conscience, speaking of God, our homeland, their children, and their relatives, living and dead. Klanya Slezkina of Magnitogorsk sent me a telegram, and the fact that she signed it with her nickname, customarily used only in a close circle of friends, warmed my heart. A Muscovite woman named Filatova wrote: "I write you on behalf of ten thousand of my friends killed in the war, the soldiers of the Second Division of the People's Volunteer Corps." Kulyukin, a "veteran of all the wars," to use his actual phrase, wrote me about all his children, grandchildren, and great-grandchildren. I received mail from the writer Viktor Konetsky; a retired schoolteacher named Khmelnitskaya; pupils from a school in Zagorsk; Colonel Skipalsky; the actor Oleg Basilashvili; the Leonov family, who survived the Leningrad blockade; and so many others I did not know. These are the very people in whose name policy is made. They are policy's main measure, which has yet to enter the flesh and blood of our life, because for too long the human being, a noble-sounding idea, was in reality the means and not the end of society and government. We were too severely indoctrinated—and indoctrinated others—with the idea that the interests of the state were paramount, and the interests of the individual and the citizen would be fitted in later.

Now that this disharmony manifests itself in the tragic disruptions of our national life, we see there is no other way to strengthen the state than by strengthening the individual. We must affirm humanity through the harmonic combination of the interests of the citizen and those of society. Only politics imbued with a strong human element can do this.

That is the message of the telegrams and letters I received after my resignation. Taking them as a sign of hope and faith, I have decided that my book cannot be only an answer to my critics, but must also be an accounting to the people for whom my colleagues and I did our work.

CHAPTER FOUR

We Carried the Ball Down the Whole Field

There is no sorrier sight than a guttering fire. The dying coals crumble into ashes, a little warmth still wafts from the embers, but as the minutes go by the cold creeps up on you. If you are lucky you have a person nearby who knows how to stir up the cold ashes, find that miraculously preserved spark, and kindle it into a cheerful flame.

There are many fireplaces in the State Department, but the biggest and the best is in the private office of the Secretary of State. I recall many long and difficult hours at that hearth.

George Shultz was among the first with whom I was able to make common cause. He loved to have talks by a blazing fire, both at work and at home. He worked at home as well, combining discussion with his duties as a gracious host and cook. He could whip up a superb barbecue. I was impressed with how well he knew the art of fire-building and his ability to keep the flame going. He did this masterfully and with unconcealed enjoyment. And I had the pleasure of watching him arrange the logs and handle the tongs so that the hearth, like a cathedral organ, sang its powerful, bright, and passionate song.

On a bright Washington day, sharp flashes of light danced on the walls through half-drawn blinds, the sun reflecting off the wings of airplanes taking off from a nearby airport. The exuberant green of Arlington Hill and the bright white columns of the memorials soothed the eye, calming the soul with a landscape of peace.

An idyll? Apparently not! I do not know a single one of our diplomats or military people who could boast of having an easy time dealing with the Americans. They drive a hard bargain, as I can testify from my own experience. Yes, I shook hands with Shultz, and it was not a ritual protocol gesture meant just for the cameras. But I cannot say that our dialog unfolded easily or simply.

Several years later in Rome, Giulio Andreotti told me how surprised he was to learn from Shultz that he had discussed criminal legislation with Shevardnadze. "So it's got to the point," the Italian Premier remarked, "where Eduard and George are getting into that kind of area. It must mean they are getting along personally. And Shultz, after all, is a very hard man."

Yes, that's right. But before matters reached a stage of normal human cordiality, we had occasion to get on each others' nerves terribly. I would have to say that character flaws were the least to blame for this. Such was the nature of Soviet–American relations themselves at that time: nervous, suspiciously hostile, vengeful. It determined the rules of the game: endless, relentless pressure all over the field. The field was the whole world, which was in a constant fever from a game that could break out in fist fights (as did happen in various parts of the world) or even a general melée.

Both we and the Americans declared the anomaly of antagonism to be the norm.

The Geneva rendezvous of Reagan and Gorbachev in November 1985 was preceded by a more than six-year hiatus in Soviet–American summits. One of my good friends, a columnist, put it very aptly: A hiatus is hardly a vacuum. This one was filled with confrontations, the arms race, and mounting tension.

That was the harsh reality. But the phantoms of an external menace, the dangers of mutual annihilation, and subversive activity were deliberately cultivated in politics, propaganda, and public opinion. And we were not the only ones to do so. For the United States and the West, the "Soviet threat" was also a convenient means for solving certain problems.

I would not want to delve deeply into history now to unearth the roots of incompatibility and hostility. Mountains of books have already been written on that subject, and more than enough mutual recriminations have been made. For the sake of my thesis, I must briefly touch upon the role of nuclear weapons. The appearance of nuclear arms and delivery systems immediately introduced a new element into East–West relations: the problem of mutual annihilation.

For Americans and others in the West, the awareness that their countries could be annihilated as a result of nuclear war was psychologically a greater shock than for Soviet citizens.

The quote from Auden about the Old Masters is especially apt here: "About suffering they understand everything." Before the new thinking was established in politics, the "old masters"— government figures, columnists, the military, political scientists, and artists—went to great lengths to depict the horrors of nuclear war and the catastrophe it entails.

In both countries, horrendous scenes of nuclear apocalypse were painted, and ideology assigned to everyone the roles of "saints," "sinners," and mere mortals or, in other words, the doomed. Such a construct is required to recreate the political atmosphere of the early 1980s, when the peril of war loomed over daily life in both East and West.

It was in such an atmosphere that the Strategic Defense Initiative took root. It alone could destroy everything that had been achieved in limiting strategic offensive arms and antimissile systems.

In short, by 1985 the situation was extremely gloomy. April of that year produced a ray of hope. We in the Soviet leadership were acutely aware of the need for fundamental changes in policy and a quest for alternatives.

Naturally, Soviet–American affairs were our central concern. But they seemed to be at such a hopeless stalemate that our ruling circles, as we like to call them, grew determined to remove the obstructions that had appeared in foreign policy because of poor relations with the United States. As a kind of end run, we came up with the idea of focusing more on Europe and intensifying our contacts with other countries.

Such a course was justified in some ways. Up to that point we had actually operated within narrow confines, concentrating our resources on relatively few problems and regions. But still, neither we nor the Americans were prepared to say anything new. They were encumbered by too many things at that time. There seemed to be no way out, except to slash the Gordian knot—and destroy the world in the process.

American sanctions imposed because of our involvement in Afghanistan were having their effect. The question of political dissidents in the Soviet Union and human rights practices in general was a sore point. Negotiations on nuclear weapons in space were stalled, with a major controversy over the fate of the ABM Treaty. No solution was in sight concerning the deployment by both sides of medium-range nuclear missiles in Europe; worse, the Soviet Union was accused of violating existing agreements on strategic arms limitation.

In such circumstances, a simple determination to clear away the huge obstacles was not enough; more complicated than that was determining where to begin.

No matter where we turned, we came up against the fact that we would achieve nothing without normalization of Soviet–American relations. We did some hard thinking, at times sinking into despair over the impasse.

In 1985 personal and psychological difficulties surfaced that seemed insurmountable. It was almost always a conversation between the deaf. All Soviet–American contacts began with mutual recriminations and accusations. It was a well-traveled road that led nowhere. We and the Americans were divided by walls built out of the rubble of distrust and the stones of ideology. We Soviet representatives were not the only ones guilty of extremely ideologized attitudes. Personal meetings with President Reagan—and I had quite a few, about a dozen—gave me ample grounds for saying this. I hope he will not be offended at my recollection of our first meetings. He began just about every one with a reading of a "bill of indictment" against the Soviet Union, whose charges were crammed with loosely interpreted quotations from the founders of Marxism. He also made liberal use of Alexis de Tocqueville and the American Founding Fathers. The number one man in the United States looked at our country through the prism of ideology and saw it as the "Evil Empire." To be disabused of such a view, he would have had to begin seeing a country made up of real people—the most exact form of political truth. At that time, he still had a long way to go, and in the beginning we were not much farther along ourselves. I retorted with my own salvos of ideological fire; for I knew there were no absolutely guilty or innocent governments, and rich, prosperous America, the "fiend of imperialism," it seemed to me, was no exception.

I had the impression that President Reagan did not quite take my statements at face value. I could read the expression on his face: "Wait a minute, am I hearing this right?" The grip of stereotypes is very tenacious. I had a feeling that the current occupant of the White House very much wanted to figure us out. After talks in the Cabinet room, he invited us to another room with a luncheon table, where we spent two more hours of lively, pointed discussion, which was fortunately spiced with a rare pinch of humor, including political humor, Neither of us held back.

An unfailing participant in these very peculiar "crossfire" negotiations was George Bush.

In the ideological sense, we were worthy of each other. The problem was to rid ourselves of this dubious worthiness and to take on new qualities. But where to begin? My entire hope rested on the innate common sense of the Americans. Surely somebody among my new counterparts would realize that we could not go on like this. Besides our common obstacles, we also had common interests and a common responsibility. Like Diogenes, I could have exclaimed when asked what I was seeking: "An honest man!" I found not just one man but many who recognized the simple truth that it was futile for our countries to be enemies and that it was vitally necessary to cooperate.

Ambassador Thomas J. Watson was a guest in my Moscow home recently. I deeply respect this outstanding American, whose heroic life's story is so closely connected to the history of my country and with its tragic wartime chapters. I was especially pleased to learn that we think alike.

"Signs of a falling standard of living have begun to appear in our country," the seasoned politician and diplomat said. "We have suddenly found that infant mortality is rising in the United States, and despite our wealth and our superior level of health care. Unfortunately, few in our country are aware that this is a consequence of the arms race. And it's the same for you. By taking the chief brunt of the arms race on ourselves, the United States and the U.S.S.R. are beginning to lose the competition in other areas."

Nodding in agreement with Ambassador Watson, I cited the

example of the Federal Republic of Germany and Japan. While we were competing in the production and stockpiling of state-of-the-art weapons, they, freed from this burden, surged ahead of us. Both of us have lost the arms race, I said.

I could have added that in our economy only the military–industrial complex has operated at peak performance, thriving at the country's expense, and has made it possible for the country to entertain illusions of its own might and power. But suddenly it has dawned on us that real power is something much more than nuclear warheads.

But that is another theme that will resound throughout this book. It is time to return to the conversation about common sense and those in the United States who have it.

I repeat: I did not lack for such people, and the first among them was George Shultz.

By the time of our first meetings, the flames in the fireplace of Soviet–American relations were guttering, the coals turning to ash. We had to stir up the embers, blow on them, and let the sparks fly. And that is what we did.

An unprecedented number of Soviet–American summits were held in five years—seven—and there were countless meetings at the ministerial level. Shultz and I lost count somewhere around thirty-five or thirty-seven meetings. My personal meetings with James Baker numbered in the dozens. These statistics would not say anything by themselves if they did not reflect the growing intensity of the Soviet–American dialog and, most important, the qualitative changes taking place in relations.

I think we could dispense with a chronology of the new Soviet–American relations. Those who wish to refresh their memory may look it up in the appropriate reference books. But as I now reach into my own memory, I draw forth alarms and joys unseen by the world, the foretastes and afterthoughts connected with the perestroika of the Soviet–American dialog.

■ ■ ■

Even before 1985 occasional periods in our relations with the United States were like windows through which the sun shone. We were able to conclude useful agreements, say, in limiting nuclear testing, strategic weaponry, and antimissile systems. Great hopes were tied to the years of "détente."

These periods of probing and discovery were enormously important for Soviet–American relations. Summits and lower-level meetings took place more frequently, negotiations were already under way or were being initiated on many issues involving security. We set about looking for an agreement on antisatellite systems, the arms trade, and a reduction of military activity in the Indian Ocean. We drafted and concluded various agreements, some of which, however, were not ratified and others of which lapsed or were not implemented for various reasons.

But in spite of all this—with the probable exception of the five years related to the Soviet invasion of Afghanistan—the frequency of contacts, negotiations, consultations, and visits grew steadily.

The potential for moving forward had built up over the years but until the beginning of perestroika in our country the opportunity was frozen.

For us—I must be frank here—one factor always prevented the development of relations with the United States, and with the West as a whole. That was the primacy of the doctrine that ideological struggle between the two social and political systems is inevitable. Any agreement, any attempt to improve our relations with the United States immediately foundered on this obstacle. In the period of "détente" at the start of the 1970s, Party ideologues had to work overtime to reconcile the warming of relations with the United States with the old hidebound dogmas. Then, as before, dogma triumphed. The ideologues came out with the conclusion that in moments of warmer relations the ideological struggle must not subside. On the contrary, it must be waged more fiercely.

To be honest, I cannot figure out how to make friends with a person and at the same time carry on an implacable struggle against him. Even long before perestroika, our propaganda and our policies (at times it was impossible to tell them apart) would get more and more entangled by trying to reconcile their contradictory ideological tenets. However no intellectually and politically tenable formulation was forthcoming. That was the kind of contradiction from which we had to find a theoretical and practical way out.

By the time I made my appearance "on the field," ministerial meetings had developed their own traditions, their own rules of the game, so to speak. The old hands tried to teach them to me. As I understood it, tradition required that every question be disputed, whether or not there was any point in doing so. It was considered especially important to insist on a "correct" agenda for such a meeting. This last rule was dictated by the fact that our positions were quite vulnerable on questions of human rights, on Afghanistan, and on certain other conflicts. Our delegation felt more confident in arguments about the necessity of nuclear disarmament.

I was probably not playing by the rules when, if I recollect, during the second meeting with George Shultz, I proposed that from then on we begin our negotiations with questions of human rights observance.

My talks with Shultz concerned four groups of issues: disarmament, regional conflicts, human rights, and bilateral relations. Later, when James Baker took the post of Secretary of State, on his initiative, a "fifth basket" was included on the agenda for our meetings: transnational problems, which meant natural disasters, the war against drugs and epidemics, international terrorism, and so on. We enlisted the appropriate institutions of our countries and foreign partners and drew up a broad plan of action.

I think my "preemptive game" surprised George. Human rights had been the Americans' favorite hobbyhorse, and a taboo for us. Suddenly, here was the Soviet minister making a move like this. After a while my suggestion became our tradition, steering our talks, to use his words, onto a two-way street.

It immediately freed us from many fruitless, unnecessary arguments. The formal approach was not the only thing that changed. We responded with deeds to the many requests at that time from the American side to review individual and family cases. In time, we ourselves began to raise questions that were hardly comfortable for the Americans.

I must admit that at first the change in disposition met with little understanding on our side of the table. Habit is second nature. The consideration of human rights issues had long been blocked with the argument that it was our internal affair, that we had always acted and would continue to act in accordance with our own laws and regulations. We did not need to be shown how to behave.

I had my own counterargument: the priorities proclaimed by the highest leadership, the necessity of following stated principles. We are building a state based on laws, I said, and in such a state the rights of man is not an empty phrase. Laws had to be changed, and for that we had to change the attitude toward freedom and the rights of the individual.

Early on in perestroika, resistance was strong. Statements about human rights and freedoms remained on paper since many of our powerful opponents "could not forgo their principles." Their logic followed the former regimen. It was one thing to make declarations, but let Andrei Sakharov and other prisoners of conscience serve out their sentences. Let the number of refusenik cases pile up, and let the divided families stay divided. Let the "loony bins" keep on working, and not a whisper from anyone about giving international experts access to these prison "hospitals." What about the stripping of citizenship and expulsion from the country of writers and artists? They are renegades, and good riddance.

It cost immense efforts to bring back from exile and banishment several outstanding scientists, writers, and theater directors—honest, conscientious people whose only offense had been refusing to accept the canon of violence and falsehood. But it was even harder to restore the good name of the country where the best people had been treated that way.

It was difficult to persuade even my colleagues on the simplest point: Since we had signed the Helsinki Final Act and had assumed obligations under international conventions and agreements, we had thereby acknowledged the right of other participants in these agreements to inquire into all issues and to insist that we observe the obligations we had undertaken. By that time it had become perfectly obvious to me that the human dimension in international security was crucial. But many of our partners had yet to believe in the sincerity of my statements on that score.

At the opening of the Vienna meeting,[2] I proposed holding an international conference on humanitarian problems in Moscow. That had been preceded by stormy debates in the Politburo. More people disagreed with me than I had expected. Meanwhile, I was convinced that the conference was essential in order to show the country and the world how far we intended to go and, beyond that, to provide an impetus for democratization and the perestroika of legislation in everything relating to human affairs.

[2] In November 1986, a follow-up meeting to review the Helsinki Final Act opened in Vienna, attended by the thirty-five signatories.—Trans.

The discrepancy between word and deed had come to the fore. People did not trust us. How many times before had various statements been made by the political leadership, a certain line of action proclaimed, while everything remained unchanged?

The problem is deeply rooted. For a whole range of reasons that did not always have to do with us, agreements with the "bourgeoisie" or with the "imperialists" were always regarded in our country as a necessary evil at best, but more often as a means to gain time, a tactical maneuver. I myself often encountered cases in which executive agencies either did not know about or did not acknowledge signed agreements and valid political contracts that required those very agencies to take clearly defined actions. An ideological struggle was on, and any means were fair. The main thing was to protect your goalposts. In a game between such teams there are no referees, at least none that can penalize the players or kick them off the field. Of course, there is world public opinion, but for the mighty it is not customary to take it seriously. The image of the Soviet Union in the eyes of the world was of little real concern. Some obsequious client, a "prominent figure" could always be found who would praise Soviet peace initiatives and condemn American imperialism.

The difference between ideological struggle and psychological warfare continues to be a mystery to me. The former is what we waged, and we were always right. The latter is what the West waged, and we denounced it vigorously.

For the sake of fairness it must be said that both in the United States and in the West forces were operating—and continue to operate—for whom there are no honest rules.

I cannot recall a time, especially in the earliest years, when my meetings with Shultz were not complicated by some unexpected incident, some scandalous affair. I even began to suspect that each time we had a chance to move forward, someone would find a way to cloud the situation, to toss some unpleasant issue onto the negotiation table.

This had happened in the past, and was the reason why little could be achieved. George and I made it a rule to remove any complications no matter what happened. We spent many hours, meeting either late at night or at the beginning of negotiations, but we did not give up seeking a mutually acceptable resolution to the problems that arose. And invariably we found it.

Looking back, I see that this experience of major battles over petty and personal situations helped us to establish the necessary confidence that we could talk things out and trust each other.

American football, they tell me, involves two kinds of play: either the forward pass, which, if successful, will gain dozens of yards at once, or carrying the ball in your hands, conquering ground a yard at a time. George Shultz and I carried the ball of Soviet–American relations toward a common goal. It was physically, intellectually, and psychologically hard work.

The first attempt to complete a pass was made at the summit in Reykjavik. I will remind the reader that the idea for the summit arose in the hiatus that had occurred in Soviet–American relations after the meeting in Geneva, when the two sides announced that nuclear war should never be unleashed and that there are no victors in such a war. But somebody tried to trip us up right before the meeting in Iceland. In order not to stumble on the "Daniloff affair," Shultz and I needed almost twenty hours of negotiations.[3] Reykjavik would never have taken place if we had not resolved this "issue" first.

I will never forget the fall of 1986, Reykjavik, and the talks in the Hofdi Mansion. When the Soviet delegation, headed by Mikhail Gorbachev, came out for the concluding press conference, our faces, as they told us back home, expressed our state more eloquently than any words. We had been one step away from agreements capable of transforming the world, but that step had not been taken!

A film was made in the West about this summit. People say that it accurately portrays the drama of the negotiations. I do not know. Probably the genres of literature and art have yet to plow the virgin land of recent political events. This is a matter for the future. But as for the genres of current political reporting and talk shows, with analysis hot on the heels of events, their masters hastened to declare Reykjavik a failure.

But was it?

---

[3] Nicholas Daniloff, a reporter for *U.S. News and World Report,* had been arrested by the KGB on trumped-up charges of espionage. The United States and the U.S.S.R. eventually arranged an agreement whereby Daniloff was released and allowed to return home, a Soviet citizen suspected of espionage in custody in the United States was returned to the U.S.S.R., and Yury Orlov, a physicist and human rights activist who was a political prisoner then in Siberian exile, was released and sent to the United States.—Trans.

In the Icelandic capital, the leaders of our governments, Gorbachev and Reagan, could not keep their hands on the ball that they themselves had passed so far forward. From today's vantage point, I think that perhaps it was a good thing that the meeting in Reykjavik ended as it did. After all, the very attempt by the two leaders to make a quick, long-distance gain frightened many people and activated forces that were alarmed by a rapprochement between the U.S.S.R. and the United States.

Nevertheless, the meeting in Reykjavik had enormous significance and exerted a strong influence on our perceptions of the dimensions of what was possible in Soviet–American relations and in world politics.

But these possibilities could hardly be explored, because there was a lack of trust in relations between East and West based on not only the perception of the intentions of each side and the predictability of its behavior, but also the machinery for verification and control.

■ ■ ■

Throughout postwar history, the question of verification occupied a central place in Soviet–American relations. As a rule, it was cynically used by each country in the propaganda war. Our refusal to accept verification and control measures ought not to be attributed entirely to our desire to gain strategic advantages. Rather, it was basically an effort to hide our weaknesses and inadequacies. The obsession with secrecy had an economic aspect too: Under the guise of secrecy, the statistics of production could be distorted, and economic indicators nudged in the necessary direction.

There were also more prosaic reasons. It was easier, say, to "close" a whole city than to clean up a local train station or repair a hotel. I believe this syndrome of secrecy had to be overcome, not only for foreign policy considerations but in order to establish a normal economy and a comfortable domestic life.

I do not know if my American partners understood this. Their efforts went in another direction. Ronald Reagan even delved into Russian folklore. He recited the Russian proverb "Trust but verify!" so often that he seemed not only to have adopted the saying as his own but also to hold monopoly on its message. Like a battering ram, the Americans beat the question of verification against our walls and, shaking them, convinced the world that the great

cause of disarmament was powerless in the face of the closed nature of the Soviet system. But as soon as we ourselves raised the
idea of monitoring, the "monopolists" scuttled backward. It turned
out that the Americans would not welcome inspection of their war-
ships.

"Our sailors don't like being verified," George Shultz told me.

"As if our missile engineers loved it themselves!" I retorted.

Nobody likes it when someone interferes in his business. If
one loves the world a little better than oneself, however, one can
accede to such an imposition. All the armed forces, including the
naval forces, should be a subject of negotiations, I told my partners. I am convinced of that even now.

Among Reagan's many good qualities, I was especially fond of
his sense of humor. He knew many jokes and was an excellent
raconteur. Every time the question of verification came up, he
would say in Russian, *"Doveryai, no proveryai!"* ("Trust, but verify!"), in a jocular way. Maybe he had a point. In laughter, mankind distances itself from its faults.

One of the main achievements of recent years was the universal recognition of the idea of verification, whereby confidence-
building measures and the possibility of monitoring are organically
combined as an unconditional norm of political reliability.

Sometimes it is not so much the declaration of some highly
effective idea that wins the day, as it is the ability to accept and
implement it. Thus we who had from infancy grown accustomed to
taboos and secrecy gained a very important victory in making
verification a genuine means to a new détente. I had always wanted
it to become a comprehensive means. Alas, this has not yet come
about.

At various disarmament forums much is said about openness
in military affairs and about the necessity of knowing precisely
where every motorized rifle or airborne battalion is stationed and
where it will be deployed. Inspectors are prepared to peer even
into army kitchen kettles in order to make sure that the right kind
of kasha is being cooked. But we must move from isolated measures of trust and glasnost in international relations to a global
policy of openness, which would become an integral part of universal security and international peace.

In Wyoming, where in September 1989 Secretary of State
James Baker proposed holding the next round of the "Open Skies"

talks outdoors, under the open sky, the weather decided to favor us. There was neither wind nor rain, nor was the sun beating down too hard. In that regard, I want to say just one thing: The idea of "open skies" is good only in good international weather, and the prerequisites for that have been created.

In recent years great strides have been made in understanding that openness is the principal factor in any sort of progress—intellectual, material, or social. Security, long an arena for a two-sided game of hide-and-seek, has not been overlooked in this process. A historical threshold was crossed when all the European governments accepted the principle of on-site inspection at the Stockholm talks.[4] Now this principle is being applied in practice through monitoring the destruction of nuclear missiles and other confidence-building measures. So far, not a single complaint has been heard that the inspections and verification have compromised anyone's security.

The success and usefulness of verification are so certain that its application has markedly increased, not only in military affairs but in the ecological, humanitarian, economic, and other areas. I would definitely say where verification is concerned, nothing is excessive. If we intend to continue on the path we have taken thus far—reducing troops and weapons, dismantling the enormous structures of military antagonism, moving to defense doctrines and support of military capabilities at a level of reasonable sufficiency for purposes of defense—then we need an even more effective, versatile, and reliable system of verification.

■ ■ ■

Stockholm opened the way to rapid advancement in other directions related to arms limitation and reduction. It led us to conclude the INF (Intermediate Nuclear Forces) Treaty. This agreement had a long, difficult, and quite dramatic history. It deserves an unhurried, subtle author and a thorough, exact portrayal. The story contains numerous sharp turns, unexpected moves, and seemingly indissoluble knots. There was an argument about some of the Pershings that belonged to the Federal Republic of Ger-

---

[4] As part of the review of the Helsinki Final Act, a conference was concluded in Stockholm in 1986 on confidence-building measures, e.g. prior notification of military maneuvers.—Trans.

many, for example. Resolving this issue became possible thanks wholly to the constructive approach of Kohl and Genscher.

Yes, there were arguments, implacability, antagonistic positions, interests, and personalities, but in the end they were transformed into a movement to meet each other halfway, to make sensible mutual compromises and agreements.

The INF Treaty was unquestionably advantageous both for the Soviet Union and for the United States, as well as all other countries. I continue to consider it a major contribution to our country's security, because we were able to push the American nuclear presence farther from Soviet borders and to foreclose opportunities in the future to deploy missiles of these two classes anywhere else in the world. Even though Soviet and American intermediate missiles make up only four percent of the entire nuclear arsenal of both countries, the agreement to dismantle them spoke to the world about the possibility of actually getting rid of the most lethal weapons of war. It translated the idea of nuclear disarmament from the realm of dreams to concrete realization.

Surely there is not a single intelligent person on the globe who would not understand that nuclear weapons threaten mankind with annihilation. But there is one unavoidable question: Why is it that to this day, people whose intellect cannot be questioned have not come to the only intelligent decision, to destroy this means of universal suicide?

■ ■ ■

Once nuclear weapons appeared in one country, they became the means for both absolute security and achievable military superiority. Since nuclear weapons could actually be used at that time, they were in fact used against Japan.

I want to note a particular subtlety here: They were used not only against Japan, but against the Soviet Union. The explosion of the atom bombs over Hiroshima and Nagasaki, not justified in any way by the military and strategic situation of the time, was also addressed to us as a demonstration of American technological and military superiority, and it set the stage for the postwar world, according to the scenario and direction of President Truman.

The demonstration was successful, but not completely. Aside from the profoundly immoral idea of destroying thousands of innocent lives, the atomic blackmail had at least two global consequences that deformed the contours and the life of mankind for decades to come. First, by sowing in our hearts the seeds of alarm, it engendered a striving to create the means for atomic self-defense and an adequate nuclear arsenal. In other words, the first explosions of American bombs also exploded the strategic stability and sparked the nuclear arms race. Second, it marked the starting line in the cold war.

In 1988, speaking in New York at the Council on Foreign Relations, I proposed joint efforts to study the reasons and sources of the most prolonged war in our century, and the most destructive, if we consider its consequences for the whole world. In interpreting the facts, each side maintained its entrenched stereotypes, but without shaking them, it was impossible to go forward together. The past tends to explode in the present, and at the most inconvenient time.

It was entirely clear to me, however, that the first line of the story of the cold war was penned in atomic ink. No one would dispute the fact that the first recipe for the bomb was not concocted in the Soviet Union; it was not our country that began the nuclear arms race or repeatedly pushed the cold war to the threshold of a hot war.

The story cannot be encompassed in this book. I have other purposes, and all of them are connected to the present and future. I will note here that the history of nuclear weapons follows the model of any other weapon of war. In 1945, to develop the atomic bomb required an immense concentration of scientific thought, the latest technology, and enormous material resources. At that moment only one country was capable of undertaking such a project. But within a few years, several countries caught up. Only a few countries, not because the others could not produce nuclear arsenals, but because most people were smart enough to realize that the proliferation of nuclear weapons would hasten the destruction of mankind.

The 1963 treaties on the banning of atomic testing in three environments and the 1968 treaty on the nonproliferation of nuclear weapons expressed the collective recognition of the need to rid the world of nuclear weapons. Article VI of the Nonproliferation Treaty directly obligated the signatories to achieve this goal. Nevertheless, in a little more than two decades, the number of these weapons had increased many times over.

In initiating nuclear weapons programs and investing enormous resources, governments understood that they were creating an enormous risk for themselves as well. Consequently, if nuclear arms exist even though the majority of people have only a negative attitude toward them, then they really must fulfill some sort of necessary function, or else this function has been erroneously ascribed to them.

But what would that function be? No one has seriously maintained that nuclear arms should be used in a strictly defensive capacity. If the attacker knows that he will face a nuclear counterstrike and yet still attacks, that means he is prepared to deal a counter-counterstrike. Consequently, either both sides will perish, or the one that shows good sense will capitulate.

But what about a war according to a "nonnuclear scenario"? Here a conflict without mutual destruction is contemplated. Can that possibly be why nuclear weapons are presented as a deterrent to war? Those who advocate keeping nuclear weapons reason that they are a deterring factor for a potential aggressor. Our attitude toward nuclear deterrence should not be simplistic, although I must admit that we ourselves frequently are guilty of this.

Giving this doctrine its due, we admit that over a fairly long historical period it played a certain role in preserving the peace. But new times require a new policy. Otherwise, we are stuck with nuclear deterrence and the confrontational relations it entails.

Nuclear weapons performed the function of deterrence mainly on one level. They created a safeguard for countries to get away with nondeterrence in their relations with others that did not possess nuclear weapons. In other words, they encouraged bullying on the part of members of the "nuclear club." This in turn fostered bullying and lawlessness by some of the nonnuclear countries, who tried to protect themselves from nuclear blackmail by developing their own nuclear capability.

If nuclear weapons were really a means of deterring war, then logically they should have restrained the conventional arms race as well. But in practice the reverse has occurred. While understanding that nuclear war is unacceptable because there would be no victors, governments have stepped up their conventional arms production, believing that "conventional war" is completely acceptable even with nuclear deterrence. The arms race that has gone on for these forty-five years proves that nuclear arms have never performed the function of deterrence.

Until quite recently, we and the United States did not have a single treaty or agreement that would reduce the danger of conventional war. We had no agreement on the reduction or limitation of conventional arms. Since that time more than two dozen treaties, agreements, and protocols have been signed to prevent nuclear war. We even opened Nuclear Threat Reduction Centers. It never seems to have occurred to anyone in either Moscow or Washington that the two countries might suddenly start shooting at each other. So why would anyone seriously consider the launching of a nuclear strike entirely possible?

I am convinced that it is time to reconsider the concepts that accumulated in the atmosphere of the cold war. "Nuclear deterrence" is the frozen legacy of that era.

I must emphasize: Nuclear weapons are dangerous not just because of their physically destructive capabilities. They are unacceptable because they widen the gulf between the national and the universal. It is impossible to speak of the equal rights of nations and the unity of the world, when someone's national selfishness, camouflaged as the interests of national security, can be sustained by ideas of wielding nuclear power over the world. Reliance on nuclear weapons, does not meet anyone's national interests. Only the complete elimination of nuclear capability could guarantee real safety.

The Soviet Union has pledged its commitment to the ideal of a nonnuclear world and has advocated a gradual abandonment of the doctrine of "nuclear deterrence." Clearly, however, it is impossible to eliminate nuclear weapons in an hour. So now it is a question of achieving an agreement on minimal deterrence. What should be the numerical expression of such an agreement? I suppose it is difficult to give an exact answer. Some specialists propose keeping 5 percent of the current nuclear stockpiles of the U.S.S.R. and the United States. This corresponds roughly to the current level of France's nuclear forces.

By preserving the idea of nuclear deterrence, we are paying excessive attention to national rights and interests to the detriment of obligations, but also perpetuating a lack of trust. How can we get out of this vicious circle? I have mentioned glasnost and openness, and the formation of a ramified infrastructure of ubiquitous control. If there is a need to deter each other, it should be an obvious and verifiable deterrence.

Now that the idea of monitoring and on-site inspection has been put into practice, we should proceed further. And of course, we must put an end once and for all to nuclear testing.

It is said that this is impossible as long as nuclear power exists. It may be needed for the peacetime economy, but it can be used in wartime as well. To deflect that argument, I refer to the International Atomic Energy Agency, which is capable of detecting and monitoring any explosions. Another rationale for nuclear testing is that nuclear arsenals must be checked for effectiveness and readiness for war, and also to improve nuclear technology.

It would seem to be commonly recognized that nuclear war cannot be allowed. So how can we speak of improving nuclear technology, and in the name of what? It is all done, I am sure, not so much for the sake of "deterrence" as for the sake of global intimidation, in order to attain nuclear superiority. But that path is unacceptable and even unnecessary today, and undoubtedly in the foreseeable future, when the new world order is in place. The events that have determined this process—the Malta and Paris summits; the talks in Wyoming, Irkutsk, and Houston; the collective rebuff to aggression in the Persian Gulf—have allowed us to approach the problem of the elimination of nuclear weapons from new positions. Realistic politicians cannot help but understand that it is now in their power to ride the world of these weapons.

■ ■ ■

To this day, the disagreements over the INF Treaty have not subsided. We are reproached with the fact that under this treaty, the Soviet Union destroyed a significantly greater number of missiles than the United States. You would be amazed how persistently this simple issue is raised. Frankly, I am more surprised by the silence of those who negotiated the treaty along with me on equal terms, and even received government awards for this.

Why don't the deputies from the Soyuz Group[5] for example, ask not just me, as they are so zealously doing, but Marshal S. F. Akhromeyev, a man I respect, about the reasons for dismantling the Oka Missile Compound? He sat next to the General Secretary

---

[5] The Soyuz, or Union, Group is a Soviet parliamentary caucus of conservatives.—Trans.

during the negotiations about this class of weapons. Surely a marshal would know much better than I who gave their consent to this and why, as he would also know that without the consent of the Minister of Defense and the Chief of the General Staff such a decision would not have been made.

Neither silence nor lying is my policy. And I am not alone; everyone, including marshals, generals, and military experts, along with the diplomats, did a great deed when they eliminated a second strategic front from our borders. Many arguments have been made in defense of the treaty. There are those who accept them and those who do not. But I have never heard anyone say that our posture, both military and political, would have been better had we not signed this treaty.

To reiterate, it was difficult to achieve, and a lot of blood was shed. In the prolonged and tense process of its drafting there were often moments when the two sides lost track of the guiding thread. Once we almost lost the treaty. Almost at the finish line, the negotiations in Moscow were nearly broken off. The reasons were purely subjective. A frustrated Shultz did not even say goodbye to us. Under the old logic we could have said: "All right, you don't want it, you don't get it." But both we and the Americans wanted the treaty. I stopped Shultz at the very steps of the airplane and told him that we had a duty to straighten out the matter. I explained how it could be done, and he agreed.

A little while later we were in Washington. We needed just a small amount of time to save the treaty. It took no more than forty hours. A similar incident occurred during the drafting of the Geneva agreements on Afghanistan. Without going into details, I shall say only that it had to do with an agreement that would permit our countries to come forward jointly with guarantees of those accords. The discussion of the appropriate formulations was long and arduous. Several times, the five-person working teams participating in the discussions retreated into separate rooms. Finally, when all the possibilities had been exhausted, the Secretary of State had a decision to make. He went off with his team somewhere and was absent for at least twenty minutes.

I waited for him in the guest room by the fireplace. By then nothing depended on me. Shultz finally appeared, paused for a moment, and then said he could not accept our alternative. To say I was disappointed would be an understatement. At such moments a kind of spiritual emptiness sets in. We had been millimeters away from an agreement, and then it was off. George was also noticeably upset. We exchanged some empty phrases and said goodbye, returning home with heavy hearts.

Unexpectedly, on the next day, back in Moscow, I received a signal from the Secretary of State that the American side was prepared to accept our proposal. Ultimately, the agreements on Afghanistan were signed.

We traversed a great path in our relations with the administration of President Ronald Reagan. When the administration changed in Washington, a definite pause occurred, and that was probably natural. That did not occur to us then, and we were worried. But the real heart of the matter was that it was clearly no longer enough by then to continue the "linear" course of development, resolving essentially bilateral problems, whether in security or in other areas relating to the interests of the two countries.

■ ■ ■

One of our domestic intellectual critics called Gorbachev and me "the Knights of Malta." How were we initiated into this august order without the sanction of its commander? Apparently by virtue of the meeting in Malta, where, in the midst of a Mediterranean storm, the cold war quietly came to an end.

I ask myself whether anyone in our country really needs the cold war, a state of constant readiness to resist the age-old "enemy." Is the very image of that enemy, frothing with imperial megalomania, necessary to somebody?

Yes, there are probably some who cannot forgive Gorbachev for his statement to President Bush: "We in the Soviet Union are prepared not to view the United States as our military opponent." By the same strange logic, George Bush should not be forgiven for his response, delivered somewhat later at Camp David: "You can count on the United States of America never to threaten the security of the Soviet nation."

Some people must find it hard to breathe when there are no longer any enemies around. As for me, I wanted this and strove for it. And it seems to me that Jim Baker met me halfway. In that regard I particularly like to recall our meeting in Irkutsk and on Lake Baikal on August 2, 1990. This was our usual prevacation meeting.

As I have already said, at each of our meetings the agenda was always fairly packed, in keeping with the overall breadth of problems in the Soviet–American dialog. Each time, we took up concrete issues, moving step by step toward a solution of problems connected with, say, the strategic arms treaty, conventional forces in Europe, and the search for compromise solutions in regional conflicts. In addition, human rights issues, economic and other ties, and transnational promises were always discussed, and individual bilateral agreements were prepared.

Aside from all this, however, each meeting had its own philosophical component. Evaluation of what had been done; forecasts of actions in various fields; mutual understanding at the level of political institutions, which engendered trust; disclosure of each other's intentions and views of the processes occurring in their own countries and in the world at large—all of this enabled us to orient ourselves on the vast plain of world politics and to define where we were and where we wanted to go.

In Wyoming, with the Rocky Mountains in the background, we had decided that relations between the two countries were normalized and had announced that we now would like to go further toward constructive cooperation. Time passed, and we were saying that now we had to move toward joint action. Thus the great philosophical meaning of the Irkutsk meeting lay in our arriving at this conclusion: Our relations had reached a level that would allow us to operate in the international arena as partners, primarily on questions related to conflicts in the Third World.

It could be called a coincidence, but I would prefer to say it was a premonition, largely based on political intuition: During the Irkutsk meeting, we spoke in a theoretical way about how the end of the cold war and the improvement of relations between the U.S.S.R. and the United States could create a certain vacuum in various regions of the world, especially during the early stage, and that crises spawned by regional hegemonic tendencies could fill it.

We were cognizant that these were no more than cautious prognoses, but we needed then to create models of responsible behavior and joint actions by way of insurance. Of course, we could not even imagine that we were two steps away from a crisis that would lead to our joint action.

After that meeting, which was our eleventh, we headed off for vacation. On the morning of August 2 we held a closing press conference and returned to the negotiation room in Retro House to wrap up several items. As was our custom, it was a private conversation between the Secretary of State and me, without staff. We were therefore surprised when Margaret Tutwiler appeared, since our team members were disciplined and would never intrude on our privacy without a special reason.

Tutwiler handed her chief a note. Baker read the note and said: "The State Department has received information that Iraq has crossed the border into Kuwait. The Kuwaiti Ambassador in Washington, however, thinks there is not yet cause for alarm."

We continued our conversation. I was not worried and I don't believe the Americans were, either. I knew that difficult talks were under way between Iraq and Kuwait but I could not imagine that Saddam Hussein would dare to invade Kuwait. There had been no signals or indications of this at all. In the past, Iraqi troops had often crossed their neighbor's borders, had stayed briefly, and then had returned to their own territory. Further, Iraq seemed unlikely to make an aggressive move, since it would have been completely irrational under the given circumstances and would have contradicted any notions of common sense.

I am willing to reiterate this even today, although similar admissions have often been a pretext for my critics to accuse me of incompetence and neglect of expert analysis. As I have already said, I never embark on anything without the advice of specialists. I would say that in the years of my work in the Foreign Ministry, the number of staff involved in analysis and recommendation has increased. I always carefully considered their opinions. Even so, I invariably correlated what they told me with my own understanding and perception of the general strategic issue.

There are people who look at events from only one "foxhole," as it were. My very position dictated that I keep the whole front line in view. But even from the trenches occupied by our experts, a senseless act like Iraq's invasion and annexation of Kuwait could never have been predicted.

I had a fairly clear impression of Saddam Hussein from my personal meetings with him. He is a willful, tough, domineering man, but of course a very astute one. Yes, he tried to "adjust" a disadvantageous political agreement by means of a war with Iran. Yes, he had used chemical weapons in Iraqi Kurdistan. Yes, he had cruelly suppressed any sign of rebellion. But all those actions occurred in conditions that absolutely precluded any organized opposition or sanctions by the world community, which was split by confrontation and hostility. Now that a new world order is being built based on cooperation and interaction, to commit an act of aggression meant to commit suicide. It was not possible, I thought, for Saddam Hussein not to understand this.

I parted with Jim at the Irkutsk airport. He was flying to Ulan Bator, and I was returning to Moscow, where I was to learn that Iraq had occupied Kuwait. On that same day Baker's proposal for a joint statement condemning the Iraqi aggression was handed to me.

I suppose it was one of the most difficult decisions I had ever had to make. I shall remain silent now on the reasons and circumstances that made it so. For the time being I shall merely outline my train of thought. I met with Baker on August 3, 1990, at Moscow's Vnukokvo-2 Airport. He had cut short his visit to Mongolia and had flown back to Moscow. For several hours I had been trying to overcome strong resistance—and not only in the Foreign Ministry. Once again, we had to carry the ball down the whole field. But it was no longer a game of American football, which I was being accused of playing, and not even a Soviet–American game. The question of the world's future was in the balance.

Clearly, the events of August 2 and their possible consequences had set limits on much of what we had achieved. They threatened to undermine the practice of the new thinking, the tendency toward disarmament, the entire course of building new international relations.

What to do? At that time I could not foresee a favorable outcome, but I had to think about our obligation, what I thought had to happen, and what could not be allowed to happen.

My colleagues reminded me of the Treaty of Friendship and Cooperation with Iraq and our special relations. I took that all under consideration. But the thought of the eight thousand Soviet citizens stationed in Iraq filled me with alarm, and I was obligated to do everything so that not a single one would be harmed. But I was obliged to help the citizens of Kuwait as well, and of other countries. And not merely because I might be questioned about this later.

Moral imperatives collided with political considerations. Once again I thought of how the moral self-definition of a society, a state, or an individual is expressed first and foremost by the attitude toward any kind of violence.

Governments punish attacks against life, dignity, and property. Analagously, governments themselves cannot exist outside the protection of the law, outside compliance with the norms of international law, because the alternative is every man for himself, which is to say lawlessness, the reign of the strong over the weak. The world community cannot tolerate predatory governments and pirate regimes, since this leads to the inevitable erosion of world law and order and the destabilization of international relations.

The question was this: Do we live by unvarying concepts of good and evil or, cynically abandoning them, allow someone to shake the foundations of peace? The suffering caused by the Persian Gulf crisis made that question timely.

The aggression against Kuwait was aggression against the tendency toward positive changes introduced into international life by the policy of the new thinking. I could not even entertain the thought of a possible solution that would not restore sovereignty, territorial integrity, and legitimate rule in Kuwait. After all, this was a state, a past and present member of the United Nations, which should continue to be one in the future.

So, to be brief, we published a joint statement. Then, in view of the very dangerous turn of events, a special meeting of the presidents of the U.S.S.R. and the United States in Helsinki was called for September 9.

All through those days we worked extremely hard to promote the formation of an international consensus and an appropriate reaction by the world community to the events in the Persian Gulf. From the onset of the crisis, we held intensive consultations with other permanent members of the Security Council—Great Britain, China, the United States, and France—and with all the rest of the member countries. Our cooperation with the United States was unprecedented. A hotline operated between Moscow, Washington, and Wyoming, where Secretary of State Baker was at the time. We maintained regular contacts with the European Community; there was an ongoing exchange of opinions with Vice Chancellor Genscher, External Relations Minister Dumas of France, and British Foreign Secretary Hurd. We kept the leaders of the Warsaw Pact countries informed and passed along information to the governments of many neighbors and countries friendly to us, including India, Yugoslavia, Turkey, and Iran.

Our dialog with all the Arab countries and with the leadership of the Arab League and the PLO continued without a break. Nor were our contacts with the Iraqi leadership broken off for a single day. Aside from political problems, we discussed with them practical questions relating to the evacuation of Soviet citizens from Kuwait and also the departure of our specialists from Iraq.

At one point I had to resort to strong words and even to promise "the use of any measures deemed necessary" to protect our citizens. Even for that I was criticized at home. But only after that did Baghdad consent to the free passage of Soviet citizens from Iraq.

Now, as I go back over the twists and turns of this story, I conclude that I have nothing for which to reproach myself. Our sharp reaction to Saddam Hussein's actions was conditioned above all by principled political and moral considerations regarding the unacceptability of lawlessness and aggression, our duty to aid victims of aggression, our duty not to allow a small, peace-loving country and its people to perish. But Kuwait was not the only concern—there was also Iraq. The concern extended to the whole region and—again I say this without the slightest exaggeration—to the world, to the lives of all countries and peoples.

When perestroika began, we advanced a number of ideas for reorganizing international relations, new methods of guaranteeing peace and security and safeguarding the rights of individuals and nations. Supported by the world community, these ideas made it possible to execute a radical turn for the better, to resolve a number of the most complex issues in world politics, and to open the way to a new world order based on law, justice, and the renunciation of violence and excessive armament.

If the world community could not stop the aggression against Kuwait, then it would have gained nothing from the end of the "cold war," from the renunciation of confrontation, from the positive initiatives in the international arena. Indeed, what then would the principle of freedom of choice be worth? Only the strong would have it, those who could impose their "choice" on their neighbors and other peoples. What would all the efforts to limit the arms race and reduce tensions be worth?

Kuwait is a wealthy country. It could simply have "bought"

itself protection, hiring the necessary armed forces and purchasing the latest munitions. Kuwait preferred to spend its money on its own development and on aid to others. It relied on the protection of the world community, on international law. Could we deny them this protection? We could not, for moral reasons, but also because it would have had disastrous consequences for the world.

What do we mean by reasonably sufficient defense, if you cannot count on help from others when your neighbor is acting like a highway man? Any country could end up in such a situation, the target of banditry and violence. If a mechanism for thwarting aggression is not created, then every nation risks becoming a victim, and the "strong" will be tempted to settle their affairs by seizing the riches of others.

No, I do not consider the events in the Persian Gulf to be a "conflict." If your home is seized by someone, you cannot say you're having a conflict. You are the victim of a crime. I would not apply the term "war" to this situation, either. The coalition forces implemented a military action sanctioned by a world tribunal, the U.N. Security Council. They simply restored law.

That, I submit, is the key point. For the first time, on strictly judicial, lawful grounds, the aggression of one state against another was halted, and halted on a mandate from the U.N. Security Council. Have there been many instances in the past when the resolutions of that body were heeded? It is hard to recall any. But thanks to the new political thinking, it happened. It happened because the U.S.S.R. and United States began to cooperate, in the United Nations and elsewhere. The unity demonstrated by the Security Council was unprecedented in modern world politics. In the larger scheme of global affairs, this was a unique chance for creating effective mechanisms to defend rights and uphold justice in international relations.

Now for the criticism aimed at me. My opponents in the Soviet Union did not like my speech at the Forty-fifth Session of the U.N. General Assembly in support of Security Council Resolution 678. They did not like the fact that so little time was allowed for persuading the aggressor to get out of Kuwait.

I was also accused of trying to drag the Soviet Union into hostilities. All my clarifications, arguments, and denials went unheard. Nor could they be heard, because the criticism, as always, was placed in the context of the "struggle between the two systems."

One critic asked me if I had any idea what I was voting for. Did I realize that force would be used against Iraq, and didn't I know where it could spread? I want to answer that I had a very good idea, and, moreover, I had precise information on that score. No one made any secret of it. I would stress that both we and the Americans, along with other members of the coalition, were mainly concerned about whether the Iraqi leadership, and Saddam Hussein personally, understood what a military operation against Iraq would really involve. We used every channel, every opportunity, to make that clear to Baghdad.

At my insistence, a "good-will pause" had been included in the U.N. resolution. We made use of it to persuade Iraq to leave Kuwait and warn of the possible consequences if Resolution 678 was not obeyed.

At my last meeting in Moscow with Tarik Aziz, I laid out for him the information I had about new weapons that could be used against Iraq. I said that I did not know how long the hostilities would last, if they should start, but I had no doubt about the outcome if they couldn't be prevented.

On that same day, Gorbachev very sternly warned Aziz that his country would be plunged into an abyss if the Iraqi leadership did not make the decision to leave Kuwait. That was the only thing we were trying to accomplish by proposing a peaceful solution to the problem.

Shortly before my resignation, on a visit to Ankara, I wanted to seize one more chance by meeting with Yasir Arafat and, through him, conveying a warning and a request to the Iraqis to end the matter peacefully. Unfortunately, Arafat did not arrive.

Who was it, then, that did not preserve peace, and chose the path of war?

We informed the Iraqi leadership that no limitations would be placed on the use of force against Iraq, since Resolution 678 did not provide for them. I do not know what Saddam Hussein was counting on, but we did all we could to let him know what he was getting into.

Five and a half months of that should have been enough. Still, at any moment, even after the start of hostilities, Saddam could have said simply "I'm going," and the actions against him would have ceased. But no, he had to be expelled from Kuwait. I also think the efforts to organize a ceasefire in the final stages of the military actions were not justified. Back before they were launched, the Soviet Foreign Ministry had produced an analogous plan, but it was not, or rather could not be, implemented. But, Hussein made his choice. And as I see it, the special emissaries who traveled to Baghdad during the crisis to try to talk to Saddam Hussein actually did harm, since they reinforced the illusion that there were options whereby Iraq could gain some kind of advantage from its aggression.

Some said that the Iraqi leader had to be provided with a chance to save face. I dare say that I too know something about the notion of honor that prevails in the East. And I understood that Hussein would not save face by looking for peace.

Iraq's actions showed what the dictator was capable of doing: the destruction of Kuwait, the spilling of oil into the Gulf, the burning of oil wells, the repression of his own people and others, the genocide of the Kurds. The world community could not countenance the appeasement of an aggressor; after all, there were the lessons of history.

The Persian Gulf crisis highlighted the urgent need to take emergency measures to prevent the nonproliferation of weapons of mass destruction and to limit the transfer and sale of modern types of weapons and the technology for their production, particularly for missile systems. It is imperative to draft an international code to regulate the sale and transfer of weapons. The signing of an international convention on the prohibition and destruction of chemical-weapons stockpiles should no longer be delayed. As for nuclear weapons, we should speed up the agreement on limiting strategic offensive arms, make much more progress on the reduction of the number and magnitude of nuclear test explosions, and, within some sort of time frame, try to reach an agreement on a complete ban. The U.N. Charter envisions mechanisms for maintaining international peace and security. We should create these as quickly as possible.

So far, there is nothing more rational and effective in the world community than the United Nations. Even in terms of the future, the U.N. is still the only possible true guarantor of international stability. It must be allowed to fulfill this function. No country will allow a single state to impose order by force. The new world order can be built only collectively. Perhaps everyone is tired of my proposals to give the Military Staff Committee of the Security Council this primary function. If that were done, the Security Council, by concluding a treaty with U.N. members, could act as a full-fledged guarantor of peace in any region, as specified in the U.N. Charter. The Security Council would do this, and no one else.

Today many claim that after the Persian Gulf crisis a Pax Americana or "American Century" will begin, and from now on the United States exclusively will keep order in the world.

If this is undesirable (and it is), then it is all the more imperative to create the appropriate U.N. mechanisms as rapidly as possible, to elevate the role of the U.N. and make it a real center for collective actions. Fears of an "Americanization" of the world are unrealistic, to put it mildly. The Persian Gulf crisis illustrated the enormous resources required to bring to order a country that is basically small in population and industrial capability. It is most likely that the United States would have won the war in any event, but was the support of the other coalition partners—above all the United Kingdom, France and Italy— really no more than symbolic? And did not the financial resources of virtually the entire Western world and a number of Arab countries have to be mobilized in order to pay the billions in expenses for the operation?

I think that no one country in the world today is capable of taking upon itself the defense of global law and order. It can be done only on a collective basis. And politically, the time has passed when it was possible to act alone, much less oppose the majority of the world community.

In the modern world a country's economic capabilities and the level of its technological and scientific development are crucial. The maintenance of excessively large armed forces and weapons stockpiles will inevitably push a country backward and make it worse off than its competitors who do without such military budgets.

Today, we are really living in a different military and political environment from that of the past, one that requires rethinking the conceptions accumulated over the decades about the nature and likelihood of purely military dangers. I am sure that the manner in which the Persian Gulf crisis was resolved will influence the

behavior of those countries that in other circumstances might have
made claims to regional hegemony.

We are still faced with a difficult adjustment to the realities of
the situation since the end of the Cold War and the transition to a
new type of relations between East and West. In my opinion, the
problem here involves a persistent tendency to approach new phenomena with the old conceptions.

The lessons of the Persian Gulf crisis will no doubt be central
to the formation of new insights and to the elaboration of new
approaches in politics and international relations. How deep the
reassessment of positions and values goes will largely depend on
whether and how soon progress is made in resolving the Middle
East problem.

If we see the United Nations as the bulwark for the future
world order, we are obliged in every conceivable way to enforce
Security Council Resolution 242. In the current situation it is
equivalent to the formula "trading territory for peace," which U.S.
President George Bush mentioned recently.

I want to specify, though: By no means can a peaceful settlement on the basis of a balance of interests and a balance of responsibility be imposed by anyone from outside, even the United
Nations. The solution must be found exclusively by those who are
involved in the conflict. Otherwise there will be no political settlement. Negotiation and dialog are necessary to bring it about. The
U.N. and any interested countries can help to facilitate such a
dialog, can persuade the two sides to begin talks, and, if necessary,
can establish incentives to do so.

I realize that this is a risky idea, but I'll voice it anyway: A
time may come when the U.N. will begin to impose some kind of
sanctions against governments that refuse to engage in dialog with
the opposite side in a conflict. Thus dialog would be recognized as
a universal and obligatory principle in resolving controversies. After all, we have established the practice of "inspection on demand."
Would it perhaps be worth introducing the principle of "negotiations on demand"?

The climate, both worldwide and in the Middle East, has
changed significantly. The antagonism between the Soviet Union
and the United States in that region has ended. This alone is a
factor that affects all the elements of the Middle East equation. It
is no longer what it once was.

I do not share the official viewpoint on the Egyptian–Israeli accord reached through the mediation of President Jimmy Carter at Camp David. It meets all the conditions of a peaceful political solution, has been durable, and has given the two sides what they wanted. Unfortunately, given the state of confrontation in the Middle East, the Soviet Union preferred to take a critical stance toward this unquestionably sensible accord. I must confess as well that at that time we had no policy geared specifically to a Middle East settlement. Our allies in the region abused our readiness to uphold their interests and all too often used us to block various peace initiatives. That was the case with the Camp David agreement. Apparently, this was also an expression of our deep offense at Anwar Sadat, and anyway, Begin seemed to be too "right-wing." Besides, we probably thought nothing would come of it, and that we would be proved right. But if we look at the Camp David accords objectively, we see they are realistic and intelligent, have withstood severe tests, and have worked perfectly well.

Our position on matters related to a Middle East settlement has also been weakened ever since the rupture of our diplomatic relations with Israel in 1967. Reviewing our foreign policy, we came to the conclusion that relations had to be restored, but cautious people said that we had to choose the "right moment." Those who are familiar with the Middle East know that something can happen there every day. That was all the more reason why we had to have normal relations with all the countries in the region. When we did restore ties with virtually everyone, however, with Israel we went no farther than an exchange of consulates general. I deeply regret that I was unable to move things forward to an exchange of ambassadors.

When it comes to the settlement proper, there is no lack of ideas, formulas, alternatives, and compromise positions. The main thing is to act in concert with the participants in the conflict themselves first of all.

By analyzing the state of affairs from all sides, people in Israel will see that they must take advantage of the current favorable situation and trade "land for peace." A solution to the Palestinian problem cannot be evaded; it will never disappear by itself. The Israelis should enter into dialog with the Palestinians, including the PLO.

There are numerous problems that Arabs and Israelis ought

to discuss. First of all, talks should be started on eliminating nuclear, chemical, and bacteriological weapons in the Middle East.
Some sort of agreement should be reached on missiles in the region, and the topic of military sufficiency for defense needs should
be addressed. Even a simple conversation at one table on these
problems would foster trust and create the necessary climate for
subsequent political decisions.

I want to underscore once again: It is time to put aside any
"nonrecognition" by one party of the other and to begin a serious
dialog on all issues requiring political settlement.

■ ■ ■

In wrapping up the topic of Soviet–American relations and the
achievements of the years of perestroika, I would like to repeat
that the changes were born in torment. They required a difficult
reevaluation of habitual assumptions. But the shift occurred,
largely facilitated by a policy statement formulated at the highest
level. The divergence of our interests should not perpetuate our
rivalry. Political reality is such that we must make additional efforts to find areas of agreement.

I suppose it has been most difficult to apply this rule to regional conflicts. But even here it was successful.

As I see it, we now have another important common understanding. We do not have the capability or the moral right to
impose our recipes for political settlement and national reconciliation on the parties to a conflict. But there is a lot we can do, by
conducting a balanced and restrained policy and by serving as an
example of constructive cooperation, to de-escalate conflicts in
progress or prevent new ones, and to create favorable conditions
for peaceful, just solutions. Much has been achieved in this regard.
Without exaggerating the significance of the Soviet–American contribution, I will say that it was quite evident in the international
efforts to stop the Iran–Iraq war, the wide-ranging set of agreements to decolonize Namibia, and the overall settlement of the
conflict in Southern Africa. The agreement among Central American governments would hardly have been possible in the old conditions of sharp confrontation between the U.S.S.R. and the
United States. Serious Soviet–American cooperation was also significant in deciding the Cambodian problem.

I have already mentioned the importance of the cooperation of our two countries in the Persian Gulf. I can only add that I would not have attempted to predict the events had they taken place in the atmosphere of the cold war. The world was fortunate that by the onset of the aggression, Soviet–American relations had reached the level of partnership.

■ ■ ■

What next? What future awaits our countries on their difficult voyage toward collaboration and joint action? Will they succeed in making further breakthroughs toward the desired "touchdown"? I am not a prophet, but I am quite certain that without cooperation, friendship, mutual understanding, and trust between our peoples, the world stands to lose a lot. We ourselves will lose, too.

I do not want that at all. In the final analysis, there is no sorrier sight than a guttering flame that you yourself managed to kindle.

CHAPTER FIVE

The New Europe and the Old Mentality

A Time of Hopes and Fears

The "window to Europe" opened for me long before my "discovery of America," in fact, several years before I was appointed to the post of Minister of Internal Affairs. It was a window to the countries of Eastern Europe or, as we put it, the countries of the socialist community. Everything that I saw through that window in one way or another left its mark on my subsequent ministerial concerns and strongly influenced the formation of my views and attitudes toward the events of 1989–90.

There was also Helsinki in 1985. The tenth anniversary of the Final Act was celebrated widely and triumphantly, but there was nevertheless a scent of alarm in the atmosphere. Before us loomed the question: "What next?" At any rate, I could not get rid of the feeling that the Helsinki process was running down, and only some groundbreaking idea could breathe life into it.

We had been giving this a lot of thought back home in the Soviet Union. Even then we had a presentiment that sooner or later a new time would arrive in Europe, and that East and West would recover their original geographical meaning, taken from them by postwar politics. In those circumstances, such a premonition could be called utopian. In the fall of that year, when in Paris Gorbachev outlined his idea of a common European home, some applauded it as an expression of pure courage; others saw it as the usual propaganda trick, and still others thought it wasn't serious. Only a few people understood then that this mature, carefully weighed idea had originated in a sober recognition that the existing order of things in Europe could not continue. Our perestroika itself contained the outlines of a new European reality. But back in 1985 few people considered that likely.

The Berlin wall seemed to have been standing for a century. The military-political alliances firmly and solidly occupied the frontiers of confrontation. The checkpoints on the border between East and West would open up only a crack. The division was such a reality of the European landscape that life without it seemed unthinkable. It possessed the consciousness of millions of people, and policy, which is supposed to be farsighted, was based on this immovable reality. Fed on the dogma of the division of the world into "coexisting systems," our Party functionaries and diplomats could not conceive of any major changes. Practically speaking, the functionary and the diplomat spoke as one person, and more often they were one person, because the ideological and political "kinship" of Party-state hierarchies in the countries of the former socialist community presupposed unquestioning subordination of diplomats to the nomenklatura. Top Party officials were appointed to ambassadorial posts in Eastern Europe, and those appointments were made exclusively by the Politburo. (Ambassadors to all other countries had to be confirmed by the Politburo as well.)

This subordination determined the way decisions were made. Former Party officials appealed to higher Party levels in all questions, bypassing the Ministry of Foreign Affairs. And in the countries where they were posted they would often act in a similar way, going directly to the top and ignoring the foreign ministries of the host country.

I shall note in passing that this way of doing things could not be changed immediately. To be precise, it could be done only after the creation of parliamentary structures. And only in 1989, after the cycle of East European revolutions, were we able to appoint ambassadors of another type and caliber.

My former colleagues will confirm that from my first days in the Foreign Ministry I persistently—at times excessively—

advanced the idea that we needed to reorganize radically our embassies and diplomatic corps in the countries of Central and Eastern Europe. I proceeded from the resolutions and decisions of the April (1985) plenary session of the Central Committee and the Twenty-seventh Party Congress, which had proclaimed new principles in interrelations with the countries of the socialist community. I knew several of those countries quite well. I traveled to them often, and during my visits, I did not limit my contacts to those at the top. I sensed that, for many people, the "model" of existence we had imposed on them was unacceptable. The symptoms of trouble were obvious. Moreover, there was history, the lessons and convulsions of 1953, 1956, 1968, 1970, and the beginning of the 1980s, which had reverberations in my personal experience and in the life of my republic and country. Finally, the general course of perestroika created an awareness of the need to establish embassies of a new type. Knowing our vision of perestroika, it was not difficult to foresee a time when the old "Party diplomacy" would be completely bankrupt.

At the outset of perestroika, Gorbachev pointedly questioned the accuracy and completeness of information coming to the center from the embassies, chiefly those in Eastern Europe. It would contain more than a few tendentious elements. On the whole, however, more or less objective information was available to us, both from the embassies themselves and through other channels.

Among my colleagues working in countries of the socialist community, there have been and still are perceptive people who accurately analyze the state of affairs. In response to the critics who accused us of having been caught unawares by events in Eastern Europe, I was telling the truth when I said that our ambassadors had been accurate and conscientious in their assessments.

But there were others, of course, who did distort the picture. It is not their fault, but their misfortune, the misfortune of the "vanguard," which condemns it to backwardness and loss of authority, since genuine power does not rely on coercion and diktat. It is no secret, for example, that Hungarian economic reform was derailed largely through the efforts of such figures. This turned out to be a misfortune for us as well, since we had been following with anticipation the somewhat successful attempts of the Hungarians to create an effective model of a working economy. We saw in those attempts an opportunity to reform our own domestic economy on healthy and rational foundations. Alas, I myself tried to do something in my home republic and know firsthand what that costs. There's no need to go even that far for examples: Quite recently, in the years of perestroika, our economic reform collapsed when it collided with the bastions of dogma.

Revolution at first occurs in minds and only later in society. The misfortune of perestroika is that while it took place in many people's minds, it did not touch the consciousness of those on whom the most depended. Usually, those on whom the least depended were the ones who wanted the changes. Rereading the minutes of our ministerial meetings with embassy staff members, I see that many of them were alarmed at the state of affairs: the ineffectiveness of economic cooperation; the inflexibility of our ministries and institutions; the dilatory reactions to proposals by potential partners; the reluctance to adopt new regulations on exchanges of people, experience, and ideas; friendship at the slogan level but nowhere near the heart; messianism and missionary zeal, the unconquerable impulse to teach, to demand "do as I do." These are the things we had warned our people against; we asked them to forswear the mania for condescension and tutelage. I could feel my skin crawl from the displeasure, if not rage, of certain high-ranking figures in Eastern Europe when listening to speeches in this vein.

I established good, trusting relations with my fellow foreign ministers in the socialist countries. Now that almost all of them have quit their posts, I can say that they were seriously alarmed by the state of affairs and spoke candidly with me about it. How can we put our relations on a new track, they asked, if your bureaucracy refuses to throw the switches? The citizens of our countries cannot communicate with one another normally. Collectives of industrial enterprises and scientific institutions who have entered into partnerships are experiencing enormous difficulties in solving the simplest problems. As in the old days—and this was said with unconcealed perplexity—a number of influential people in our countries, critically inclined toward perestroika, find allies among your emissaries who come from Moscow or work in your embassies.

My colleagues did not have to tell me this. Even a superficial analysis led me to the conclusion that the majority of leaders of these countries did not wish changes and would resist them. They supported our course in words, but they dragged their heels on reforms at home. This created a dilemma for us. Since we had rejected the "export of ideas," the interference in the internal affairs of neighbors and allies, we could not invoke the old methods to push them vigorously toward reforms. Still, we clearly saw that in almost all the countries of Eastern Europe the political leadership was rapidly losing control over the situation and was not finding adequate responses to demands for democratic changes. In some instances, stubbornly rejecting reform, conservatives employed methods and measures that, against their intention, solidified the unorganized opposition, facilitating its formation into a broad, nationwide democratic movement.

Paradoxically, the conservative backlash to this movement looked toward Moscow or, more precisely, toward our domestic opponents. Here the socialist "community" showed its true face, and we saw what it had always been: a fraternal alliance of Party-state elites. Now in greater danger than ever, they sought one another out, easily found a common language, and consolidated into a club for those disgruntled with Soviet perestroika, and pledged to fight against it.

Aside from the general political scene, the developing events provided a personal cross-section, as it were, direct impressions from contacts with the leaders of the socialist countries. Outwardly, everything looked normal: the embraces, the kisses, the awarding of medals back and forth, the cordial receptions, the attending of congresses—the almost ritual movements of the chosen. Our liberal and radical "leftist" press could not forgive us for those embraces, honorary citations, or phrases of hospitality—in essence, they were manifestations of slavish adherence to the old ways. But it was only an outward, purely decorative display. Then the décor collapsed, the gold leaf began to flake away, and new, previously inconceivable details appeared on the façade. They were put there by the opposition, if it is permissible to call the broad popular masses "the opposition." Probably it is both permissible and necessary, because during Gorbachev's trips to the socialist countries, the population's reception spilled over into mass popular demonstrations. People welcomed him not only as the initiator of renewal in the country that had once liberated them from the horrors of fascist enslavement (although it had brutally established its own quisling regimes), but even more, they welcomed him as a natural ally in their resistance against their own leaders. This was easy to see in the mood of the crowds, in the shouts and greetings, and on the posters, signs, and banners. As a counterdemonstration the authorities in certain countries held congresses, where the cult of the leader prevailed. There was an almost religious ecstasy in these displays of loyalty and support. But behind this façade, heart-rending dramas were unfolding. I myself did not dare to instruct anyone, but simply presented our positions and tried to explain the principles behind them. Most often the response was not abuse, criticism, or deferential expressions of disagreement, but rather a stream of statistics about the successes of true socialism. The subtext was perfectly transparent: "Everything's fine with us, and we don't need perestroika."

In conversations with East European colleagues, Gorbachev was very tactful and cautious in his recommendations. With reference to our country's experience, he gave them to understand that if they did not take steps toward democratic transformations, they would inevitably face very serious problems. They politely heard him out and tried to justify themselves with barely relevant examples. They were at ease, because they knew that this Soviet leader would not send tanks to uphold democracy, as his predecessors had done to crush it.

However, there were long, noisy sessions with head-on clashes and bitter disputes turning into personal confrontations. In Bucharest, for example, the discussion became so heated that security people felt compelled to violate the secrecy of the negotiation room: They opened the doors to see what was going on. Nothing was going on, just an argument between people holding diametrically opposed views.

Things started happening later, in January 1990. First in Timişoara, then in Bucharest. I was in Brussels at that time. Deputies to the European Parliament asked me how I interpreted the events in Romania. I did not yet have a full and clear picture of what had happened there, besides which an "alliance instinct" was operating and diplomatic circumspection took over. Anyway, I said that I condemned violence and grieved for the victims. Can it be socialism, a British Labourite asked me, when they shoot their own people and murder their own citizens? No, I replied, it is not socialism, and it never will be socialism. I also compared the events in Timişoara with the tragedy in Tbilisi—they had the same background, the same reason, the same forces inciting them.

I then found it impossible to heed diplomatic caution, and expressed my opinion on what was happening in our country. Unfortunately, no one was listening back home.

I still think today, as I did then, that neither foreign nor domestic policy can defend a cause that in principle is indefensible. It goes against the grain of history, against national aspirations and passions, and against the human desire to live in dignity and freedom. No policy, even the most inventive and sophisticated, even with the loftiest words emblazoned on its banners, can defend a wall dividing a people and a continent on the principle of different camps or systems. No matter how strong an ideological mortar has cemented the bricks in this wall, the popular will is stronger and can break down any barriers. The most intimate, the finest human feelings—the love of a woman and a man, love for children, family, parents, the yearning to live with one's people, to reunite with relatives—are stronger than the steely heartlessness of ideological dogma. If a policy cannot respond to these feelings it is doomed.

The mass exodus of Germans from East to West could be stopped only in the way that the first few brave souls who hurled themselves at the wall had been stopped: with bullets. But if shooting had started in the atmosphere of the fall of 1989 and the winter of 1990, the political objective itself would have perished along with hundreds of people. And I do not rule out the possibility that the entire world would have been at risk.

A few months later, Jim Baker made a remarkable statement: "In the rubble of the Berlin Wall, I have seen a Europe becoming united." I saw that as well, but more—a multitude of extremely difficult foreign policy problems, directly linked to the internal situation in our country. It was clear to me that both the changes in Eastern Europe and the prospects for building a united continent without blocs, bound up with the processes of German unification—to which the Vienna talks on conventional weapons limitation was a prerequisite—would directly reverberate in domestic walls and cause cracks; by the law of reciprocal relation, those cracks might open deep fissures in our path. And that is what happened. The external situation aggravated the internal situation, which in turn placed further hurdles in the path of foreign policy.

■ ■ ■

The most disturbing thing about the criticism that engulfed us was not the incendiary speeches, the hatred they expressed, the use of labels and clichés from the familiar lexicon, or the symptoms of home-grown imperialism found in slogans about class struggle and the conflict between two systems. It was rather the lack of a rational alternative. The moribund and exhausted condition of the old thinking displays itself first of all in an inability to put forward any kind of sensible idea, which, if implemented, might prove the insolvency of our decisions. Essentially, the whole argument comes down to one point: The process must be stopped, or at least delayed.

A columnist I greatly respect remarked that history creates opportunities, while politics takes advantage of them. I would add: Or else politics does not take advantage of them, but instead tries to "arrange" history according to preferred ideological patterns. The ensuing temptation to wipe the board clean is precisely what our critics are proposing when they say we have to "risk complications with our partners in the diplomatic and military-diplomatic process." They prefer to remain silent about the price of such a risk.

The opponents themselves risk nothing when they assert:

"You have demolished the geopolitical structure in Europe."

"You have cost the country its allies and ruined the external security buffer."

"You have brought the opposing bloc's sphere of influence closer to our borders and removed the counterweight of the Warsaw Pact."

"You have cooperated in the unification of Germany."

Counterarguments fail to produce a constructive response. The desire to put perestroika in the dock is so strong that the accusers are entirely unconcerned about witnesses and evidence. In the past rendering judgment meant hauling somebody into a kangaroo court. Why then should one look for proof, when what the system needs is not the triumph of truth, but confirmation of its own rightness—by whatever means? It would seem that in the present circumstances, "any and all means" would not be acceptable. But the soil has been tilled for so long that it is receptive to all kinds of seeds.

Was there no alternative? There was one, we were told. I recall seething moods—not only in our country—in which calls were heard for the use of force according to the scenarios of 1956 and 1968. History, it seems, had instilled strains of repressive thinking in the genes, a resistance to rational evaluation of contemporary events. Leaving aside the impossibility of operating in the new conditions with the old methods, we could not sacrifice our own principles regarding the right of peoples to freedom of choice, noninterference in internal affairs, and the common European home.

But by the logic of our critics, it was our duty to sacrifice them, in other words, to sacrifice perestroika, its policies and principles. That is the key point of the accusations, their alpha and omega, their once concealed but now plainly visible pathos: Had it not been for perestroika, nothing like this would have happened in the socialist camp.

So the root of all misfortune and evil is perestroika. As if the system had not long been receiving signals, since the end of the 1940s and the beginning of the 1950s, that all was not well in the camp, that for the majority of its inhabitants, camp life was unbearable. I won't recapitulate the examples of Hungary in 1956 and Czechoslovakia in 1968. Let us recall the relatively recent times that preceded perestroika. Poland at the beginning of the 1980s. The Solidarity movement, supported by the working class and the intelligentsia, seriously threatened to destabilize the regime. Was it really perestroika that enabled this movement to emerge? This is a rhetorical question, of course, but it has to be raised, because the answer is far more complicated than one might suppose, and will make clear the futility of the "alternative" now being proposed.

The Polish leadership was faced with a double threat. The first I have noted, and the second was embedded in the "tradition" of restoring order through the use of force. Fears were widespread—and, as I know for a fact, not without grounds—that the Soviet Union would be sending that force. Poland itself at the time, understanding where this would lead, decided to employ an alternative: to declare martial law. This alternative worked and saved Poland from the "second threat." But it could have failed.

There were some serious reasons to explain why it worked. First, there was Afghanistan. Before 1979 the use of force by the Soviet Union in neighboring countries had helped to stabilize the situation at a relatively low (as it seemed at the time) political, military, and economic cost. This quick "solution" did not work in Afghanistan. The invasion of that country provoked a strong negative reaction that grew daily in our society and abroad. Whereas only a few people in the Soviet Union openly protested the sending of troops into Prague in 1968, after 1979 the majority condemned the Afghan adventure, either directly or indirectly.

In those circumstances the political leadership of that time was compelled to take seriously the risk involved in any action on our part in Poland. Many had come to realize that the armored fist could not strike. Here is an example: On one of those days I happened to be in Mikhail A. Suslov's office. Someone phoned him to report about the worsening situation in Poland and to insist, as I understood it, on an "activation of forces." Suslov repeated firmly several times, "There is no way that we are going to use force in Poland."

The situation was "multifaceted" and extremely ambiguous. A whole range of factors operated: Afghanistan, the Soviet domestic situation, the possible negative reaction from the West. But that was not all. I think Moscow was given pause by serious and, I suppose, correct fears that the Poles would fight back, that full-scale military actions would have to be unleashed. In my view, the personality of General Jaruzelski played a decisive role. It was he who saved his country from invasion by convincing the Soviet leadership that the Poles would cope with the situation themselves. By dressing martial law in a Polish uniform, he deflected outside intervention.

But let us ask ourselves: Did martial law end the internal ferment? Not at all. On the contrary, it did much to stimulate it, so that it ultimately led to a change of government and of orientation in Poland. So there is no reason to hiss at perestroika and cheer for military force. It would not be a bad idea for us to learn the lessons of martial law in Poland ourselves.

After April 1985 the possibility of military intervention was completely ruled out. In making that decision, we understood very well that the development of the political processes in neighboring countries would depend on the realism and flexibility of their leadership. Unfortunately, little of either was in evidence.

In those conditions the issue of the Soviet military presence in Eastern Europe became urgent. We figured that the problem could be eased within the framework of an interbloc agreement on the

reduction of conventional weapons and with our unilateral reduction of troops and armaments in the region. Events unfolded in
such a way, however, that they threatened to render any agreement about reduction of arms in Europe meaningless. The Soviet
Union, the United States, and other European countries had to
make strenuous efforts in order to draft a treaty on conventional
armed forces reduction.

I intend to discuss this topic more thoroughly in another chapter. For now I shall say that our military presence in Eastern
Europe was questioned long before the start of events in 1989–90.
And it was not just the governments that came to power in those
years that demanded the withdrawal of Soviet troops, but their
predecessors as well. Some of them told us in strictest confidence,
using very cautious formulations, that the continued presence of
Soviet troops in their countries would create serious problems for
them. It would be better for us to take steps ourselves in this
direction, they said, than to be forced later to move in haste under
the pressure of events. The content of these conversations was
reported to our highest leadership. The subject was reflected in
the appropriate policy statements. It was thought that by raising
the question seriously, joint government programs would be
drafted and implemented to bring the troops painlessly back to
their homeland.

None of it was done, unless recriminations against our diplomacy about the "hasty exit of Soviet troops from Eastern Europe,
which looks like a retreat," can be counted as an "accomplish-
ment."

I am often asked today: Did your country's leadership miscal-
culate the difficulties involved in removing thousands of Soviet
troops from European countries? Yes, we in the Foreign Ministry
underestimated the problems. After Gorbachev's declaration made
at the start of perestroika that our forces were not to remain in
Europe forever, we drafted our recommendations and forecasts,
including the social, economic, psychological, and material impact
of the withdrawal, and passed them "upstairs." I don't know if this
type of analysis was done in other ministries. Anyway, the fact
remains that the declaration and the practical actions diverged,
and people suffered as a result. That is why I have very serious
claims to make against the government, the planning agencies, the
ministries—including my own—and finally myself. At my age, it is

time to absorb one simple truth: Any statement, even one made at the highest level, is perceived in our country as mere rhetoric which you have to applaud, and leave it at that. That is how we were raised.

It had seemed that the dizzying upheavals in Europe would force others besides diplomats to face difficult issues. A government is not a sum of ministries, each of which can "push its own line." We have only one line—at least, that's what I thought. But as I see now, the attitudes toward the line can be different. And on the issue of troop withdrawal and reduction of armed forces, the clan or camp philosophy gained the upper hand. It was served up as a defense of state interests.

All the postwar realities now appeared in another light, in new dimensions: the confrontation of the two military-political alliances; the high cost of the cold war; the attempts to overcome the division of the continent; the emergence and development of the Helsinki process. Possibilities that had previously been unthinkable unfolded, but along with them came new problems demanding a new perspective on the European political landscape, a rethinking of many habitual conceptions about the foundations of security and cooperation on the continent.

"We cannot stand still, when the whole world is in motion," Jean Monet said. Sadly, many of us did stand still, stuck in the old pattern where deception and fraud are elevated to the highest honor, in the spirit of the saying, "you can't sell anything if you don't lie." But you cannot hide tanks, or the truth—you'll lose your shirt.

Did we lose our "friends" and "allies"? Were they really friends and allies in the usual, normal sense? Did we perhaps, on the contrary, acquire true friends by convincing the world that a threat no longer emanated from our country? There is no state today that does not wish to develop orderly ties with us, to enlarge and enrich contacts, to exchange ideas, information, and experience.

Who will deny that we now maintain decent, normal ties with all countries? We do not have tense, much less hostile, relations with any state. We have not worsened relations with a single state, and with many we have improved them.

We have told the difficult and bitter truth about ourselves. And we waited for the leaders of the allied countries to do the same. Where they preferred to remain silent, their peoples took the floor.

New forces have now emerged in the political arena of Eastern Europe. Popular will, not outside forces, put them there. The East European states will not cease to be either neighbors or friends for that reason. At any rate, we want them to be both.

We have clearly expressed our attitude toward past events. The logic of perestroika itself shaped those evaluations. It was perestroika also that ordained our break with the forces retarding change in those countries. Change occurred when people were completely free to choose their own path, their own methods for building a new society. Our respect for that choice is respect for the full sovereignty of the countries of Eastern Europe, unconstrained by ideology. It is a respect for their striving toward independence, and it does not exclude the possibility of transformations of socio-economic and political institutions.

I understand perfectly the complex reaction in our country to the processes in Eastern Europe. I do not dismiss it or condemn it. The loss of habitual reference points is painful for closed minds. The "collapse of socialism" in Eastern Europe was especially hard to take. People reasoned: Not so long ago the U.S.S.R. was a great country that enjoyed authority and was admired by the whole world. World socialism was the guarantor of our security. They suspect—or assert outright—that we have ruined it all, both the greatness and the guarantees.

Much was contained in such expressions: alarm that the developing events would have a negative impact on the security provided by the chain of "allied" countries that protect us from the West and by the deployment of large Soviet troop contingents in those countries. Also, I suppose, nostalgia for the time when the countries of Eastern Europe were regarded as merely satellites to our Colossus. Weren't these the emotions behind the allegations that the "buffer zone" in Eastern Europe was collapsing and our troops were leaving "without a fight"?

It is painful and bitter for me to hear such judgments, which imply that the Soviet Army did not liberate certain countries of Europe, but seized them as war trophies. It is painful and bitter for me to hear statements that offend the dignity of sovereign states. Eventually I came to consider it my moral duty to apologize for such offensive and intolerant statements from some of my compatriots. I am prepared to do so here and now.

Frankly, I could understand those people, because they have

a deep-rooted belief, as I do, that we are a great country and must be respected as one. But what makes us great? Territory? Size of population? The number of weapons? Or is it national disasters? The lack of human rights? The disorder of life? What do we have to be proud of if our infant mortality is almost the highest on the planet? It is not easy to answer the question of who we are and what we would like to be. A country that people are afraid of, or a country they respect? A country of force or a country of good will?

It is not easy for me to answer these questions. But when deputies from the Soyuz Group publish their famous fourteen questions under the title "Are There Patriots in the Foreign Ministry?" I pity their peculiar idea of patriotism.

What is true patriotism? Indulging the arrogance of state power? Sending other people's children to their death in a foreign country? Or courageously admitting mistakes and preventing new ones, sparing the young people and restoring the good name of the country?

We exist in the world of realities and in the world of emotions. Realities dictate one line of behavior, and feelings rebel against it.

Let us now speak of whom the world admires, and for what reason. Did the world admire Soviet forces when they "brought order" to Hungary? Or when they crushed the "Prague Spring"? Was the world delighted when we entered Afghanistan to fulfill our "international duty"? It is time to recognize that neither socialism nor friendship, neither neighborliness nor respect can be founded on bayonets, tanks, and blood. Relations with any country must be built on mutual interests, mutual advantage, and the principle of free choice. We have now begun to conduct business in just this way, and significant changes for the better have taken place in the world. Yes, problems have arisen, but it could have ended in tragedy had the changes been delayed.

Today we could speak of the defeat of our diplomacy only if we had been trying to stop changes in neighboring countries, only if our relations with them worsened and grew bitter as a consequence, and the risk of a military conflict resulted.

I am always interested to hear my name among the "culprits in the collapse of the socialist camp." It would behoove the accusers to consider the fact that it was not just this or that person but they themselves who hastened the collapse, with their ideological conservatism, their refusal to understand the sentiments of other peoples, and their mania for molding life to their ideas and for seeing sovereign states as a "buffer," as one of our "true internationalists" phrased it.

Among the many explanations for the recent events in Eastern Europe there is one that I believe has merit. The wave of democratic renewal was propelled by apprehension that Soviet perestroika would be cut short. Not a fear of perestroika itself, but a fear that it would be stopped and everything would return to what it was, including the former doctrines and old ways. A fear that our troops and weaponry would remain in these countries forever, that the traditions of tutelage, imposition, and interference in internal affairs would be retained and would bring on the breakdown and collapse of the economies of those countries along the ultimately compromised road of pseudosocialism.

That road did not serve the interests of our security. On the contrary, our interests are served only when the Soviet Union is surrounded by free, democratic, flourishing countries, equally open to the East and to the West, and not when a "cordon sanitaire" of utterly dubious and shaky regimes is artificially created around us. Our interests are served by the democratic nature of the social and political transformations in these countries, and not the propping up of governments that hide behind their own and others' bayonets.

I have mentioned the withdrawal of troops. It could have been done not rapidly, but gradually, in a carefully regulated fashion. Proposals and statements were made back in 1987 to that effect. We could have shown some concern for the social infrastructure. There was time enough for that. And if the moment was lost, diplomacy bears the least blame. Rhetorical patriotism, charging onstage with its accusatory questions, is fruitless. If it is true patriotism, it should do something. Sadly, inaction is revered by the "patriots" as a good deed. The worse, the better. And they stall.

All the stalling is for one and the same reason: They did not believe that word would become deed. They thought, as in the past, that an enormous distance would lie between statements and their fulfillment. And when they saw they had miscalculated, they demanded blood. Most grievous of all, they invoked the blood shed by the Soviet people in the name of liberating Europe from fascism.

While preparing my speech for the Twenty-eighth Party Congress, I could barely restrain myself from including a confession. It would have been about the feelings I experienced in Brest at the monument bearing the names of the fallen defenders of the fortress, which included the name of my older brother. I stood at the memorial stone and thought about how I was being reproached with his blood, as if I had betrayed his sacrifice and memory, by "allowing the reunification of Germany."

I refrained from speaking about that, although I could have, because the problem was a personal one for me. We would have betrayed the memory of millions, however, had we flouted the ideals for which Soviet people fought and died, and had it caused a new threat to our country's and Europe's security. Such a statement of policy is far closer to the human truth than accusations of "giving away the victory." In fact, they don't contain a drop of humanity, but there is a particular type of politics that I cannot pursue.

■ ■ ■

The Berlin Wall fell on a November night in 1989. A year later the Charter for a new Europe was signed in Paris.

It is not true that the collapse of the wall caused alarm only in the Soviet Union. The event aroused serious concern in the West as well. When Michel Roquard, the Prime Minister of France, said that the fall of the "iron curtain" destroyed a certain comfort in which everyone on both sides of the wall had been living, it was easy to understand that "comfort" meant stability. Although unambiguously positive, changes of such magnitude and rapid pace undoubtedly had a destabilizing effect, which no sane person could desire.

The new danger that the process just begun would wipe out existing boundaries and bring chaos and collapse to this vital region, forced us to act, to look for the correct formula, which could not be other than this: dynamism within a framework of stability. This formula demanded extremely close attention, imagination, and a coordinated policy.

The year that passed between the fall of the Berlin Wall and the Paris Summit was a year of such policy. We paid attention to all levels of our foreign political contacts and took actions on a broad front of bilateral and multilateral diplomacy. Our imagination was stimulated by the desire to determine the forms of a common European order that would be rational, viable, and above all, secure. History laid the groundwork for establishing a new Europe, and so did we, the contemporaries of the process.

The idea of European unity, of creating a Europe that would follow a path of integration and form common approaches to legal, economic, humanitarian, cultural, and ecological issues, attracted broad support. This was wonderful, but it was not enough.

The idea of a European community has a long history. All its permutations in scholarship and politics, signified by the term "the European idea" (or the "idea of Europe"), applied in some instances to various designs for unifying Europe, and in others to a complex of international economic and cultural conditions of European life, seemed to belong to the past. I have already cited Jean-Jacques Rousseau on the "Grand Design" of the Duke of Sully. Yes, the Europe of that epoch was not ready to realize the plan of unification. I suppose that none of the plans for a unified Europe before or since have had any basis in reality.

Is there any now, we ask ourselves? Or, in the words of Rousseau, is today's Europe good enough for us? These questions are not idle when the postwar structures have rapidly broken down and a movement has begun to overcome the division of the continent. The very pace of events has brought the idea of a common European home into the realm of practical policy. Now we must ask whether the proposed projects are good enough for the contemporary state of Europe? Will they really solve the problems of stability and security?

The new political thinking worked very hard to remove the ideological component, and the spirit of implacable confrontation that accompanied it, from intergovernmental relations. The new thinking was advanced not by the nobility of its spokesmen and exponents but by the recognition of a common threat to the continent and the responsibility of European countries for their own fate in the face of a nuclear and conventional arms race, poor economic performance, and ecological disasters. The new thinking also had to keep its sights on objective prerequisites for economic integration and on the political structures that emerged, radiating throughout the continent and in many cases leading toward rapprochement.

The basis for such rapprochement was the common European

process, the crucial strategic concept in the array of visions for the possible building of a unified community of nations with equal rights, whose statehood and borders would be recognized as unshakable constants. The Conference on Security and Cooperation in Europe paved the way toward that goal. Building upon it, perestroika in the Soviet Union widened the path and moved closer to the goal.

The pan-European meeting in Vienna, which concluded in January 1989, was a watershed. Europe had never known such a dialog—intense, at times dramatic, but purposeful and democratic in a way that was without precedent. The Vienna agreements were a major step in the development of the common European process, raising the continent to a new level of security and cooperation. The meeting was a turning point not only for Europe, however. Our continent is not an island. The process begun in Helsinki has become central to East–West relations. Through the United States and Canada, our multilevel dialog and versatile collaboration have entered the New World, and crossed the Urals into Asia. For the Helsinki principles of security, humanity, and cooperation are at work on the Asian territory of the Soviet Union as well.

The formula for the community we want to create from the Atlantic to the Urals contains the very golden mean of Europeanism, in which all the nations of the earth, both great and small, can find their place.

After the Vienna meeting, there were a number of multilateral meetings devoted to various aspects of cooperation in Europe, from information policy to ideology. Finally, negotiations were concluded on the reduction of troops and the improvement of confidence-building measures. The formation of a unified economic and legal zone in Europe, integrating the existing systems, seemed within our grasp. The visit to Brussels was an example. We had meetings and talks with the leaders of Belgium, the European Economic Community, the European Parliament, and NATO. I came away with a firmer belief in the viability of the design for a united Europe. The visit convinced me that we were justified in acknowledging the integration of Western Europe and establishing active collaboration with the European Community and its Parliament.

The agreement on trade and commercial and economic cooperation between the U.S.S.R. and the European Community was a great step in the direction of mutual East and West European accommodation, overcoming their alienation and creating a common European economic zone.

At no other time in the past has the European idea had such a chance to come to fruition, even if gradually. But what will be its final form?

A cluster of ideas and approaches on this score has long been in formation. Virtually all of these ideas are in the same vein. France's President Mitterand has proposed a European confederation; U.S. President George Bush sees an integrated democratic Europe; Foreign Minister Genscher of Germany speaks of a new world order in Europe; Enskens, the Belgian Minister of Foreign Affairs, envisions the confederative community of Europe; the one-time Polish Prime Minister, Mazowiecki, called for a Council of European Cooperation; the Czech Foreign Minister, Dienstbier, proposed a Commission of European Security; and there have been others.

We ourselves envisioned the creation of permanent institutions for the pan-European process, and new structures of security for the continent. Under the powerful influence of events in Europe, the necessity of collective discussion came to be generally acknowledged. Gorbachev's proposal in Rome for a 1990 pan-European meeting at the highest level met with unanimous support.

We saw clearly from the very beginning how closely interconnected were the prospects for a new Europe and the problem of Germany, the possible results of the Vienna negotiations and the agreements on reduction of military concentrations in the center of Europe, the overcoming of the division into military and political alliances and the formation of permanent pan-European structures of security. Never had history offered such a complex knot of interconnected problems, and never had it demanded that they be untangled so quickly.

In Greek mythology, Europa was abducted by a monster from the East. In history, Europe has long been dominated by the very real monsters of enmity and opposition. Now at last she has a chance to be restored to herself and to become what her best minds have always hoped for her. But many matters still had to be settled. Frankly, at times they seemed beyond our strength.

CHAPTER SIX

From Ottawa to Arkhiz

The Road to German Reunification

"When did you realize that reunification of Germany was inevitable?" Hans-Dietrich Genscher asked me. We were talking at my home in Moscow, after my resignation. Since I was no longer bound by any official or political strictures, and since agreements had already been ratified, I could be very frank.

"As far back as 1986. In a conversation with one of our top Germany specialists, I suggested that this issue would surface very soon. I said that in the near future the German question would define Europe. When a people has been divided for almost half a century, it is a nationality question, a question of the unity of a nation refusing to be divided by the walls of ideology, weapons, and concrete."

At first glance this view may seem the fruit of an emotional and moralistic outlook. But recent events at home and abroad had once again convinced us that national sentiment is a serious factor and that policy must take account of it. The existence of two Germanys in the center of Europe had become a dangerous anomaly, seriously threatening security. We had to devise a political means to keep the ongoing process from becoming unmanageable.

At the time I made that forecast, however, it seemed impossible to frame the issue at the level of principle. The conviction that the existence of two Germanys maintained the security of the Soviet Union and the whole continent was too deeply rooted. We had paid an enormous price for it, and to write it off was inconceivable. The memory of the war was stronger than the new concepts about the limits of security.

Even when we were forced to face facts by the pace of events, none of us dared to ignore the inborn wariness of our people about German unity. Along with negotiation documents, my portfolio contained much heavier baggage. These were our history and national experience: the memory of the two world wars unleashed by Germany, especially the last war, which cost our country 27 million lives. It was useless to appeal to forgiveness or to argue that every nation has the right to self-determination, especially one with an immense creative potential, which it has converted into peaceful development. Useless too were attempts to point out that despite forty-five years without war, only because of the order established in Europe after 1945, hostilities continued. And we bore many casualties. Fear, mistrust, hatred, constant expectation of a violent eruption, and enormous military expenses, leading at last to material privation and a consistently low standard of living. The victors had thus become losers.

When the heart is in such pain political rationality has little chance. It can succeed only by easing the pain with irrefutable proof that the measures it proposes will not undermine the triumph of justice, and the memory of the victims will not be desecrated. That was the moral and emotional imperative. And the political perspective moved guarantees of security to center stage.

Thus, from the outset we linked the German unity issue with the problem of forming new structures of European security. We wished to see the unification of Germany take place over a fairly extended period. We needed to bring Soviet public opinion around to the realization that it was really happening. That is why for so long we did not consent to Germany's membership in NATO. That is why we sought a mutually acceptable solution providing a guarantee against the remilitarization of Germany and against the recurrence of the *Drang nach Osten* policy.

I have one answer to all the questions about our position and its background: Look at the shape our country was in at the beginning of 1990. Look at the people and note how cruelly the enemies of perestroika played on their heartstrings. Those strings could easily snap.

■ ■ ■

An international conference on "Open Skies" convened in snowy Ottawa in February 1990 in a building converted from an old train station into a social and political conference center. We arrived at the conference like an overloaded train weighed down with much more baggage than the ideas on the agenda. "Open Skies" was blocked by the German unification problem. All the speakers dealt with it in some form, and there was talk in the corridors that the "train was running late." Events in East Germany were such that we had to move quickly.

We embarked on what then seemed a long road. We began the hasty formulation of the "two-plus-four" mechanism.

Hans-Dietrich Genscher said that in overcoming its division, his country sought a European Germany, not a German Europe. Secretary of State James Baker spoke of the certainty that all European nations would profit from the creation of a sovereign, democratic, unified Germany. I naturally wanted that as well, and believed that guarantees would be found in the very atmosphere and outcome of the "Ottawa Six" meeting.

There were meetings in Bonn, Berlin, Paris, and Moscow, as well as my own talks with Genscher in Geneva, Windhoek, Brest, and Munster. Although they were businesslike and productive, and although hundreds of people were drawn into our discussions, what worries and ordeals were involved, what an effort of will, mind and heart, were needed to calm our fears and sustain our hopes! Aside from the pace and rhythm, this high-speed diplomacy was saddled with a colossal burden. And this is one case where I can say without fear of contradiction that the burden was placed squarely on my shoulders. I suppose that each one of the six ministers sensed this when we met at that round table with sharp corners.

Now a word about how we sanded down and finally removed those corners. Naturally, I shall speak first of all about the Soviet contribution.

First, our starting position differed substantially from our finishing one. Some in the West thought we were deliberately

being stubborn in dragging out a decision. Some of our compatriots, on the other hand, accused us of excessive compliance in fail-
ing to derail or at least stall the reunification of the two Germanys,
which, in their opinion, did not serve the "authentic interests" of
the Soviet Union.

Second, it was clear from the outset that we would not resist
the unification of Germany. Such opposition would run counter to
our own political principles, but this was by no means the only
reason. It would have contravened elementary morality to tolerate
the division of a people and a country for the sake of political
interests. But, as I have said, the other option always before us,
related to the tragic experience of history and our responsibility to
our own people, was no less serious.

From the beginning, we asked ourselves what kind of Germany would better serve our interests. Dismembered, harboring
bitter and potentially explosive grievances, with a dangerous in-
feriority complex, so out of keeping with its spiritual, intellectual,
economic, and cultural potential? Or a united, democratic Germany, taking its rightful place among the other nations as master
of its own destiny? The answer to this question is now well known.

As for the stubbornness, it is worth mentioning that we really
had only two alternatives. The first was to achieve, within the
framework of the "two-plus-four" mechanism and the pan-
European process, an agreement on a final legal settlement of the
German question, which would serve our security interests and
the cause of stability in Europe. That seemed within reach. The
second alternative was to use our half-million troops in East Germany to block unification. We can imagine what that would have
entailed.

I learned later that not everyone saw things this way. What
did our domestic opponents offer? To forestall us, they would have
to think up something, but what? Block the borders with troops, as
some were saying? Start up the tanks? But that would put us on
the brink of World War III. Given the concentration of troops and
armaments in Central Europe, any resistance by force would run
that risk. This conclusion rests on serious analysis and firsthand
information. We chose the other road, certain of the support of
everyone who refused to doom Europe and our nation to catastrophe. That's how I respond to those who continue to say that we
should not have consented to reunification.

■ ■ ■

It would be an offense against the truth for me to say that "the Six" had a smooth path from the first step. We got to the starting line quickly, but not so easily. I believe it was Genscher who in Ottawa first complained about my hardness. We argued relentlessly. But, we had too many reasons for alarm and apprehension to accept all the offers and formulations of our partners right away. Recall the autumn of 1989. After the Berlin Wall fell, the drive for unification overwhelmed both Germanies. The euphoria seized the whole population, including certain circles in West Germany. Despite the harsh political realities, people moved quickly from calls for the self-determination of East Germany to advice, if not prescriptions, on how to change its state structure and on what timetable. The lawful interests of the U.S.S.R. and other European states were clearly ignored and the implications of unilaterally deciding the German question through a fait accompli were overlooked.

All of this couldn't help but provoke a reaction from the Soviet Union. The response to Moscow's objections was rhetoric about the right of the German people to self-determination. We had never denied the Germans that right. But we saw in this rhetoric an effort to question the U.S.S.R.'s participation in settling the issue of German reunification or, at least, to force us to reconcile ourselves to the outcome.

On Gorbachev's behalf, speaking before the political commission of the European Parliament in Brussels, I carefully outlined our position. The events in East Germany had pushed many things to the top of the agenda, for Europe and for ourselves. We knew from the start that the reunification of Germany was not such a remote possibility. Naturally, aware of our responsibility, we did not intend to remain in the background. Our purpose was clear: to guarantee the security of the U.S.S.R. and all of Europe. Our partners in the West did not understand that at first, but they came to see it very quickly.

What kind of guarantees were we talking about? The first was a real reduction of armaments in Europe, including those on German soil. The second was to combine the process of unification with the formation of pan-European structures of security. The third was a reorganization of NATO and new relations between the allies. To reiterate, we believed the resolution of this triad of is-

sues would serve the interests of the U.S.S.R. and all the other
countries of Europe.

In my Brussels speech, I stressed that it was wrong to raise
the question of German reunification without taking the lawful
interests of other countries into account and without clarifying
many important issues. What was threatening about that? Did we
not have the right to ask the Europeans and ourselves the questions on which our future depended?

We were interested first of all in political, legal, and material
guarantees. Second, in the readiness of the united Germany to
recognize the existing borders in Europe. Third, in the military
and political status of the new Germany. Fourth, in coordinating
the building of a unified Germany with the Helsinki process to
overcome the division of Europe.

We also had other issues in mind: the demilitarization of Germany, its neutral status, its attitude toward the presence of Soviet
troops on German soil and toward the four-power agreement on
Berlin, and so on. We hadn't heard answers to these concerns and
could not help but be alarmed. On the other hand, we had no doubt
that we were within our rights to raise them and said as much to our
partners. Accordingly, these issues were included in the agenda.

But I think the most significant point of my Brussels speech
was that it put Moscow at the table on German unification.

The meeting in Ottawa on February 13, 1990, was one I shall
never forget, since it was the midwife, so to speak, of the "two-
plus-four" mechanism. There were five talks with Baker, three
with Genscher (the most difficult for both of us), and talks with
Dumas, Hurd, Subushevsky, and the ministers of the other Warsaw Pact countries—all in one day, which culminated in the birth
of the Six.

I had said in the past, addressing the Canadian Parliament:
"We can have different attitudes toward the existing state of affairs in the world. But we must recognize that, for the first time,
there is an acceptable level of political stability and security. Thus
we must weigh each step, acting cautiously and with eyes wide
open."

Some politicians want to play political matches with a five-
minute time limit on each move. But is that intelligent when, without exaggeration, the stakes are peace and the security of all
peoples?

I quote myself here for two reasons. First, to emphasize the political context as we approached the German settlement. Second, what I said in Ottawa is in many respects universally applicable. Thus, again in Ottawa, we first realized that the German question should be one of the main items on the agenda for the summits of European countries, the United States, and Canada at the end of 1990.

In an interview for *Izvestia* soon after returning to Moscow from Ottawa, I noted that the process of building German unity was likely to take several years. It was a perfect pretext for accusing me of short-sightedness. Well, I am willing to take the heat, but with one significant reservation: The practice of foreign policy should be seen as a process that at each moment has a certain purpose for all parties and is directed toward the results they need. But the main thing—and here I have nothing to reproach myself for—is that the restoration of German unity had its own internal dynamics, which kept pushing up the negotiation timetable, overtaking it, and forcing it to go faster.

On May 5, 1990, the first scheduled meeting of the Six took place in Bonn. We were to outline the positions of our countries and draw up the agenda. This was a difficult job—and continued to be—but in the end we reached a consensus.

One of our most important tasks was to synchronize a solution of the German question with the formation of new structures for pan-European security. Everyone recognized the solution we had proposed as having merit. The consensus had been reached long before that day, and I could not help noting this in Bonn. All the members of the Six were saying that Europe needed new security structures, and that the Helsinki process would enable us to tie the unification of Europe to the unification of Germany.

Genscher, who chaired the meeting, noted that all the speakers had recognized the desire of the Germans for unity and that the border question would be decided with the participation of Poland. But despite these statements, the overall situation was, to put it mildly, complicated. The stumbling block was Germany's future military and political status. On the eve of the meeting, the newspapers had written that on this issue, a "one-plus-five" mechanism would operate rather than a "two-plus-four." The one-to-five ratio in fact did operate, and it was not hard to guess that the Soviet representative was the "one."

"Of course," I said in Bonn, "we understand that the decision can only be the result of a mutual consensus by all six countries. But we must keep in mind that in deciding the external aspects of German reunification we cannot abstract ourselves from the internal conditions in our own country. Here we are talking about an issue that is especially important to Soviet people, our entire society. If we are put in straightened circumstances in matters affecting our security, then this will lead to a situation—and I will say this openly—where the degree of our political flexibility will be greatly restricted, since emotions will boil over in our country, the ghosts of the past will come forward, and nationalistic tendencies will be reborn, all of which are rooted in the tragic pages of our history. I would ask my colleagues to understand: We are not fooling and we are not bluffing."

I must admit that I re-read these statements now with mixed feelings. It seems that not even three months went by and we turned our attitude around 180 degrees. Ought we to have been breaking our lances? Wouldn't it have been better to consent right away to Germany's membership in NATO?

No, I am convinced that it would not have been better. Remember that in the beginning of May the question of the transformation of the military blocs, although under vigorous discussion, was still short of the stage of intentions, so to speak. NATO remained what it had always been for us, an opposing military block with a definite doctrine which depended on the possibility of delivering the first nuclear strike. And naturally, given these factors, united Germany's membership in NATO would substantially affect our security interests. It would tip the balance of forces in Europe and create a dangerous strategic situation for us. Thus, we simply had to express our negative attitude toward a united Germany in NATO.

More, our firm position on this issue clearly motivated the Western countries to step up the process of transforming NATO. So in that sense, the goal we established and then attained determined our tactics within the "two-plus-four" mechanism.

In Bonn I called my colleagues' attention to the insufficient pace at which the talks on conventional arms in Europe were proceeding. Could we resolve the military political issues around a German settlement if we had no agreement on the reduction of troops and arms in Europe? Our answer was negative; the Vienna talks had objectively blended the process of German reunification with pan-European interests. And I was glad when this position received a positive response from our Western partners.

Without getting into a close analysis of my Bonn speech, I will say that it raised other issues: the borders of Germany; the necessity of Poland's participation in reviewing the border issue, as well as security problems relating to Polish national interests; the imperative for a united Germany to forswear nuclear, chemical, and other weapons of mass destruction; and the expiration of the four powers' rights and duties with regard to Germany and Berlin as both a component and an outcome of a final settlement. With these and all other issues, a common understanding was slowly but surely evolving, although the search for compromise was often troubled.

Still, I must note that at our first Bonn meeting, my partners in the Six displayed enormous tolerance, tact, and flexibility which prevented the "Ottawa formula" from irrevocably turning into the unpleasant "one-plus-five" equation. They constantly assured me that they understood the special sensitivity of the Soviet Union to the events. I recall how Baker mentioned this factor, then said, "We must find a solution where there won't be any winners and losers, but where everybody wins."

I think the critical factor here was that we openly and clearly expressed our problems and indicated on what basis an acceptable solution could be found.

Berlin in June 1990 was an entirely different situation after the Washington Gorbachev–Bush summit, where the German question had naturally moved to the center of attention. The Warsaw Pact Political Consultative Committee had met in Moscow and had issued a Declaration that initiated far-reaching transformations of our alliance in all areas. We had genuine hopes that NATO would now move in that direction as well. We received a positive response in that regard from Turnbury, where a NATO council meeting at the foreign minister level was under way. In a word, realistic possibilities that the military-political division of the Old World would be breached could be discerned. We waited impatiently for the outcome of the NATO session in London, having every reason to hope that it would enhance the process. Now the question of a united Germany's membership in NATO took on another coloration. Thus I did not touch upon it in my Berlin speech.

In Berlin, the Soviet delegation submitted for the consideration of its partners in the Six a draft document, "Fundamental Principles of the Final International Legal Settlement in Germany." I find little point in repeating its entire text, so I shall simply list its essential proposals and the issues it covered.

First, the question of the borders of a future Germany. (I will note here that a consensus had virtually been reached on this point by then.)

Second, an agreement that a future Germany would not launch military actions against anyone, except to exercise its right to self-defense. On their part, the four powers would be guided in their relation with a united Germany by the same principles.

Third, measures aimed at reducing the military presence on German soil, which in the years of the cold war had become an arsenal of highly advanced weapons. Its most important component was Germany's obligation, like the majority of other countries, to renounce the production, possession, receipt, and deployment of nuclear, chemical, and biological weapons.

Fourth, a reaffirmation that all international treaties and agreements signed by East and West Germany would be valid for a period of five years. This would mean that the actual situation at the moment of unification—East Germany's responsibility to the Warsaw Pact and West Germany's to NATO—would be preserved, but that NATO's and the Warsaw Pact's jurisdiction would not extend beyond their present zone of activity.

Finally, the principle of synchronization was again put forward. Much of this list was supported by my partners in the Six. Meanwhile, during the ensuing discussion we substantially adjusted our approach on several points. Again, I want to emphasize that it was a mutually acceptable decision that in no way infringed the interests of the Soviet Union.

Politics is the art of the possible. We may like or dislike this, but it is an axiom that has no need of proof. In the real world of politics we could not escape the need for a constant and scrupulous reading of the changing political context. But the internal situation of the Soviet Union was the crucial factor. Our position had to coincide with the will of our people.

We moved toward this for nine months and did not arrive—I can say this now—until June 1990, at the Twenty-seventh Congress of the Communist Party. We scaled this peak with enormous effort. Strong winds blow at such great heights. Here the gusts seemed more than we could stand. There was ferocious resistance, but support was just as strong. The clash of passions and opinions reflected the complex spectrum of attitudes toward the German question. But one idea prevailed: It was wrong, and even impossible, to build one's own security on the division of another people. We finally received a mandate of trust and support.

I shall not hide the fact that in the extremely inflamed atmosphere of the Congress it was difficult to breathe. My personal fate was on the line. About eight hundred delegates had voted against my election to the ruling body of the Party. I had been included on the list of nominees without my consent or wish. The Congress gave vivid testimony to the growth of opposition to our policy. In my circumstances, it was especially important to see some encouraging response from "the other side" [the West]. Otherwise, we would be in an untenable position.

When the news came out about the NATO session in London, I knew there had been a response. The declaration passed in London indicated that NATO too was embarking on the path of transformation, decreasing its purely military emphasis, and changing its strategy. Most importantly, the declaration expressed a readiness to announce that the two alliances were no longer enemies and would refrain from the threat or the use of force. No less so was the statement that the Vienna talks on conventional armaments must be brought to a conclusion and that new negotiations should be initiated on the reduction of forces in Europe.

NATO also spoke in favor of limiting the offensive capabilities of armed forces in Europe and of opening talks on reduction of tactical nuclear arms. There was also mention of a reevaluation of the "forward-based defense" strategy and the doctrine of "flexible response," along with the announcement that the doctrine that contemplated the possibility of using nuclear weapons was changing.

In mid-July of 1990 there were meetings in Moscow and Arkhiz, a town in the North Caucasus, between President Gorbachev and Chancellor Kohl. The changes brought about by that time enabled the leaders of the two countries to look at things differently and to resolve the difficult issues of German reunification. Views were compared in Arkhiz, and a search was made for ways to disentangle the issues reviewed within the "two-plus-four" mechanism. In other words, bilateral diplomacy promoted the successful outcome of multilateral talks.

The two sides came to a mutual understanding, which opened up the possibility now of accelerating a draft agreement within the framework of the Six for an international legal settlement of the external aspects of German unification. In addition, we discussed a whole range of issues related to the signing of important bilateral agreements. Their basis was to become the so-called Great Treaty, the idea for which had originated in 1987 but in the conditions of that time could not be implemented.

■ ■ ■

On July 16, 1990, I flew to Paris directly from Mineralnye Vody for a meeting of the Six that was to take place the following day. No sooner had I boarded the airplane than my assistants and some journalists put me through a cross-examination: Why had all the issues been resolved so swiftly?

"Was that really so swift?" I said. Much had been determined by recent events and the rapidly changing situation, which created an atmosphere in which such advances became possible. The statement by the top leadership of the NATO countries in London had bolstered our confidence. What we wanted was happening, so we took the appropriate measures. Besides, I said, matters could have come to a dead end. We could not stop the reunification of Germany, except by force. And that would have meant disaster. Had we withdrawn from the process, we could have lost a great deal. If we had not laid the foundations for new relations with Germany, it would have had a negative effect on the pan-European situation.

Even so, I was showered with questions. They kept coming back at me later, in Paris and other cities. Recently a group of German historians and political scientists raised them again in Moscow. I feel I ought to recount that lengthy interview. The questions and answers explain a great deal.

QUESTION: Critics in the Soviet Union reproach you for agreeing to the reunification of Germany. You "lost" the Victory of 1945. What are the guarantees, commensurate with the Victory of 1945, that Germany will not start a new war?

ANSWER: It's impossible to "lose" the Victory of 1945, either for me or for anyone else in the Soviet Union or beyond its borders. It was, is, and will be a victory—in our memory, in the history of our country, Europe, humankind, and, if you like, in our current affairs.

The word "lost" is in quotation marks, but even in this high-lighted form, none of my critics, even the most fierce, would dare to use the word. The moral and political risk is too great in suggesting that there was some kind of "game," since the stakes were so exceptionally high.

In that sense, there can be no "guarantees" equivalent to the Victory—you see, I am using quotation marks now. The Victory of 1945 and the unification of Germany are different, incomparable events.

I would prefer simply to speak of the guarantees that Germany will not start a war. In these recent months, starting from the end of last year, the goal of our efforts was to formulate and obtain such guarantees. I think we have obtained them. What are they? Briefly, they are the correct solution to the external aspects of the German settlement, its linkage to the pan-European process, to the design of institutions for European security, and to the transformation of the military-political alliances; the formation of effective contractual-legal mechanisms; and finally, the will of the Germans themselves.

Europe is no longer what it was before World War II, when the effort to create a system of collective security met with no success. The lessons of history are worth something.

QUESTION: At the end of 1989, you said that the death of 27 million Soviet people was the price of existing European stability, the price of the existing division of Germany. It was a strong argument. But didn't these people die not for the freedom of their homeland, but for Stalin's empire, and not for the freedom of their neighbors, but for their suppression?

ANSWER: You have answered your own question. It is largely rhetorical. Yes, in saving the country, Europe, and the world, they did die for the freedom of their homeland and neighboring countries. But since you have brought up Stalin, let me remind you that the Soviet leadership of that time was originally against the division of Germany. The anti-Hitler coalition was made up of several countries, and the question was decided jointly according to the concerted will of the Allies and the traditional practice of that time.

On the whole I am against retrospective judgments upon history, against the attempt to divide it into the "correct" and the "mistaken." What's done is done. Twice in this century alone, the leaders of Germany unleashed world war. In the struggle to prevent this from recurring, we hit upon the method used in 1945. In the light of prevailing conceptions, it has outlived itself, but it would be absurd to apply those to the past and to ask why they did it that way.

One more thing: We were not the ones to explode the atom bomb. We were not the ones to call for a cold war against our recent allies. We were not the ones to start this war, which divided Europe and Germany with an iron curtain for so long.

I am not sure you will quote me correctly, but a strong argument does not lose force even now. We would be betraying the memory of the fallen and the interests of the living if we ignored the danger of the reemergence of German militarism. Not a single politician, especially not a Soviet politician, or at least one like me, in whose life to this day the war has left the pain of personal losses, has the right to conduct himself without some generosity.

Personally, I prefer to analyze the full range of possibilities, including the negative ones.

At that moment I had grounds for speaking and thinking that way.

QUESTION: You also stated back then that it was wrong to expect the status of the G.D.R. to change radically, and the status of the F.R.G. to remain the same. How will the status of the future Germany differ from the status of the F.R.G.? Would you be satisfied with the reduction of the Bundeswehr to 370,000 people?

ANSWER: See, you're saying "back then." Back then it was a different situation in which a forecast like that was completely justified.

The reality is that a new state has emerged—Germany. It will exist in conditions of transformed military-political alliances, the reduction of the level of hostility, and the creation of pan-European security structures. Taking into account these conditions, the comparison of Germany and the F.R.G. has no point.

Unified Germany will have fewer troops than the F.R.G. The level of 370,000 is a ceiling for the forces of the Bundeswehr. In the framework of European disarmament it would be lowered. I am very satisfied with this, just as the other partners are.

QUESTION: Not long ago you called the unification of Germany in accordance with Article 23 of the Constitution a very dangerous path and said that membership of united Germany in NATO does not serve the interests of the U.S.S.R. You also remarked that the merger of the G.D.R. with the F.R.G. would present a direct threat to the neighboring countries of both German states. Why is it that you are now satisfied with NATO's statement that it will no longer view the U.S.S.R. as its enemy? Is the U.S.S.R. interested in the presence of American troops in West Germany?

ANSWER: Allow me to note that contrasts such as "then" and "now" outside a concrete historical political context seem weak to me, not to mention methodologically incorrect.

Unification on the basis of Article 23 of the Constitution will happen after a final settlement of the border question is reached. That removes your concerns on that score. Without the decisions passed by the NATO Council in London, membership of Germany in NATO would have been unacceptable to us. We are now satisfied with the process developing in NATO.

The NATO statement to the effect that it would no longer view us as an enemy is a serious gesture of *bona fides* and acquires the significance of a guarantee.

Today we have more substantial guarantees that enable us to look calmly upon the unification of Germany.

As for the presence of American troops in Germany, we do not see any threat to us in that. It is a problem of German–American relations.

QUESTION: Were you surprised by the events in the G.D.R. or do you think the Soviet Union itself facilitated such developments? The U.S.S.R. did not send troops to suppress the people, who were in rebellion against the dictatorship of the regime. The U.S.S.R. also did not stand in the way of the opening in November 1989 of the Berlin Wall. Was Moscow informed of these events ahead of time? What do you think, does the G.D.R. owe its liberation to perestroika?

ANSWER: I have already spoken on this. The changes were not unexpected for me. At the end of April 1990, Ambassador Yuly Kvitsinsky, now Deputy Minister, sent the report: "The fall of the G.D.R. is a matter of days." Many considered this a capitulation.

All the changes could have been predicted, if not their rapidity. Perhaps a miscalculation occurred here. There was no miscalculation, however, in the refusal to stop them by force.

The question of our interference in the G.D.R. or anywhere else was not posed, nor will it be. That's the end of it.

The Soviet Union did not facilitate events there in any direct way. Indirectly, mediated through the influence of its perestroika—yes. But on the whole, it would be more correct to say that the people of the G.D.R. made their own choice. That was their right, and they need answer to no one here.

■ ■ ■

On July 17, 1990, in Paris, I informed my colleagues about the agreements reached during the meeting of Gorbachev and Kohl. They created the immediate prerequisites for the settlement of the external aspects of German unification. The parties stipulated that the unification of Germany entailed a cancellation of the rights and obligations of the four powers, which meant the restoration of complete sovereignty. Germany thereby obtained the opportunity to decide independently the issue of its membership in either military-political bloc. The parties also determined the timetables and conditions for the presence of Soviet troops on the territory of the present G.D.R., to which the NATO structures would not extend. United Germany would renounce the production, deployment, and stockpiling of nuclear, chemical, and bacteriological weapons and would comply with the Treaty on Non-Proliferation. While the Vienna negotiations were still in progress, the government of the F.R.G. would pledge to reduce the numerical strength of the Bundeswehr to 370,000 officers and soldiers.

That very day the question of the borders was resolved with the participation of Polish Foreign Minister Skubiszewski. We also pledged to begin work on a concluding document so that it would be adopted during a meeting in Moscow in September 1990.

There was a hitch at the finish line, however, which threatened to derail the treaty on the final settlement of the external aspects of German unification. I would not mention it, except for the fact that the information has already been leaked to the German press.

The night of September 11–12, 1990, on the eve of the concluding session, I was informed that one of the partners was demanding the addition of a clause extending the zone of possible NATO maneuvers to the territory of the former G.D.R. I asked that the message be conveyed to my colleagues that if they adopted this article, the meeting the next day would be off. In other words, there would be no treaty, and it would be their responsibility. Toward morning I was informed that the proposal had been withdrawn. On September 12 we met at the appointed time and signed the final document. Two months later in Bonn, a package of agreements was signed with Germany in Bonn.

We are fully justified in affirming that the security of the Soviet Union was not lessened but in fact was enhanced, as a result of the "two-plus-four" talks. If the right of peoples to the exercise of free choice does not harm other peoples, then we cannot deny it to anyone.

The movement toward German unification laid the groundwork for new relations between the Soviet Union and united Germany, reinforced in the Treaty on Good-Neighborliness, Partnership, and Cooperation and other agreements that cover the areas of politics, economy, culture, and science, as well as issues of mutual security.

I was happy to read in the paper the announcement from the U.S.S.R. Supreme Soviet on March 5, 1991, that it "views this set of documents as having historic significance, putting an end to World War II, taking account of the new realities in Europe and the world, and opening up a new era of stable peace and large-scale cooperation between the Soviet and German peoples." That was precisely my goal.

European history has known quite a few "settlements." Some were based on a balance of dynastic interests, others on a balance of power. This time, a legal settlement was drafted based on new principles governing international relations, specifically the observance of natural and human rights and freedoms, and of the indivisibility of security, with an emphasis on collective, cooperative mechanisms for the support of peace and stability.

■ ■ ■

To all appearances, my account of the difficult days of 1990 could not have ended on a brighter note. Everything that was intended at the beginning—the incredibly difficult, multi-layered design— was brought to fruition. The levels and parameters for the reduction of conventional armaments were coordinated. The high-level CSCE meeting in Paris was convened. The "Charter for a New Europe" was signed. It would seem that there was no longer a threat that the vacuum formed as a result of the breakdown of the postwar structures would be filled by a kind of chaotic Brownian movement. The process has been developing in two dimensions, both across the continent and bilaterally between countries. The Soviet Union has concluded its first treaty with France in history, a treaty on cooperation and consent. A treaty has been signed with Italy. Soviet–Spanish and Soviet–Finnish declarations have been signed, and a corresponding Soviet–British agreement is in the works.

I would like to make separate mention of Soviet relations with Eastern Europe. To their credit, they are passing through a difficult period without sliding toward a hostile, tense relationship. Having safely skirted a dangerous intersection, we should pause, since we are obliged to establish ties on new beginnings and principles.

As the structures of our relations are being dismantled, as the Warsaw Pact has virtually ceased to exist, and as economic relations demand fundamental perestroika, we are engaged in an intense exploration of paths to new relations with our nearest neighbors, chiefly on a bilateral basis. This work was begun on my watch. A new Soviet–Romanian agreement has been signed. Agreements with Poland, Hungary, Bulgaria, and Czechoslovakia are in preparation. This cycle must be completed, and then we can think of how to go further, either in the framework of the pan-European process or on a regional basis. Thus, the outlines of a new structure are fairly distinct.

Yet that bright note was not sounded, for a variety of reasons. Chief among them was the situation in my own country and several other European countries. The outcome is difficult to predict, but we may be confronting a serious, destructive, destabilizing phenomenon.

In the broader, global scheme of things, the danger could come from deteriorating relations between Europe and the South. The gap in the levels of economic and social development will inevitably spark conflicts against the background of growing migration from South to North and from East to West. A solution can be found in increased economic cooperation on a broader scale.

The problems are obvious and not difficult to enumerate. It is far more difficult to propose some effective and realistic programs, and to find the necessary capital and other resources. We are also threatened with backsliding in the area of human rights, for problems here most often cross over into the realm of securing social and economic rights, not political freedoms. All of this can have a serious impact on the fate of the Helsinki process just at the moment when it can become a rallying point for the actions of European governments.

A more serious threat brewing in the Soviet Union is the noticeable brake on perestroika.

■ ■ ■

After the signing in Paris of the Treaty on Conventional Arms Limitation, circumstances arose that placed its ratification in doubt. This problem is now the subject of negotiations, and it would be improper on my part to interfere in this already complicated process. I hope that by the time this book appears it will be resolved.[1] For now I can say only that the breakdown of this very important agreement, which for the first time in history establishes limitations on the levels of arms in Europe as a whole and in separate zones, and also defines separate quotas for each of twenty-two countries signing the treaty, would have catastrophic consequences—political, economic, and military. With the deepening crisis in our country, when a favorable international atmosphere and support from outside are so necessary, the failure of the treaty would be a betrayal of our real interests. Such an outcome would destroy everything that has been done to start the building of a common European home and the formation of Europe-wide areas of cooperation.

Of course, a dignified way out of what I would call a deliberately created deadlock will be found, and the treaty will survive, because it serves the interests of all the countries signing it. Some people, however, assert that the treaty does not serve our interests, that Soviet diplomacy has betrayed the interests of its government, which explains why the desperate attempt was made to save the country's military hardware, on the questionable assumption that tons of metal are more valuable than trust in our country and its good name.

[1] The Treaty on Conventional Arms Limitation was signed in November 1990 but not ratified. In June 1991, the United States and the U.S.S.R. resolved the dispute over whether some Soviet forces should be exempt. Subject to approval by other nations, the treaty should go into force.—Trans.

I consider the demagogic attacks by certain military and non-military experts on the conditions and parameters for the reduction of conventional armed forces in Europe to be the height of irresponsibility. Those conditions were set forth at the Paris summit. Behind that completely groundless criticism I see a naked desire to leave everything the way it was in the years of hostility and ideological confrontation.

The treaty is vitally necessary for the maintenance of stability in Europe. As far as I know, there was never a case in history where twenty-two countries agreed on the international regulation of their armaments and approved a reliable system of verification and control. This treaty is essentially one of the pillars of the new united Europe. It is the material basis for the declared new relations between states. It embodies the very idea of overcoming military hostility on the continent. That is why we, Europe, and the world cannot allow ourselves to lose this treaty because of those "discrepancies" that have come to light after its signing.

I want to say the following to whoever tries to dispute this treaty or the disarmament measures: All right, I agree with you. We don't need to reduce arms and troops. No, we should escalate them and continue the arms race. But just answer one question: Is the country able to bear such a burden without being crushed under the weight, with our current budget and finances, and with inflation threatening to leave us without the means to pay our generals and officers their salaries? An honest answer will suffice to judge their patriotism. Only genuine patriotism—not ministerial loyalty—will motivate us to think seriously about the kind of army we need.

The Persian Gulf, where the electronic technology of the twenty-first century exposed the utter flimsiness of mere fortifications, should have told us what real security is and how to provide it. Not the quantity of weapons and the number of troops, but their quality and human resourcefulness, with the capacity to absorb and operate the latest technology.

We need a professional army, and for a professional army a democratic society is necessary, one where a citizen in uniform knows himself to be an individual living a decent life in all respects—social, material, and spiritual. We need a different training system that will produce a cast of mind not cramped by authoritarian regulations.

It is not hard to understand why people so fiercely oppose the changeover to market relations. The process, after all, is linked to the need to dismantle the centralized command system, and will entail reduction of the military budget and conversion of the defense industry, which will be profound and comprehensive, not a feeble imitation that compromises the very idea. The way to economic perestroika inevitably leads through a reduction in the size of the armed forces, the introduction of a professional army, and its exclusively defensive use.

The changeover to a professional army means more than just higher spending on personnel. It means a "natural selection" process, resulting in a loss of status and rank for some, but a higher level of competency and professionalism overall.

A hasty arithmetical approach to arms reduction ("Are we giving up more than they are?!") predominates in people's minds. The criticism of treaties and agreements covers up the fact that our reductions were accompanied by reductions on the other side. If we are reducing more in a given number of classes, that is only because we have stockpiled much more than was required for parity. The "arithmetical thinking" is static, and incapable of looking ahead. Most of the time it is concerned with the consequences of agreements reached and not with what will happen if there are no agreements. What a loss is in store for the militarized economy of the country.

We must reject the phantoms of "numerical superiority" and aim to plan and manufacture goods of maximum quality. When we were proud of trying to reach 100 percent capacity or more in our industries, we lost sight of the fact that this inhibits the design and assimilation of new machinery, production mechanisms, and consumer goods.

Our army also needs to make quality a priority in everything, first of all in the standard of living for military personnel. The highest-ranking Party officials have passed resolutions on this issue; I voted for them, because they fitted precisely my conceptions of the country's future.

I might be asked what this has to do with the problem of German reunification. I would reply that the two are directly related. For those who rebel against the changes of the system, disarmament agreements and a German settlement are phenomena of the same order.

CHAPTER SEVEN

The Great Silk Way

Closing the Past, Opening the Future

I do my best thinking on airplane flights.

Before the visit, my aides looked at the map and slapped their heads: "Another ten-hour flight!" The exception was becoming the rule, and we were becoming familiar with regions that had once been neglected by our foreign policy.

After a long and difficult trip, you go over it again mentally from the beginning. You retrace the most difficult parts of the route, wondering if you went the right way, or if you should have done it differently. I am going through something like this now, mentally flying over the expanses of Asia. The time is quite specific, and so is the occasion: the visits to Japan and China, and a trip to Vladivostok. I suspect this mental traveling has been conjured up by the Soviet President's visit to Japan.

■ ■ ■

The trip was packed with reading and contemplation of documents, preparation of materials, polishing of negotiating positions, and editing of official statements and speeches. This time the usual load was increased by an upcoming event, the international conference in Vladivostok on "Dialog, Peace, and Cooperation."

I was to deliver a speech about Soviet policy in the Asian Pacific region. The situation in our country was engendering complicated reflections about the future. I had long entertained an idea in this regard for which conditions now appeared favorable. The Soviet Union had unique opportunities to form a Eurasian zone of security and stability, and to bring about the rapprochement of the West and East, of Europe and Asia.

I reflected on the phenomenon of Japan, on the rapid progress of China and other countries of the region, and tried to outline some answers to the question of whether new economic and political power centers meant rivalry or cooperation. At the same time, despite my wish to think of something else, I was preoccupied with thoughts about the coming September 1990 meeting in Moscow of the Six and about everything related to German reunification, the Europe-wide summits, and their significance for peace.

Although these thoughts seemed scattered, they shared a single axis: our common future. The world was on the brink of the twenty-first century. Now, when it was just a step away, all our reflections and questions took on a thoroughly practical character.

Prediction is a thankless, risky business, and dangerous besides. The twentieth century humbled so many prophets because it turned out so dramatically different from their wonderful visions. Contemporary futurology claims, not without some basis, to have the status of an exact science, but even its most exact computer calculations and mathematical models collide with the unpredictable nature of life. The clairvoyance of the medieval Nostradamuses elicits a mixed feeling of mystical horror and amazement; however, contemporary magic, whether white or black, is making substantive revisions in the path foretold for humanity.

I do not intend to be a seer and will refrain from prognoses. My thoughts on that flight merely reflect the questions everyone is asking. Almost all of them grow out of our current concerns and affairs and are permeated with a hope for a better day. For all its "universality," the scale we apply has one notch, small in size but great for all times, the principal unit of measurement against which everything should be checked: the human being. And I shall apply this scale to all the following issues.

How will the world enter the third millennium? What inheritance will we, today's generation, leave to our children and grand-children? Mountains of superdestructive weapons capable of blowing everything apart, enmity and confrontation, ecological collapse, and a suicidal economic order? Or a world of good-neighbor relations and global cooperation, a world where war and other dangers have no place, where peoples can freely work, live, and, most important, enjoy life?

We need answers today. We need not simply to formulate them, but to generate the material prerequisites for the achievement of the right goals. Without risk of being mistaken, I can say that the fate of the twenty-first century will largely be decided today. Whether the coming generations even have a future depends on us, on how we understand the world in which we live, on whether we correctly see the trends determining its development and, especially, whether we choose the right standards for our behavior.

It has lately become a commonplace in political analysis to observe that the world is changing at an unprecedented pace. But did it not change ten or thirty years ago? Is the whole difference perhaps just a matter of speed? I don't think so. Well, then, what is so different about today?

The world now finds itself on the cutting edge of a civilizing process, where, in the words of one great thinker, "the body of humankind is growing up." Possibly for the first time, the world has reached the final limit of its natural boundaries. For the first time, we are beginning to realize that many vital resources are exhaustible, and many types of human activity should be regulated at the global level.

Politically, almost everything has remained the same. Efforts to change things meet with collective resistance. There are very few states that do not maintain formal diplomatic ties. And there are no countries physically isolated from the life of the world community and its problems.

There is no more "Wild West" or "Siberian remoteness." The Third World is losing its ordinal number. Instead, there are common problems and threats and a common effort to find points of agreement and a balance of interests.

If the world has a body in common, then any sore point hurts everyone. The pain of the world and the threats against it are inseparable from the standpoint of security. The very logic and drama of the world, united in their multiplicity, lead us to search for a common philosophy of world development and the building of new international relations capable of securing the contemporary and future world order. But what can be done about those sore points that divide peoples and countries?

■ ■ ■

I write these lines as President Gorbachev is completing his trip to Japan. Starting back in 1985, my colleagues and I had methodically and persistently steered matters toward the point where this event would become possible. Hence I have the right to make an unbiased judgment about it.

On the eve of this visit, many people asked what I expected from it. I answered that there would be no major changes—the conditions are not ripe for that. In my opinion, people in the Soviet Union, Japan, and elsewhere were mistaken in predicting sensational results. Politics flies by very quickly in our day, but no more quickly than the opportunities offered by the real state of affairs. The rate of change is restricted by them. Politics is dramatic at its base and in its concrete manifestations, but that is not a reason to turn it into the handmaiden of sensation.

Something happened that should have happened long ago: The head of the Soviet Union visited a neighboring country with which good relations are of great mutual importance. It was the first visit, which already means a step forward. A dialog took place at the highest level, and a number of agreements were signed. But I categorically disagree with those who maintain that this visit began a new stage in Soviet–Japanese relations.

We have been talking about a new stage since 1985, when we began regular discussions with the Japanese. During my first visit to Tokyo in January 1986, Sintaro Abe and I agreed that we would discuss all the issues—the territorial problem, bilateral relations. The mere fact that the islands captured by Soviet forces during World War II were finally opened for Japanese who wished to visit the graves of their ancestors and relatives was an enormous moral and political achievement. The human scale was applied to relations that in the past had been clouded with inhumanity.

Afterward, I visited Japan twice again and met with many Japanese colleagues and government figures. Each meeting was a step forward.

In the course of my second visit to Tokyo, at my suggestion, a working mechanism was created for holding talks on the signing of a peace treaty that would resolve the territorial issue. On the third visit, in 1990, our Japanese colleagues agreed for the first time to discuss the question of security and stability in the Asian Pacific region. Thanks to the efforts of my colleague Taro Nakayama, this dialog became multilateral; that year in New York, ministers from a number of the key countries in the region met to exchange opinions.

All three visits to Japan were primarily concerned with the "territorial problem," and despite the fact that I made no compromises, we were at least able to break the ice.

The traditional hospitality of the Japanese does not prevent them from raising hard questions. In 1986 the noise of demonstrations raging on distant streets in Tokyo could be heard in the Soviet Embassy. Matters eased somewhat after that, but even at the time I had no complaints about the protest. It is all too easy to bang your fist on the table; they say this indicates strength and commands respect. I don't want that kind of "respect."

Still, I was forced to be inflexible. We were separated by a negotiation table, and behind us were our peoples and countries; the positions we took were dictated by their interests. Neither I nor my counterparts had the right to back down one iota. But how could a balance of interests be sought in this atmosphere of disequilibrium? Were our critics right in asserting that the rhetoric of universal human values is not always an adequate defense of national interest?

For me they were not rhetoric at all, however, but practical guidelines. The proclamation of this principle motivates us to look at the problem through the prism of humanity. If we are called upon to understand the feelings of the Japanese, then by the same token we must not deny the Russians the same understanding. And we shall never understand each other by standing still.

One of my Japanese partners remarked that the longtime refusal to move from "dead" positions would end if we looked at the problem "not from the North or South," but from above. We had to grasp its true meaning and scale in the mosaic of the region and the world and finally decide what to do. But we need a long-term approach, he added.

I agreed. That was exactly what I was proposing to my Japanese colleagues. We could not stand still. Moscow and Tokyo were not competitors; we could complement each other very well on the world scene. We had to resolve those problems that could be solved. This would create the preconditions for solving others in the future, which today we were approaching from a position of realism, each in his own way.

On my last trip to Tokyo, the discussion centered on the territorial issue. But I said, as I had before: Even if a compromise is not found, we have to develop ties. They would be the basis for a mutually acceptable solution. We had to meet each other halfway, so that in coming together, we would find a balance of interests. For that, perhaps, it was worth declaring a decade of rapprochement between the Soviet Union and Japan, taking us up to the year 2000.

Times changed, and the situations changed in the world and the region. In 1986, speaking with Sintaro Abe, I had constantly sensed the presence of the American–Japanese treaty as a dividing line. Changes in relations between the U.S.S.R. and the United States significantly improved the climate for a Soviet–Japanese dialog. Now it was much easier to talk to each other, easier to find a common language, and that was the best guarantee for the future.

Suddenly, during my third visit to Tokyo, Taro Nakayama and I managed, for the first time, to introduce into the talks issues that the Japanese side earlier had categorically refused to consider. In addition, we discussed a series of documents on humanitarian, scientific, and technical cooperation between Japan and the Soviet Union. These were signed during Gorbachev's first visit to Japan.

So there was some movement. It was dictated by the change in the general situation made possible as a result of the policy of new thinking.

I am convinced that as we develop Soviet–Japanese relations, we shall reach a balance of interests.

Here is my case. My argument is Kostya Skoropyshny, a little boy from Yuzhno-Sakhalinsk, saved by Japanese doctors from a lethal burn, saved by the people of Japan, who had come to the aid of Kostya and his parents at a moment when they had nowhere else to turn. If there really are universal human values, I do not know a more convincing example. Kostya, his relatives, and his fellow citizens are their future. The little boy will grow up with those values, and what once helped him and his fellow citizens to overcome the division between them and the Japanese will mature as well.

Both sides have to work for this. The excessively politicized territorial issue has inflamed stormy nationalist passions. The room to maneuver, already small, is narrowed even more. We must enlarge it with patience and strive to meet each other halfway. Undoubtedly, Gorbachev's visit to Japan will serve this aim. That is the only amendment I would make to the evaluation of the visit. We are not starting with a blank page. It is already filled with much that is promising. It must be continued.

In 1990, speaking before a Japanese audience, I proposed that to broaden the framework of the dialog on the territorial issue, we should remove it from the narrow circle of professional politicians and diplomatic bureaucrats. A joint commission of historians, lawyers, and military people from both countries should be established, and other prominent foreign academics and specialists should be invited to participate. The scholarly discussion would stimulate the political process and would prepare public opinion.

At the time, this idea could not be carried out. I would like to raise it at a practical level in our Foreign Policy Association and review the problem in a calm atmosphere. I think it would be good to start this before Tosiki Kaifu's visit to Moscow.

■　■　■

Shanghai, February 4, 1989. In eleven days, the last Soviet soldier would leave Afghanistan. In a few minutes, Deng Xiaoping will receive the Soviet Foreign Minister. The meeting is in preparation for the Soviet–Chinese summit. In other words, the beginning of normalization of Soviet–Chinese relations.

I know what the decades-long confrontation has cost us and China. Billions were wasted on military hostility. Blood was shed at the border. A sharp deterioration in relations between the two great powers caused the strong of the world to play the "China card" in their own interests. Soviet–Chinese relations, once a powerful factor of positive influence on world affairs, became decidedly negative. In the big game of world politics conducted under the rules of the cold war, the West managed to score points where it hadn't before. The correlation of forces between West and East was disrupted. In the political sense, the West had become "greater" than the East.

On top of all this, I had my own strictly personal motives for desiring the normalization of our relations. For my generation, the People's Republic of China was our youth. Many of us had directly participated in the establishment of the P.R.C., had worked on its grand construction projects, had helped to supply plants with Soviet equipment, had worked on the state farms, and had shared our experience. We had learned much from the Chinese and had kept the memory of our friends for life. And I suppose for many it was a personal shock when relations between the P.R.C. and the U.S.S.R. then chilled and deteriorated. Their normalization was my own personal cause, my political and moral duty.

So we were at the threshold of a summit. But we were blocked from opening the doors wide because of several stubborn obstacles. Not everything depended on us, I assured my colleague Deng Xiaoping. The knots of contradictions are tightened by the incompatibility of the interests of our two countries. It is customary to believe that if we tied them, we must cut them. But they arose as the result of the hostility and conflict in which each side strove to affirm its "model" and canon. "Cold" and "hot" wars in this region are the consequence of this logic.

The key problem was Cambodia and the military presence of Vietnam in that country. From the beginning of our talks with Deng Xiaoping on ways to normalize Soviet–Chinese relations, we invariably stumbled over this issue. It seemed insurmountable. It was not the military presence at our borders or the settlement of complex boundary issues, but the Cambodian question that kept the door firmly locked.

How we opened the door is a long story. I will only say that this was an independent effort with broader implications, and that the Soviet Union actively cooperated in its resolution—and continues to cooperate—not only with China. As a factor of world magnitude, it takes on a scale commensurate with the global rivalry of systems, and with the policy of the new thinking that is overcoming that gigantic schism.

On the eve of the meeting with Deng Xiaoping, the lock seemed to give way. In a small, modestly appointed house in the suburbs of Shanghai, Deng Xiaoping proposed a formula for the normalization of Soviet–Chinese relations.

"There have been periods in history when our relations zig-zagged. There was a time when we knew and understood each other better. Then there was a break for twenty years. . . . This is an exceptionally difficult task, the resolution of which touches upon exceptionally complex issues."

It was not hard to guess which questions Deng Xiaoping had in mind.

"The better to accomplish this task," he continued, "we need to know the past. But that does not mean we have to stir it up. Knowledge of the past must have limits."

"Yes," I said, picking up his last phrase and carrying it forward with my own favorite maxim from Jaurès: "Take from the past not the ashes, but the fire."

Deng Xiaoping nodded in assent. From what he said further, an entire picture of the world emerged in its historical and present dimensions, directly related to the interests of China and its place and role in the world. In my respected partner's mind, he had done almost everything that he had intended in order to create the best conditions for his country's development. Everything except restore relations with the Soviet Union.

"The exchange of visits by our Foreign Ministers means that the process of normalization has begun. The main event in this process is the summit. We must normalize our relations. And I must meet Gorbachev for that. As I understand it, our meeting should close the past and open the future."

Everything went according to that formula three and a half months later, as we intended. But that occurred only because Deng Xiaoping and I managed to remove the major obstacles.

At one point I expressed confidence that Vietnam would remove its forces from Cambodia. Comrade Deng looked at me doubtfully but refrained from comment. Naturally, I was pleased to learn soon afterward that I was not mistaken.

Deng Xiaoping spoke of the difficulties, but only in the most general way. Having defined the strategic task, he presented us with an opportunity to wrack our brains over the insoluble parts of the equation. Two hours of conversation about political philosophy flew by quickly. Slow, difficult movement began beyond the walls of the house in Shanghai. The exact date of the summit was not scheduled, only the period: mid-May 1989. In order to set an exact date, we had to compromise. Neither we nor the Chinese backed down, but we did find a mutually acceptable result. How? I shall leave that for future textbooks on diplomacy.

The summit did take place and indeed opened up the future for new relations. But the events on Tiananmen Square meant that the fragile sprout of dialog had been planted in very inhospitable soil. In my view, we came out of this trial with dignity, although in all conscience I must say that I was deeply wounded by the tragedy, which added directly to my concerns about our own domestic affairs.

In a short time we managed to overcome suspicion and distrust and entered into talks on the dismantling of the structure of military hostility. During the crisis in the Persian Gulf, we were essentially on the same side. The active multilevel political dialog, and the meetings with Deng Xiaoping in Peking, Harbin, and Urumchi, developed relations in the direction needed by our countries and the world.

■ ■ ■

Vladivostok is a closed city, shut up by years of confrontation, division, military rivalry, and mistrust. It is closed to cooperation, exchanges, and the normal, peaceful, harmless life of citizens. This otherwise beautiful city is defaced by signs that the vital fabric of human life is subordinated to the "interests of the state," and the needs of the people to the maintenance of the state's might. Yet it is also an amazingly kind city, yearning for open communication with the world.

I considered it extremely important to speak there. It was just the place to present ideas about possible paths for the region to take toward unifying political ideas. Such ideas are well known in the history of continents, I said. Even at the level of political philosophy, these ideas served to bring countries and peoples together and preserved their commonality. Today, at a time of the greatest trials, they are at the foundation of our common home of peoples.

I had in mind the idea of Europe. And I maintained that an Asian idea existed, the idea of Asia.

Orientalists will dispute this assertion. I say, however, that it lives in the great teachings of the ancients, whose common legacy we accept as a unified conception of humanism. The idea of Asia lives also in the insights of our time, in political figures' appeals addressed to the vast Asian and human community, in the philosophy of nonviolence, in the principles of "Pancha Shila," in the Bandung declaration. Soviet–Indian summits were of great significance, culminating in the Delhi declaration of the principles of a nonviolent, nuclear-free world.

Now is the time for the idea of Asia to work at full strength, as the idea of Europe has been working.

I place these two great continents together for a reason. Rather, it is not I who place them together, but history itself and contemporary life, politics, geography, and culture. Europe and Asia, West and East have long been traveling toward each other. They move, surmounting walls and the isolation of some countries, the nightmares of colonial occupation and enslavement, regional conflicts and material inequality. On the shores of the Pacific Ocean, a path begins; it passes through the expanses of the Far East and Siberia, the European part of the Soviet Union, and Eastern and Western Europe, and emerges on the shores of the Atlantic. "The Great Silk Way" closed off the pathways of war and violence; it was a thin, silk thread of history woven through space and time. To do the same is all the more possible now, as the slow silk caravans have been replaced by lightning-swift electronics, merging the disconnected worlds into a single whole.

If our political scientists and columnists are correct in thinking that the great Eurasian tract called the Soviet Union is the "world of worlds," then it must also be correct that it does not separate these formerly divided worlds, but joins them. As the noted Russian philosopher Georgy Fedotov said, Russia should live politically in the complex world of both the European and the Asian peoples. I would add that Russia and the others that compose the "world of worlds" of Soviet Eurasia wish to serve politically the establishment of peace and neighborliness between them.

The unique location of the Soviet Union can play an invaluable role in establishing the most diverse ties between Asia and Europe. If trans-Atlantic cables could be laid, then with modern technology we can implement the project of trans-Eurasian communication. The potential of the Soviet Union to integrate Asia and Europe is enormous.

The alienation of continents was predicated largely on the cold war. Its lines bisected not just Europe. Now, with complete assurance, we can speak about the formation of a united Eurasian zone of security and stability. We are entitled to speak of this, I submit, by virtue of favorable preconditions for encouraging the formation of unified zones embracing continents: political, economic, scientific, humanitarian, and cultural.

The Soviet Union is an organic part of this united Euro-American-Asian belt. For several decades, the country was largely isolated from the rest of the world. Traditional trade routes were interrupted, and spiritual, cultural, and simply human ties were broken. Now, at last, they are being restored.

We can look forward to a time in the near future when there will no longer be a Soviet military presence beyond our national borders in Asia, or in any other part of the world, for that matter. Positive changes in the Asian Pacific are at hand. Countries that not long ago were suspicious of each other are now establishing normal, neighborly ties: China with India, Laos, and Mongolia; the countries of Indochina with Thailand and other members of ASEAN. The restoration of ties between China and Indonesia, and China and Saudi Arabia, as well as the United States with Mongolia, were great events.

The countries of the region are actively promoting a settlement of regional conflicts, chiefly in Cambodia. They are taking steps to lower the level of tension in South Asia, home to more than a billion people. China has reduced its armed forces. Vietnamese troops were withdrawn from Cambodia. The United States has announced plans to reduce somewhat its military presence in the Asian Pacific. Agreements have been drafted for an all-encompassing Cambodian settlement. We can take satisfaction from the fact that the five permanent members of the U.N. Security Council now hold the same position on this question.

There is no lack of productive ideas in the region. I would like to make special note of India's wide-ranging proposals to create a nuclear-free and nonviolent world; the Chinese idea for a new international political order; the Mongolian initiative for dialog between countries of Northeast Asia; the signing of a treaty on a nuclear-free zone in the South Pacific; the ASEAN and Indochinese proposals for similar zones in Southeast Asia; New Zealand's antinuclear legislation; Australian confidence-building initiatives in the Northeast Pacific; Thailand's formulation of principles of "positive coexistence" in Southeast Asia; and Indonesia's proposals for security in the South Chinese Sea basin.

The Soviet Union supports North Korea's initiatives for a peace settlement on the Korean Peninsula: the North and South Declaration on nonaggression; measures to prevent accidental conflict; gradual reduction of troops in both Koreas; and making the peninsula a nuclear-free zone. These are all steps that may actually create a different atmosphere in this powderkeg region. There are also proposals from South Korea. It is important to coordinate the points each side's proposals have in common and then to implement them in practice.

The infamous walls of division were erected not only in Europe. Beside the Berlin Wall there is the wall separating the two Koreas. I would like to believe that in the near future, the concrete barrier that stands in the way of Korean unification will meet the same fate as the Berlin Wall.

Several days later in Pyongyong, I tried to convince the leaders of North Korea that the forthcoming establishment of diplomatic ties between the Soviet Union and South Korea would serve to overcome division and reunite the country. Unfortunately, that did not come about, but it was hardly our fault.

The degree of mistrust and even enmity is still too high, and it is fueled by territorial disputes and ideological, ethnic, and religious factors. A dangerously high level of military hostility remains, especially on the Korean Peninsula. The production of nuclear missiles continues, and naval activity has increased.

Having graduated from the "academy of Europe," the school of the Helsinki process, we are hoping for an extension of this unique experience to other parts of the world. True, this experience is not universal. We cannot measure Asia by the European yardstick. But it does serve as an example of how harmony can be established where discord once reigned.

I find it hard to agree with those who emphasize the uniqueness of the Asian Pacific and try to slow down the process of introducing to this region the positive trends of world politics. By appreciating the multicolored picture of the region and the way in which its composition differs from others in the world, we can search for a specific "Asian format" to resolve the problems of security and cooperation. I believe we can apply the principle of reliable security to Asian realities, with a serious reduction of arms to the level of sufficiency, by making effective use of political means.

Must we repeat here the road already traveled by others, the accumulation of weapons, the creation of military alliances and coalitions, and the building of new military bases—only to find out later that it could have been avoided and our resources directed to solving acute social and economic problems?

In reflecting on how we might initiate talks in the region, I am more and more convinced of the necessity of a broad dialog on regional problems. Almost everywhere, with the exception of the Asian Pacific, there are general forums for discussing the most burning issues. In Europe, there is the Conference on Security and Cooperation in Europe; in America, there is the Organization of American States; in Africa, there is the Organization for African Unity. Of course, not all of their activities run smoothly, but the utility of these organizations is not questioned.

Interest in convening a pan-Asian forum of some type is growing. The idea of scheduling a meeting at the foreign minister level for these purposes is taking hold. Scientists and public figures are playing an important role in forming an infrastructure to stimulate movement toward convening an Asian Pacific forum. The Williamsburg conferences, the Kuala Lumpur round-tables, the New Zealand symposiums, and the Vladivostok meetings all prove that a congress of representatives of Pacific Rim countries, including government officials, to discuss regional problems in concert is possible and increasingly timely.

No doubt the time is ripe for wider and more regular parliamentary exchanges. Given the well-known difficulties, an approach toward an Asian Pacific conference could be made gradually, using various political and diplomatic methods. I believe it would not be productive to set any preconditions for this conference. There is no sense in waiting until all disputes and disagreements disappear. A more effective approach would be to intensify efforts at conflict-resolution, the reduction of hostility, the elimination of friction, and stepping up bilateral contacts, while simultaneously making the transition to the multilateral talks.

How could it be set in motion? It is worth considering a meeting of the countries with the largest military potentials. This could be a working meeting of foreign ministers open to observers from other countries. I think the Soviet Union would be prepared to engage in the necessary consultations in order to prepare such a meeting and work out the agenda with its participants.

Given the overall interest in free and secure seas, we need to

think through the idea of an international regional Center for the
Security of Sea Lanes. No country, no matter what the size of its
navy, is capable by itself of guaranteeing stability and defending
the freedom and security of ocean passages. Moreover, any such
undertaking would provoke suspicion in other countries.

I believe the best solution of the problem of security on the sea
and in the air, including the war against terrorism and piracy,
would be a system of international safeguards. I proposed to the
Ministers of Foreign Affairs of those Asian countries willing to
accept our invitation a meeting in Vladivostok in the autumn of
1993. It could be an open meeting, both as to participants and as to
agenda.

It should be possible to draft a joint document announcing the
policy principles agreed upon by the participants, and affirming a
renunciation of confrontation and a transition to relations of partnership.

As I emphasized in Vladivostok, the Soviet Union is prepared
to begin a dialog on military problems and confidence-building measures with all the countries of Asia and the Pacific Ocean. We are
not calling for the destruction of existing military and political
structures. Each country determines for itself, in keeping with its
national interests, how it must arrange its relations with other
countries, including the question of security.

Economic development is as much a concern in the region as
military and political dangers. Recently there have been forecasts
of an "economic cold war" among Asia, Europe, and America as
well as within the Pacific Rim. We cannot allow a new front of
hostility to emerge between North and South. For the first time in
history, conditions are ripe for an integrated development of the
world economy on principles of equality, mutual benefit, and mutual aid. Economic cooperation between East and West has noticeably increased, which deepens the integrational process. Countries
show a growing interest in strengthening and increasing the effectiveness of multilateral trade and hard-currency finance mechanisms.

Such trends are fully present as well in the region, which
today largely determines the "economic weather" of the planet.
Processes of economic integration are accelerating. It is important
that we make these processes harmonious and democratic through
our joint efforts, so that they do not lead into the blind alley of

insular trade groupings, constantly causing friction, conflict, and sometimes even outright trade wars.

I realize that much remains to be done so that the economic presence of the Soviet Union in the Asian Pacific will reach the level commensurate with its economic possibilities. Here active economic diplomacy and new forms of incorporation into the economic life of the region are needed on our part. That will require internal measures to speed the development of the economy and the market in the Asian part of the Soviet Union and the Soviet Far East, and measures to create a favorable political and legal environment for investments.

The Union republics are actively developing direct ties with countries in the region. The Russian Republic is taking the lead. The Russian Supreme Soviet passed a resolution to create free enterprise zones in the Far East. Uzbekistan is reaching out to countries in Southeast Asia, and Kazakhstan is working with provinces in China. Soviet representatives are taking an active part in a number of programs within the Conference on Pacific Economic Cooperation. They are willing to participate in analogous programs in the framework of an intergovernmental forum of Asian Pacific economic cooperation.

Realities are such that the transition of our economy to the market, its increased accessibility, and the introduction of mutually advantageous forms of external economic ties are creating the basis for incorporating the Soviet economy into the economic architecture of the Asian Pacific. To overlook this would mean to reduce significantly the potential for economic integration and to underestimate the enormous prospects of the Soviet Far East and the unlimited possibilities for profitable capital investment, with an eye to the twenty-first century.

The Soviet Union does not conceive of its future development without a greater participation in the world economy. Accordingly, it will find partners and will organically link the economy of its Far East and Siberia with the Asian Pacific economic complex.

As they say in the East, many roads lead to the summit. Of course everyone is free to choose his own road according to his taste and opportunities. But if we unite our resources, determine the optimal path, and help one another, we will reach the summit faster, and with fewer losses.

We propose moving toward the summit together, guided by

such interconnected ideas as respect, trust, and cooperation. Only in respecting our partners, their choice of social and political systems and their lawful interests, can we create an atmosphere of trust so needed to implement measures in the political, military, and economic fields, so as to eliminate suspicion and introduce predictability, reliability, and mutual understanding into intergovernmental relations. I believe that many of these proposals are still timely.

■ ■ ■

After my resignation, I had a rare opportunity to learn what the people I had met at the negotiation table thought of me. I will leave aside the compliments, without leaving out, however, my gratitude for the sympathy, support, and fond memories. Now I think it is more productive to look at the critical remarks.

When a journalist asked a certain ambassador of a great Asian country what he thought of my resignation, he said that of course he regretted that Shevardnadze was leaving.

"However," he added, "in fairness I have to say that the former Soviet minister was an 'Americanist' and 'Europeanist' and gave less attention to Asian affairs."

I dispute this assertion. It is factually wrong. The point is not that we paid no attention to Asian or African affairs, but that today all these affairs are so interconnected that it is impossible to focus on just one. And experience and practice should not be neglected. There was the experience of Afghanistan; the peaceful settlement in Namibia and the declaration of its independence; the expansion of ties with Indonesia and other ASEAN countries; the active participation in the ending of the Iran–Iraq war.

The visit to Iran took place during a very difficult time. After the meeting with the Ayatollah Khomeini, the Soviet–Iranian dialog, virtually broken off in past years, was renewed.

We see very positive movement in our relations with Turkey. Now good-neighbor relations are not a goal, but a reality.

In the countries of Indochina, ASEAN, and Australia, we persistently sought ways to settle conflicts that the world had inherited from the era of the "great opposition of systems" and the cold war, which had extended to the Asian Pacific region.

The transformation of Soviet–American relations served the cause of peace. The signing of the INF Treaty had significance for

Asia, since we removed missiles of this class from the Asian part of the U.S.S.R. when we dismantled them in Europe.

I am not merely listing my own Asian accomplishments here. If anything deserves credit, it is the policy of the new thinking. In beginning perestroika with a rejection of the politics of global confrontation and the primacy of class warfare in intergovernmental relations, we did not limit our political horizons to America, Europe, and the Far East. We proceeded from the political, historical, and geographical reality that the Soviet Union is the only country on earth that has borders with Europe, America, and Asia. This reality places special obligations upon us, requiring a special, increased responsibility in Asian Pacific affairs. The objective need for regional cooperation in the Asian Pacific, the acute problems of stability and security, the relentless arms race, and the danger of nuclear proliferation were the motives for the initiatives outlined by Gorbachev in Vladivostok and Krasnoyarsk.

We set a true course when we embarked on this path, the course of the policy of new thinking. The geographic span of this path was immense, the load of responsibility heavy, but we knew where we were headed.

I had my own personal baggage, the historical memory of the centuries my people had lived on the border between Europe and Asia. This brought us many troubles in the past, and peace is still not at hand, but the complicated interaction of civilizations, cultures, faiths, and languages has fused in our souls a precious bond with the rest of the world.

In my list of priorities, the Third World was not tertiary. The path of the new thinking was extended around the world so that our foreign policy linked its problems both with perestroika and with global affairs. The Third World, after all, is the first to pay for the impoverished state of nature, the arms race, and the growth of debt. It is also the most vulnerable in terms of regional conflicts. Our ability to meet the global challenges depends on how the world economy will develop and whether we will find the resources for environmental protection, development, and the elimination of poverty, epidemics, and the consequences of economic catastrophe.

My visits to the countries of Africa and to Central and South America have persuaded me that the idea of reasonable sufficiency for defense could be applied in these regions. Without disarmament, reduction of military expenditure, conversion of military industries, and release of resources for developmental needs, it will be very difficult to manage increasingly grave global problems.

In the years of perestroika, we renewed a dialog with countries whose role, weight, and influence in international affairs would increase at the close of the century.

I found the ministers and leaders of these countries to be wonderful partners and in some cases, even friends. Unfortunately, many of the agreements we reached remain unfulfilled. But I always returned my debts. I will try to do this in my new career in the Foreign Policy Association.

Even the most exact and elegant formula for the improvement of the world may be applied only by our common efforts. Perhaps one or two countries will attempt to shoulder the burden, but as matters proceed they will discover that their achievements will be nullified because of international disfavor. We need a global effort at cooperation, not islands of limited agreement. Only in this way can we open a path to the future for ourselves and others.

I know this is difficult. The past does not allow itself to be forgotten. I have been reminded of this every step of the way. But we have no other choice.

CHAPTER EIGHT

Which Road Leads
to the Cathedral?

I Make My Choice

On that morning, the telephones jangled at an hour when they are normally silent. I postponed my usual Monday meeting to answer all the agitated questions. They all boiled down to one: What had happened? I had no answer. During those first morning hours I didn't yet know that an accident had occurred at one of our nuclear power stations. My efforts to extract news from the sources I could reach produced little. "Yes," they told me. "Something's happened in the Ukraine, but so far we can't get any clear information." Scraps of news trickled in, but did not give the full picture of what had happened.

Gorbachev telephoned and asked me to come right over. By that time more than a dozen foreign ambassadors had requested emergency meetings with me or my deputies. Their governments had urgently ordered them to find out which radioactive elements were spewing into their countries' atmosphere, soil and water. Once they had ascertained that their own reactors were functioning normally, they had traced the leak to the Soviet Union. The affair was turning into a scandal.

I was just leaving my office when my aide informed me of

another call. This time it was about Tenghiz Abuladze's film *Repentance*, which had languished in the can since 1984. Like many good films, it had been banned, and he hadn't been able to screen it. Abuladze was now requesting my advice. Could he ask Gorbachev for help and appeal to the Congress of Cinematographers on May 12?

This story is fairly well known; Abuladze himself has often mentioned my role in getting his film shown. The movie had to be financed from the republic's dwindling coffers. Even at the editing stage, we had discussed its future at length and in detail. Knowing the director's abilities, I was certain of his picture's artistic merits. But I was no less interested in its sociopolitical resonance. The film promised to break the conspiracy of silence about the tyranny, lawlessness, and persecution to which millions of people in our country had been subjected. My intuition told me that the time was approaching when we would have to go much further than Khrushchev himself had gone nearly thirty years ago. Solzhenitsyn's *One Day in the Life of Ivan Denisovich* remained an isolated phenomenon.

I did not think, nor do I now, that a dead ideology should muzzle creativity. In all respects, this film was a question of principle for me. When Abuladze had confided his concept to me, I doubted that the film would ever find wide distribution. I had even shared my misgivings with the director, but urged him to shoot the film anyway. It was a risk, but a carefully calculated one in every detail from the financing to the choice of a studio lot where the filming could take place without fear of a shutdown on orders from Moscow.

Shortly before my transfer to Moscow, Abuladze showed me and some comrades a rough cut of the film. We sensed its power. My doubts about its reaching the screen were all the stronger.

Just as the finishing touches were being put on the film, I left Tbilisi. Immediately, demands were sent to the appropriate offices to destroy the only copy of the film and the order came down to "punish" the author. Alarmed at his brainchild's fate, Abuladze hurried to videotape it. The people who helped him make the copy were charged with duplicating an anti-Soviet work and fired from their jobs. The film was "arrested."

In my first few months in the Foreign Ministry on Smolensk Square, my conscience pricked me now and then. I had incited a man to commit an out-of-the-ordinary act, had supported his idea, had helped him to shoot the film, and had now left him hanging out to dry. Finally, I couldn't hold out any longer and spoke to Gorbachev. "I owe a lot of people back home and I can't repay them all now. But there is one debt I must pay no matter what happens, and you can help me."

Gorbachev saw *Repentance* and said he would have to give it the green light. In fairness, may people of all sorts played a role in the film's destiny. Not even counting Abuladze's filmmaker colleagues, Aleksandr Yakovlev had been involved and I am told, Yegor Ligachev. *Repentance* garnered strong support but incited equally strong opposition. The consensus of the Politburo was that if we entangled ourselves in the past, we'd never extract ourselves from the swamp we were in today. Accommodating the numerous demands for the Party to exonerate past prominent figures would spark a chain reaction of historical reevaluation. The fate of *Repentance* was understood in this light. Any repentance presumed an admission of personal responsibility. A public condemnation of the past threatened an inevitable break with its "methods."

I sent word to Abuladze that Gorbachev knew about the film and had definitely given it the green light, but that he just had to wait a little.

The truth about Chernobyl couldn't wait, but publicizing it proved to be terribly difficult, and for the very same reasons that *Repentance* had been censored.

The Twenty-seventh Party Congress two months prior to this had been called the "lessons of truth." We really told the truth about the country's state of affairs and solemnly vowed our loyalty to glasnost.

Three days before the Chernobyl disaster, at a meeting to commemorate the 116th anniversary of Lenin's birthday, I quoted Gorbachev: "We categorically oppose those who call for releasing public information in doses; there can never be too much truth." Now, four days later, I was forced to denounce those who had tried to hide the truth in the system's patented safe of secrecy.

It was profoundly absurd from the standpoint of common sense. How can you conceal something that can't be hidden? How could people complain about "washing our dirty linen in public," when it was radioactive and had slipped out in spite of us? From the standpoint of morality, it was outrageous. How can you hide from millions of people the truth about a threat to their lives and health, when the criminal suppression of the facts about the impending danger would leave whole nations in the dark and deprive them of a chance to take preventative measures? From the standpoint of politics, it was outright sabotage at the highest level of the principles of the new thinking, and of the hard-won domestic and international trust in the Soviet leadership's new course.

Although I had been raised in a spirit of mystical veneration for the "top secret" stamp, I did nevertheless everything I could so that the truth about Chernobyl would be known to the country and to the whole world in the first days after the accident. I was not able to do much, but even that unsheathed the claws of some of my colleagues in the Politburo. To use the lexicon of the political patriarchate, my colleagues and I took a lot of heat for passing information onto our foreign partners. And I'll be damned if they weren't doing business as usual, by the worn-out scripts of the past, despite our proclamations of honest openness. The absence of full and accurate information was compensated with a massive invocation of the "ideological safeguard" of unprovability, and with the automatic, reflexive denial of "the provocative propagandistic ballyhoo raised in the West about an accident at our nuclear power station."

Gorbachev spoke on Central Television on May 15 and dotted all the i's.

Today, five years later, when the total number of victims has reached the tens of thousands, when not just a 30-kilometer "circle of hell" is contaminated with cesium and strontium, but whole provinces and republics, the meaning of the battle for the truth back then is more distinct for me than it was in April 1986. In losing the battle then, we lost people's trust in us today, since for the nth time we were disregarding the highest stakes there are: human life.

"Chernobyl Day," as I privately called April 26, 1986, marked a watershed in world history, a new criterion for foreign policy. We hadn't managed to pronounce this phrase yet and had not clarified the real dimensions of the catastrophe, but in one second, the explosion heralded an era when no ecological disaster caused by a breakdown in technology could be kept within rational borders. In the modern world, the boundaries and radius of various natural disasters were very conditional. There was an unconditional need for outside international resistance to a threat no less horrible than thermonuclear war: the ecological collapse of the planet. And if we are going to use the word "war," then I shall say that the ecological war has already been unleashed, first in the unrestrained and uncontrolled encroachment of the technosphere into the biosphere, then, in our time, the deliberate use of military resources against life-sustaining natural resources. The clouds of smoke from the burning oil wells in Kuwait could darken the horizon for all humankind. This war against one nation was deliberately escalated to aggression against nature, which belongs to all humanity.

The ecological imperative of survival has laid bare numerous previously unseen and unrecognized values. First is the factor of the integrity of the world. As Ronald Reagan said about Chernobyl, "Rarely has the interdependence of modern industrial countries seemed more obvious than in these days." The American President spoke the same language as the Communist Party's General Secretary, whose thesis concerning a single interdependent world was a key concept in the new political thinking. "Chernobyl Day" instantly placed the common human value of life above "class consciousness." And again, the protection of the human being, the chief purpose of any policy, including environmental, was revealed, liberated from the masks of ideological shamanism. It was the defense of that "unit of measurement" by which we must gauge the authentic security of nations and peoples. But even so, a more inclusive ratio must be used here. Only in defending each person along with his natural environment can we give all of humankind a chance for survival. And the converse: By acting as a whole world—under the banner "Peoples of the world, unite!"—we can save one person.

This would all have seemed a sophisticated game if the dying Black Sea had not been before our very eyes, and a desert had not replaced the Aral Sea. I knew that this ecological disaster placed an entire nation on the verge of extinction. I knew the genuine danger of the rich Volga region's deterioration. I had run up against a dilemma in my home republic: the ferrous smelting works in Zestafoni, which were poisoning Western Georgia with dangerous wastes but could not be shut down because of "the significance of its production in especially important state interests." The health, life, and future of our children, who were being born with terrible disabilities, was at stake.

"Chernobyl Day" tore the blindfold from our eyes and persuaded us that politics and morals could not diverge. We had to gauge our politics constantly by moral criteria. Lest I be thought too sanctimonious, I shall say that moral politics is the credo of the pragmatist, a person whom life has taught that immoral politics goes nowhere. The Chernobyl story, which was a battle for glasnost and disclosure of the facts, the causes, and the consequences of the accident, is the surest argument in favor of that principle. The question of truth, of accurate information, not owned or doled out according to class, caste, clan, or ethnic attributes, is a crucial test of the morality or immorality of politics.

It also became the crucial test of my personal destiny, and of my work in the Foreign Ministry. The problem of truth and deception was central to my resignation. I began to contemplate leaving approximately a year before December 20, 1990. But even at the early stages of my activity as a member of the Politburo and as Foreign Minister, when I constantly encountered throwbacks to the old double standard, backsliding from stated principles, and attempts to operate in the old fashion, I was compelled to reflect upon my role and its limitations. Back in 1986 I asked myself how long I could go on speaking as an exporter of the new thinking while other people and groups inside the country were obviously oriented toward the old thinking.

I am not blaming anyone for adhering to old thinking, and my reason is by no means a desire to come across as the righteous type who overlooks the sins of others. All of us were cut from the same cloth. To put it more accurately, we all meant to be, in words at least. But although some genuinely wanted to throw off the totalitarian mantle, others could not, and still others found it suited them just fine, as if it had been custom-tailored. I remember how they demanded that words about the class struggle be included in the Party's program, and Gorbachev said to them: "We remember about the class struggle when we want to force people to starve." It was naïve to think that generations raised for decades on barracks socialism could quickly adjust their consciousness. But I would like to believe that it is possible, because it is vitally necessary, and I have kept assuring myself and those close to me that the time will come when we will learn how to speak the truth, and speak it in time.

Chernobyl was the first test of glasnost, and it failed. Now it's all up ahead, I told myself, we're just starting. But ahead lay the tragedies in Alma-Ata, Sumgait, Stepanakert, Baku, Tbilisi, Vilnius, and Riga, and the old mechanisms kicked in, simplifying, distorting, or just eliminating the truth about events. I myself ran into a clear attempt to conceal from the country's leadership important details of the April execution in Tbilisi, so I can back Gorbachev's statement that he knew about the events in Vilnius only after they happened. But that means a theory of some "shadow" authority inevitably surfaces, a force operating at cross purposes with the lawful authorities, sending out disinformation along with the tanks. Or there was a desire to "cover for" this power and keep it out of the glasnost zone, something that is harder for me to believe.

■ ■ ■

The monopoly on power is a monopoly on information, on the means and methods of its production and dissemination. The rejection of the monopoly on power entails the admission of pluralism, including information, opinion, analysis, and ideas. Sadly, the years of enforced political monopolism hindered the growth of a political culture capable of translating centrifugal discord into normal, civilized, constructive public dialog.

We all remain prisoners of our past, continuing to rely on such past means of escape as an armed breakout or tunneling under the walls. I understand those who do not see any other way; the decades of violence ruled out any other means of overcoming oppression. But there are other methods of shaking off a burdensome legacy: reflection, sober analysis, separating the wheat from the chaff, dialog, a cease-fire, the signing of an armistice, and finally peace. Unfortunately, here too we encounter a deficit of political culture, which is clearly being exploited by pretenders to the role of "leader" and candidates for the new dictatorship who yearn for the old ways. "We will witness how ancient, underground monsters will be awakened by the air of freedom and will crawl out from their underground."[1] These are words of Adam Michnik, the Polish human rights activist and historian and one of the theoreticians of Solidarity. At one time some of my comrades in the Party used his name to scare little children. In 1989 he interviewed me for his *Gazeta Wyborcza*. We had a photograph taken together for

[1] Adam Michnik, "Nationalism: The Monster Awakens," *The Twentieth Century and the World*, no. 10, 1990.

a memento, and the picture ended up on the cover of the journal. The Poles rubbed their eyes in disbelief—a dissident side by side with, almost embracing, a member of the Communist Politburo!

It was not deception. The deception, or self-deception, is to barricade yourself from a person with a wall of "ideological" incompatibility on the sole grounds that he thinks differently from you. On closer scrutiny, it turns out more often than not that he thinks no worse than you, if not sometimes in unison. At any rate, some of Michnik's ideas on the nature of nationalism and chauvinism are consonant with my own conceptions. For example, I agree with the words of a thinker Adam cites that the victory of national chauvinism over humanism leaves the way to power open for tyrants. It's a paradox, isn't it? But no more so than the partially successful attempts of some "national patriots" coming to power to arm themselves with the dirtiest methods from the arsenal of dying pseudo-Communist regimes: the persecution of dissent, the suppression of national minorities, projection on mythical enemies of responsibility for their own mistakes, the creation of phantom "enemies of the people," and so on.

After my resignation, I was able to meet again with Michnik, this time in Moscow. We discussed the situation in the Soviet Union and Eastern Europe with the idea of possibly influencing events that sadly were not always positive; about European stability; about the processes transforming the new Europe; and about the sorely needed structures of security. Again, we agreed that the tendency toward the awakening of national chauvinism endangers the establishment of new democratic societies and threatens to undermine hard-won peaceful European revolutions. Essentially, Michnik said, it's a question of what course the revolution will take in each country. And again our reflections led to the conclusion that the natural desire to put an end to the past is clothed in forms that threaten nations with a contraction of historical prospects. Placing the guilt for their troubles and misfortunes on the "aliens" or the "collaborationists," chauvinism and nationalism evade responsibility for the present and the future.

All of this has already happened. As always in a time of troubles, the Sharikovs and the Kvarkvare Tutaberis[2] emerge on the

---

[2] Sharikov is the protagonist of *Heart of a Dog*, a novel by the Russian author Mikhail Bulgakov. Kvarkvare Tutaberi is the title character of a play by the same name by the Georgian playwright Polikarpe Kakabadze. Both personify the political opportunist.

scene, along with the *lumpen*-opportunists, and the hoisting of "sacred banners" distracts attentive eyes from their true face. Meanwhile, the intelligentsia, which has done so much to awaken national consciousness, can be forced off the road of social and political life.

Why? There is something to reflect on here. Historically, in countries where the imperial psychology is embodied in official state doctrine, where the postulates of power require unswerving subordination of intellect and spirit to some universal idea, the intelligentsia enters into opposition to authority. It is a natural pose, since the intellect and spirit always rebel against restriction. For democratic countries, this is the norm: Reined in by culture and responsibility, freedom always finds a way to express disagreement. Intelligent leaders should not only listen to dissent but encourage it. But if there are no such leaders, and if the democratic idea has no tradition, then the intellectual enters not into opposition, but confrontation with authority. It usually becomes a permanent state of war, in which the two sides exchange heavy blows, trying to knock each other out of commission. Finally, the intelligentsia plunges into a revolutionary struggle and takes on a function of destruction alien to it, and thus undermines itself. It stops being what it should be. Unable to inspire, enlighten, and incite the masses, it unwillingly loses its ability for practical creative work. And when the elements awakened by its will enter the arena of battle, the intelligentsia can only be horrified by its demonic creation. Or, as throughout our history, it becomes the victim of repression and terror.

■ ■ ■

Journalists in Rome from *La Stampa* and *Repubblica* asked me recently about the social basis for perestroika. Who were we aiming at when we began it? I replied that the support had been nationwide. Perhaps few knew the truth about the economic consequences of the stagnation period, which had slowed development and increasingly caused the Soviet Union to lag behind the leading countries of the world. But dissatisfaction with the existing state of affairs was widespread. It was felt in the Party, both among its leaders and in local branches, in industry and agriculture, and among people in the arts and sciences. The Party-state gerontocracy stunted the growth of at least two generations of the most active part of the population. People with brains and talent got a late start in life, and when they did start, they discovered cramped opportunities for expressing their abilities. The century of the "Kremlin Methuselahs" seemed endless, and their impotence, finding its reflection in the inertia of the enormous country, seemed everlasting.

Gorbachev's contrast with his predecessors was so marked that many saw him as their sole chance for survival. And the first to seize this chance were those whose intellect could not accept the deepening stagnation of the country.

In speaking of intellect, I would not limit myself to fixed social groups—workers, peasants, people in science and culture—for the boundaries here are as mobile as the line between people's mentality and their internal principles. I would not make an absolute classification according to social criteria; the changing means of production arising from the scientific and technological revolution have altered previous definitions. The new technologies have placed increased demands on the individual. They require greater freedom and responsibility. Some are ready and willing to accept this challenge, but others are incapable of meeting it. This demarcation could be recognized as the only possible and correct one if it were not far more complicated. For example, in agriculture, we have collective farms that have achieved a high degree of efficiency in communal labor and accordingly have provided a wide range of social and economic benefits to their workers. But there are farms in the mountainous regions of Georgia where it is hard to make ends meet. While those in the first group are fearful of transferring the land to private ownership, since this could upset a well-run life, those in the latter group are happy to rent haying machines and pastures, since this form of land use is for them the most intelligent and promises a greater profit.

I draw another example, more cogent for me, from the sphere of international relations and national state policy. The constitutional norm of national state sovereignty guaranteed the republics *de jure* status of sovereign nations. But this was nullified by *de facto* unitarism and the harsh canons of subordination to the Center, which always had force behind it. Perestroika eliminated that or, at least at the level of the proclaimed principle of freedom of choice, awakened hopes for a restoration of real statehood. In many republics, perestroika was seen by the national majority as a long-awaited chance to acquire real sovereignty. But the interests of the non-native part of the population in these republics diverged greatly from the interests of those striving for national statehood.

Perestroika was perceived and widely supported as a universal idea of renewal and democratization. But the expectations it raised varied widely in certain sectors of society, and too often people's intentions differed. Thus unintentionally the "Brownian motion" intensified, pushing the reforms toward a reorganization of the political system, with its key component, power. And when that occurred, the accumulated critical mass neared explosion.

The Chernobyl accident is explained by a fateful combination of many unforeseeable factors. Each of them taken in isolation did not lead to the catastrophe, but when they combined, the explosion occurred. By analogy, I could say that the "accident" threatening our country was also caused by an agglomeration of many opposing tendencies. People will tell me we should have been able to foresee them, and I agree. The blueprint for perestroika was based on correct and progressive principles capable of finding support in all sectors of the population. But that was just an overall intention that did not take into account the real burden of all the complex problems we inherited. Why speak about conflicting interests in a society, if its leading nucleus has also turned out to be so diverse, with people of such differing views? Again, I am not blaming anyone. A few people got together and decided that they couldn't go on like this, but when they tried to figure out how they could go on, they disagreed. And large social groups, to use the language of the sociologist, also differed in their reference points, conceptions, and paths.

I wanted to outline my views in this chapter on the relationship among politics, ecology, and the environmental collapse. I shall tell what I achieved and what remains to be done.

There was, of course, some success. For example, we were able to turn foreign policy toward the problem of protecting the biosphere. We were able to articulate the principles of ecological diplomacy or political ecology and to find people capable of implementing them. We were able to draw the attention of the world community to the consequences of the Chernobyl disaster and, now, to make efforts to create a World Ecological Foundation for rapid response to environmental catastrophes.

This was my thesis, but, against my will, reflections about environmental protection through consolidated efforts by the world community go off on a tangent, and now all my thoughts are about the ecology of the soul, about the preservation and expression of moral resources, the predatory exploitation of which has placed the nature of the human being and humanity on the brink of destruction.

All of our present problems intersect this focal point. We can differ in our value systems and disagree with one another in advocating our cherished ideas, can dispute others' opinions, can try to prove our views, but we have no right to forget that to be a human being means to recognize the humanity in everyone else. We cannot build our happiness on others' misfortunes; we must do unto others as we would have them do unto us.

Do you want to be alone, living within the borders of a single nation-state? Then acknowledge and secure the right to the same existence for another nation.

I am disturbed by all the groaning about the destruction of the Berlin Wall and the unification of Germany. I am amazed by the moral blindness that seizes peoples' minds and hearts when they avert their eyes from the real reasons for the division and its elimination. The Berlin Wall was built not as an obstacle in the enemy's path, but as a barrier to its own citizens who did not want to live according to the imposed canon. People who tried to scale this barrier were killed. What do the accusers of perestroika, those who call it a "betrayal of class values," say to that? I suppose they will trot out their strongest argument: The reunification of Germany brought on social discomfort for the residents of the former G.D.R. They clearly take a certain glee in the reports of recent demonstrations and protests: "Look where your policy has led!" So that means thousands didn't flock over the wall, and hundreds of corpses weren't left hanging on barbed wire, shot dead for trying to cross the border between the two Germanies? So was it more comfortable to stay locked up, rather than look for happiness even in a foreign land?

It is astonishing that some fail to see that people in the former G.D.R. are now having difficulty not because they are reunited with their compatriots, but because the previous regime programmed into them a difficulty in adapting to life in a dynamic, highly developed society.

I am disturbed by the television coverage of the devastation and casualties of the recent bombing of Baghdad. The subtext of the anchorman's script seems to be: "Look where Resolution 678 has led!" It is painful to look at the dead and wounded, but they were murdered by the leaders of Iraq, to whom the world community had offered the choice of peace for many months. They always had the opportunity, but they chose war. They chose it long before January 17, 1991, by killing 12,000 Kuwaiti citizens. But the "pacifists" don't count that as part of the war. They exempt themselves from any moral considerations in favor of great-power and pseudo-class preferences. Is that why this chorus is silent in the face of the Kurdish tragedy, because it doesn't fit their libretto?

I am disturbed by accusations about the "hasty withdrawal of Soviet troops from Eastern Europe," and not only for the reasons mentioned earlier. An objective analysis of Soviet and U.S. defense spending and a comparison of the figures for investment in pension rights and material compensation for the officers corps in the two countries will suffice to draw a conclusion. The "human factor" in our army receives far less attention than in America. The United States spends twice as much on the maintenance of their troops as we do. Those who attempt to change the accents and distort the real picture in order to place the blame on others' shoulders are distracting attention from years of statutory disregard for the real needs of the man in uniform. The withdrawal of troops in Eastern Europe, undertaken at the demand of sovereign governments, exposed this outrageous discrepancy. To cover it up, people are waging a "war of words" with the policy of the new thinking.

■ ■ ■

The Chernobyl of the moral sphere took place long before the explosion of April 1986. It was planned and executed by the system, which thus undermined its own future. Now that its time has come, it has to pay. Having no other means at its disposal than those it used to safeguard its existence in the past, it is once again resorting to them. Recent events vividly confirm this. Two parallel processes, the application of force and the suppression of glasnost, are most indicative. These processes are combined into a single stream of antiperestroika tendencies. The events in January in the Baltic republics coincided with the "perestroika" of state television, whereby progressive programs were canceled and popular reporters were expelled from the studios.

In my first interview after my resignation, I felt I should mention this. But Moscow television viewers did not hear what I said in support of those expelled; that part was cut out. Once again, I must admit to having underestimated the forces arrayed against perestroika and glasnost.

From an acknowledgement of this type I am one step away from a repentance, and I am ready now. I shall take to heart the statements about the naïveté of the initiators of perestroika. I believed that truth was all-powerful, that one need only give it a voice, and it would have its own productive effect. Now I see that I was cruelly mistaken. The productivity of truth largely depends on society's readiness to demand it, and on the state of the hearts and minds of the people who find the courage to disseminate the true word. The publicists, as A. Lunacharsky said, write letters to society.

What letters? Letters of hatred, enmity, and irreconcilability, or appeals for consolidation, civic peace, and constructive cooperation? The answer is before our eyes, preordained by the condition of those same hearts and minds, formed by years of internal war of each against all. Hence the "constraints on the profession," both the burning hatred of "democrats" in newspaper columns and the annihilating counter-barrages in the fledgling uncensored press. Attacks on the free press disgust me, but I am no less alarmed at the clear tendency of the liberal democratic press to exploit the methods and means of the propaganda of hatred. This kind of "truth" is as unproductive as a lie. Richard Nixon is right when he says that the "potential for perestroika will be wasted in an atmosphere of mutual accusations, intolerance, and open personal enmity."[3]

We are in the firm grip of our own past. The power monopoly played a bad joke on us by teaching us to affirm our understanding of the truth only in a style of attack and ambush. Both tactics are capable of demolishing the edifice which perestroika was intended to rebuild. In removing censorship restrictions, there was no way we could put into effect the restraints forged by freedom, culture, and responsibility. We did not and could not have these restraints,

---

[3] *New Times*, no. 13, 1991, p. 12.

raised as we were in total unfreedom. And now, thinking that we have liberated ourselves, we nurture slavery within ourselves. It's not enough to say that glasnost didn't pass the test; we failed the test of glasnost. The Chernobyl of the moral realm combined with a Chernobyl in the realm of ideas. By virtue of the same mentality, warnings are sounded in the form of shouts and labels. Only recently a scholarly attempt was made to understand the phenomenon of the "liberation of unfreedom."[4] "Today's newspaper commentary is often confused with political opposition," a sociologist writes. I agree with him that these are different things. The opposition is an element of a democratic state order, providing society with the dynamism of political alternatives. It exists within the framework of the state and is loyal to the state and its institutions.

Loyalty is alien to journalistic political commentary. Such writing sees no alternative within the framework of the existing state and considers it necessary to destroy it in order to start all over again. We must destroy the Union, "the prison of the peoples," and only when it's gone will all peoples come together on their own and live as one happy family.

What motivation does such commentary have? There is no simple answer: thirst for popularity, personal vanity, and a well-meaning delusion that one may quickly build a new society from scratch. Taken together, it forms a revolutionary syndrome, the most dangerous disease for society today.[5]

■ ■ ■

Our perestroika has been called a peaceful revolution, and I myself have readily used that characterization. But now that such embryos of violence have so visibly grown within the womb of the "peaceful revolution," I shall refrain from such definitions. The Russian philosopher Nikolai Berdyayev singles out revolution as one of the ailments of society and government that will either renew the country or kill it. Naturally, I advocate renewal and reorganization of the Union of states, but only on a basis that will simultaneously ensure both its strength and the authentic sovereignty of its peoples.

---

[4] *New Times*, no. 13, 1991, p. 12.
[5] Leonid Ionin, "What Makes Famusov Pleasant?" *New Times*, no. 12, p. 10.

Knowing the role and significance of the Soviet Union for Europe and the rest of the world, I cannot help but think that when upheavals in a country like ours reach their crest, they will send destructive shock waves to all corners of the world. But mainly, they will destabilize Europe.

We have been speaking of the creation of pan-European zones, a significant part of which will be the present unified economic, legal, and political zone of the Soviet Union. Its destruction will bring enormous deprivation and suffering into the lives of millions of people. The economic and ecological problems will increase by leaps and bounds. The existence of enormous stockpiles of nuclear and chemical weapons as yet untouched and the dozens of Chernobyls concealed within the remaining nuclear power stations vulnerable to the chaos will place all of world civilization at the brink of deadly risk.

I think advocates of secession from the Union should adopt such a geostrategic perspective. They should appreciate the threat to the existence of nations when there is a sharp break from established ties. A smooth, regulated legal procedure is needed for the transition from one condition to another, with strict, binding consideration of the interests of all sides.

True, independence means the Constitutional right of each nation to freedom of choice and self-determination. When a national majority speaks out for such a choice, the people's will must be respected. But how to implement it is another question. How will everything look now in real life? How will it turn out? Therefore, I advocate a serious, patient dialog between the Center and the republics.

Recently nine republics of the Union arrived at a long-awaited agreement. Negotiations over the basis for a special status must be held with those others who do not wish to join the Union Treaty. Although I accept the principles of the right to self-determination and freedom of choice, I find it hard not to ask: At what cost?

Once again we are faced with the same issue. We are hostage to traditional conceptions. One of them is that it is possible to obtain happiness through misfortune—"Through the thorns to the stars!" But this is the credo of a genius who, by virtue of his titanic sense of self, is able to withstand adversity and, more important, makes the choice as an individual, not for a whole nation. The thorns could bleed an entire nation white, depriving it of the stars forever, or at least for a long time. We must agree that a nation is not simply the "sum of its parts" but a complex interrelation of individuals, whose rights and welfare should not be sacrificed on the altar of even the most exalted idea. I mean the rights to life, to personal integrity, to freedom from infringement of peace, welfare, and the opportunity for self-determination without becoming a toy in the hands of the elements.

One aspect of the history of revolutions has always bothered me. Although carried out in the name of the people's welfare, they have threatened the sovereignty of the individual. The guillotine hung over the head of those who dared to hold a contrary idea. The massive moral and physical terror used against dissent destroyed the nucleus of the elite, thus narrowing the people's historical prospects.

I first acquired this point of view intellectually, from abstract examples. Then suddenly, it all directly touched the lives of people in the present and imposed a harsh question: Does anyone really have the right to lead an individual or a people to doom according to his own will and conceptions? My life is my own, as is yours, and let us dispose of them sovereignly. Otherwise, it is the same totalitarianism. It comes in a different package, but that does not prevent it from being totalitarianism.

This has all happened before, and how it ended is well known. But where then is an escape to be sought? In the example of an intellect that produced the idea of strengthening and developing national sovereignty through integration in supernational structures. In the examples of Western European countries with fully developed economies and rich democratic institutions and traditions, that nevertheless recognize the need for an alliance in the face of the multiple challenges of the day. Nations weakened by decades of suppression are even more in need of a union.

The kernels of the new thinking were planted in the soil of humanity long ago, but they have sprouted only now. Why? Because only our era has brought humankind to an awareness of the dangers that threaten it. I want to believe—and do believe—that an awareness of such perils will inevitably persuade the Union republics of the need for unification, but on a qualitatively new basis. The very force and nature of realities that cannot be ignored will lead them to this conclusion. If only the new thinking were not delayed, if only their minds would absorb it faster!

Politicians are obliged to consider all possible choices and their consequences and never to base their decisions solely on the most favorable outcome. That is how I weighed the problem of German unification. Further, there are the lessons and experiences of history. As a historian, I know well where cataclysms lead nations. I find intolerable the idea of the sacrifices of the defenseless little man, extracted from him in the name of an idea. How many innocent victims were buried under the Berlin Wall! Are we to tear down the walls of Europe, only to erect them on the enormous Eurasian plain? That has already been done, and it should never be done again.

■ ■ ■

With all its dramatic turns, perestroika created conditions for the formation of a new coalition of sovereign states. It removed the force holding together wholly heterogeneous components. Now that this "cement" has crumbled, we must speak of another force, the force of vital necessity. This force will be the basis for a union of sovereign countries, that is, an economy capable of binding them into one through a commonality of vital interests. In our case, that is a normal market economy.

But here again, we face the problem of intelligence. The sleep of reason produces monsters. Yet an awakening reason risks the same, if the lethargy has been as long as ours. Did the architects of perestroika take that into account? Did they in fact consider everything, in order to prevent dangerous warps in the reconstructed building? Were they even capable of such reckoning, while remaining products of their time, with its dominant attitudes and assumptions?

I have only one answer to these questions: No! If we call a spade a spade, it is impossible not to admit that the highly brutal mechanism of the system, built for confrontation, failed to withstand the overload of the warfare of each one against all which it produced, and broke down before our eyes. This began long before perestroika.

When I ask myself where we went wrong, I keep coming back to the conclusion that in the main there were no mistakes. Perestroika was necessary, but the choice of means and of the tools and pace of work was limited by a set of misguided assumptions. The condition of minds that grew up in unfreedom was to blame. The biblical tale about decades of wandering in the wilderness so that a generation of free people might come to maturity now sounds to me entirely realistic.

Does that mean perestroika should have stretched out over decades? Not at all, although clearly the exodus from the desert of totalitarianism could not be rapid. We began this movement, but too often we swerved off course. And most often it happened in the internal sphere.

■ ■ ■

My account of perestroika's tragic failures has no self-justifying motive. I am constantly emphasizing my own role and responsibility. In speaking of the achievements, I do not say they are to my credit; they became possible thanks to a consciousness of necessity that had matured in the minds of many people. When I criticize the administrative command system, I am not, like it, striving to locate yet another phantom enemy. My analysis has tried to be sober and unbiased.

The three whales, the three pillars of the system—a centralized economy; the political system with its main unit, the Party-state apparatus; and the unitary state—were objectively unable to reform themselves or to give up their "conquests" voluntarily. Just as objectively, an inadequate regard for the interests of the establishment that represented those pillars could not help but provoke a reaction—first dislike of perestroika, then resistance to it.

The attacks on perestroika or the attempts to subvert the politics of the new thinking can be explained by the fact that both its theory and its practice destroyed this monolith from the inside. The renunciation of global confrontation and class struggle, and the priority given to universal human values, pluralism of opinions, and political freedoms are rightly viewed by the system as explosive devices. The system's main task was to smash them.

For all my desire to see a different kind of country, I did not volunteer for the role of a destroyer. Destruction is always fraught with the risk of perishing under the rubble. From the standpoint of both ordinary life and politics, it is not sensible to close one's eyes to the real interests of various groups and pretend they don't exist.

That was the main miscalculation. I have spoken of the well-known naïveté of the reformers. I could put it more harshly: We fell victim to political illiteracy. We tried to create a new reality by the old methods, sending out directives from above. After all, directives, whether statutes or decrees, are only accepted by a community that is connected with the command center either by a unity of interests or by ties of obedience and fear. When these are absent, the directive does not work.

But where could political literacy come from if there was no need for it in the conditions of a power monopoly? If the art of governance had been casually replaced by the habits of coercion by decree? And how were we to operate without cutting off the branch on which the system had us sitting?

The example of the conversion of the defense industry comes to mind in this connection. It struck a painful blow at the interests and positions of hundreds and thousands of people. The foundation of our industry, the military-industrial complex, which had accumulated countless inventories of intellect, knowledge, experience, and the latest technology, began to crumble. I am familiar with many of the factories and their managers—they are excellent enterprises and remarkable leaders—and I share their dissatisfaction with their situation. It could have been avoided by designing a nationwide, scientifically based program for profound conversion and elaborating social safety nets for defense employees. Instead, there was an order from on high and hasty, ill-conceived actions to win "merit badges."

I have already spoken about the army. The time had come to engage in the practical implementation of political statements.

And the apparatus? They too were not treated as people, either in the propaganda exposés or in matters of living conditions. After all, the government apparatus is also thousands of intelligent workers and their families, people who were turned into pariahs in one stroke, under the laws of total revenge. Just as in the bad old days, using the methods of the same nomenklatura, they were treated in a heap, as if they all fitted into one pattern. On top of that, it was forgotten that besides the apparatus there is a 19-million-member Party, the majority of whom wanted change and should have been the bulwark of perestroika. But for that to happen, both the Party majority and the apparatus would have had to undergo perestroika.

That was deferred, and we lost the opportunity to create a true democratic foundation that could have passed in a relatively painless fashion through the phase of dismantling the power monopoly. Only under public pressure was Article 6 of the Constitution, which had safeguarded the "leading role of the Party," repealed.

And the unitary state? The transition to democratic forms of government should have been made smoothly, without friction, not breaking the structures but transforming them gradually. Overall, my priority is gradual evolution, and I fought for a stage-by-stage strategy. It did not happen. It turned out that a correct step toward a law-based state struck a blow at executive power. Now we speak of its paralysis.

When we proclaimed freedom of choice, we did not concern ourselves at the time about the forms in which it might be realized. As early as 1989 mass demands for reorganization of the national-state system were voiced. But they were ignored, and only the reality of the Union's collapse brought the issue to the plane of practical decisions.

It was clear from the very start that the centralized administrative command economy was incompatible with a free, self-regulating economy. The programs for transition to the market, however, did not begin to be designed until economic links were already breaking down.

The need to fix the monetary system and to readjust price-setting mechanisms was obvious, but we were afraid of popular displeasure and the loss of broad support for perestroika. Yet at the same time we made absolutely unpopular and, more important, incorrect decisions dictated by the same administrative-command mentality. "Let's order the production and consumption of alcohol to stop, and the country will obey."

Institutions of representative democracy were formed, but with the obvious intention of building into them "working parts" of the state mechanism. This was done fairly selectively. Not a single diplomat became a member of parliament, which seemed right to me, although the army and the military-industrial complex gained broad representation out of proportion to their numbers. A fairly large number of parliamentary deputies bypassed direct election in receiving their mandates. The results of this type of symbiosis, unknown to a single developed democracy, are now known.

Thus we ourselves created the situation in which we ended up. It forced us to act while looking over our shoulders, to delay, to take half-measures, to tack against the wind. The moment was lost when we could have relied on truly democratic forces. At the same time, we were afraid to enter an alliance with them.

Again, I am prepared to lay all of it, all the miscalculations and mistakes, at my own door. And even my resignation—to call it by its real name, it was an act of disagreement and protest, and simultaneously a warning—does not exonerate me. Much of what was happening around me provoked alarm and the premonition of unavoidable collapse, and I said this to the General Secretary and, later, to the President. But even so, not for an instant did I forget how complicated his position was, how contradictory and many-sided the pressure he was under. He had to make choices constantly, and not every choice was to my liking. I also told him that in our confidential talks, but I did not dream it possible to come out in direct and open opposition, for many reasons. First, Gorbachev personified perestroika. To oppose any of his decisions would be to oppose perestroika. Understanding how difficult it was for the leader, I did not want to and could not deprive him of my support. Second, intense concentration on foreign policy matters did not allow me to divert my energy and attention to internal affairs for long, and, I suppose more important, narrowed my opportunities as Minister of Foreign Affairs. Most of my work day was taken up with negotiations at home or abroad, in harmonizing positions with my partners in the country's foreign policy community, and with the structural perestroika of the Ministry of Foreign Affairs. We worked at an intense pace that could only be called hellish. The load was enormous.

Of course, the quantities of work are not the point. Visiting about sixty countries during this period, we tried to imbue our foreign policy with a new character, new qualities. Each of these missions demanded great effort, but the most difficult was that connected with domestic affairs. I suppose I should talk about that since my decision to resign began to ripen just at that time.

■ ■ ■

On the evening of April 7, 1989, Gorbachev and I returned to Moscow from England. We were told at Vnukovo-II Airport that after repeated requests from the leaders of Georgia, units of internal troops that had been relocated from Tbilisi to Armenia were being ordered back to Tbilisi. The requests, we were told, were motivated by the need to maintain order, threatened by an unauthorized rally on April 7 on Rustaveli Avenue in front of Government House. I was alarmed by the report, since memory and experience are stronger than any words or assertions. The events of 1956 and 1978[6] had given me a categorical aversion to the use of force as a means for resolving political conflict, especially against masses of people. Thus, Gorbachev's words gladdened me: "No matter what, the situation must be settled by political means. For that, if we need to, we'll send Shevardnadze and Razumovsky to Tbilisi."

I made a telephone call, and was told that "the situation is under control. You don't need to come down here." I reported back to Gorbachev. Later I learned that at that moment military units—and not only internal forces—were being rushed to Tbilisi. They were already there by the morning of April 8, and they made a show of force on Rustaveli Avenue that afternoon. It had an opposite effect to that intended. Instead of intimidating, it provoked an explosion of dissatisfaction, a desire to band together and obtain deliverance in solidarity. It takes an absolutely distorted perception of the national mentality to resort unafraid to such a measure as a "stroll" of tanks and personnel carriers down the main avenue of the capital. People threw themselves under the tanks, because their genes no longer carried the fear implanted by past repression. Without fear, the fury was stronger, because people who believed in perestroika could see for themselves that in 1989 the same methods were being used against them as had been used against their fathers in 1956.

They can be labeled "extremists," "separatists," or "anti-Soviet activists" in the old way, but I would hesitate to draw upon this arsenal of old epithets when confronted by the sight of an eighteen-year-old girl fearlessly lying down on the asphalt under the looming steel treads. In this case, you must first of all clarify what you are dealing with: one person who is an anomaly, or the spontaneous protest of a soul yearning for freedom in the face of the pathology of power.

I was supposed to have flown to Berlin on April 10 for the next meeting of the Committee of Foreign Ministers of the Warsaw Pact nations. But on the morning of April 9 I was informed that people had been killed at dawn during a forcible dispersal of the

---

[6] Periods of mass unrest in Georgia.—Trans.

rally in Tbilisi, and that I had to fly there immediately. By the afternoon of the same day, I was at the site of the tragedy.

I shall pass over what I experienced during those first hours in a city so dear to me. For a number of reasons I intend in time to recount scrupulously the details of this, the most difficult mission in my life, and my knowledge and ideas about the reasons for the events of April 9. For now I shall speak of them only as they pertain to the theme of this chapter.

What conclusions did I reach after acquainting myself with the circumstances of the event?

First, the number and composition of the demonstrators, which included many women and adolescents, completely precluded the option of using force to disperse the rally.

Second, the "crowd control" forces used means absolutely unacceptable in such cases.

Third, the persons responsible for this concealed, over the entire duration of my stay in Tbilisi, the fact that chemical weapons had been employed. Only on the eighth day, under pressure of indisputable evidence, were they compelled to admit it, claiming, however, that they "had not known of the presence of such devices" in the military units.

Fourth, the commander of the operation violated an order instructing him to guard a number of sites, and not to disperse the rally with force.

Fifth, whatever decisions about military measures were taken by local Party and state agencies, they could not have been implemented without the sanction of the Ministry of Defense. Thus it was improper to blame only the local leadership.

Finally, and this is perhaps the most significant point, at all stages leading up to the tragedy and after it, information about the events was either distorted or censored. News reaching the center was fabricated by the apparatus, which was attuned to giving out information in the customary clichés. The slogan of truth and glasnost was cast down and discarded by a machine absolutely incapable of adapting to it. In other words, the system went into its usual mode fighting to win back the territory lost to perestroika. It struck a blow against perestroika, but as later events illustrated, it was a Pyrrhic victory. Another Chernobyl.

I reported my findings to the Politburo and demanded the most thorough, impartial investigation into the reasons for the tragedy. At my suggestion, a special commission had already been formed in Tbilisi, for which, at my insistence, the most authoritative and qualified lawyers and public figures were enlisted. Subsequently a similar parliamentary commission was created in Moscow, headed by Anatoly Sobchak. It was to give a political evaluation of the April 9 events. Parallel to this, the chief military prosecutor's office was carrying out an investigation.

The Sobchak commission report was included in the agenda of the Second U.S.S.R. Congress of People's Deputies. The commission was charged not only with finding the reasons for the tragedy; it was to establish the limits on the use of force, in this case by the army against the people, and was to formulate the legal bases for resolving future critical situations. In other words, the commission was supposed to decide how to respond in the future, given the changed sociopolitical circumstances, which demand renunciation of the former methods of restoring order and the devising of new measures acceptable to a democratic society. At any rate, that was the purpose of the parliamentary charge as I saw it. As for the criminal justice aspects of the tragedy, the military investigation, as yet not completed, would deal with those.

All parties to the conflict were acquainted with the commission's findings, and all accepted them. As far as I know, even the Georgian deputies had expressed their agreement with the report. It was stipulated that the report and the commission's findings would be accepted without debate and would form the basis for a Congressional resolution. But on the following day, December 24, 1989, after the chairman of the parliamentary commission made his speech, the floor was given to the chief military prosecutor. All his premises and evaluations differed completely from the parliamentary report. He blamed the victims of the tragedy, and the actions of those who attacked the demonstration were called lawful. I was outraged, not just by the theorems of his proof, but by the very atmosphere in which it was expounded. He was applauded with fervent joy, with unconcealed vengeance, just as Academician Andrei Sakharov had been pilloried not so long ago in the same hall. Not just deputies applauded, but my neighbors in the government. I was shaken by what this vigorous clapping revealed. My colleagues were not celebrating the truth, but force and lies, injustice and the triumph of clan interests. "We won!" was the sentiment behind the ovation for the military prosecutor.

During the break I demanded to be given the floor. I wanted to express my attitude toward what was going on and to show how poisonous it was for our young democracy. Without beating around the bush, I wanted to speak to those who were threatening perestroika and its leaders with the fist, and to prevent the possible consequences. I wanted to reveal that only by promising an objective investigation of the tragedy and a prosecution of those responsible, no matter who they were, had we managed to normalize the situation in Tbilisi, returning pupils to schools, students to lecture halls, workers to shops, and women to hearth and home. But the promise had not been fulfilled, and in the eyes of the people to whom it had been made, I looked as if I had not kept my word. This was not a question of being in a vulnerable position; it was a question of the government's authority and people's trust in it.

Gorbachev refused to give me the floor. Perhaps he just wanted to put out the fire. But I think the fire had started earlier and was only now burning through to the surface. All the backing and filling had not quenched it. We should have defined the scale of the impending danger and warned the country. But I did not get the opportunity to do that. I left the Congress hall and dictated my resignation statement the very same day. It did not contain words about a dictatorship, but there were words about a coming reactionary movement and a protest against it. I thought that those words should be taken seriously. I also thought at the time that they were heard by my friend. That was the only reason why I acceded to his persuasion and remained. But the further unfolding of events, a whole series of major and minor Chernobyls, showed me that we were dealing here not with some accidental excesses, but with a stubborn tendency, worsening from day to day. From day to day the pressure from the right increased, as support from the left weakened, and it was necessary either to freeze solid into the iceberg and drift along with it, or to maneuver between the floes, at the risk of being crushed to death. Or else—and this was the only possible choice for me—we had to find a way through to the open sea, where we could set sail on our charted course.

The first and second alternatives did not suit me. I tried the third until all chances were exhausted, and then I did what I had to do. It was unbearable to think that if I did not take that step, I would be forced to participate in something that went utterly against my beliefs. I also wanted to sound a warning and force people to think:

Where are we going and what are we doing? Will we remain faithful to perestroika, or do we want to return to the past?

No hyperbole, even the most exact and capacious, can take the place of facts. I do not consider it necessary, however, to cite and analyze the facts in the realm of domestic politics that determined my decision. They are too obvious to bear repeating. Dictatorship is born in a power vacuum, anarchy, chaos, and the effort to subvert lawful authority from within and force it to behave as dictated or else be replaced. With the worsening economic crisis and the falling standard of living, there was no reason to expect a broad resistance to the restoration of totalitarianism.

As for the facts relating to the sphere of our foreign policy, the facts of internal resistance to it, and the no less successful efforts to change it, I do not feel it is yet time to discuss them. While talks are still under way and there is a chance to save the agreements that have been subjected to freewheeling internal amendment, I do not have the right to speak of them. Everything has its time and place. Now I must resort to the language of hyperbole: Because I did not want either to freeze onto an iceberg or retreat before it, I preferred to stand in its way. Even if I could not stop it, at least I delayed the crash for a short time—that is no mean feat for one person. But the main thing for me is that I openly expressed the refusal to be suffocated in the ice. I warned many good people against this fate and called them to rally together and form a barrier in its path.

■ ■ ■

Unfortunately, my intuition had not deceived me. Recall the events of January 1991 in the Baltics, the March 28 demonstration opposed by troops in Moscow, the demands for martial law heard in various forums.

Fortunately, the democratic movement came out of its frozen state, began to consolidate, and formed structures capable of withstanding the united forces of reaction.

■ ■ ■

Very early on the morning of December 20, 1990, I wrote out my resignation statement. I had had a sleepless night. At dawn I called my daughter in Tbilisi and told her about my decision. Then, before leaving for the Kremlin, I told my two closest aides and heard the same words of support.

They say my speech was unprepared, rambling, and emotional. Perhaps that's true. But frankly, I said everything I wanted to say, and most likely I could not have said it in any other way. Many people thought my speech left something out, and they hastened to read between the lines. One very good columnist even made an addition to what he considered my unpolished speech:

"Politics is the art of the possible. In my professional activity I illustrated fairly well my adherence to the method of compromise. But there cannot be a compromise at the expense of the politics themselves, their essence, their sacred aim. And we cannot lose speed—that would simply be dangerous. Not personal caprice, but urgent public demand dictates the necessity in the current conditions to provide clear, uncompromising support of our line in foreign policy. That's not happening.

"That's how I see the situation. And since I see it that way, I have no other choice but to resign."[7]

That's all true. That is precisely what I said, but in other words. And my text was not so "obscure," if the journalist was able to read this into it.

"Plato is dear, but truth is dearer." And the truth is that I did not leave a friend; more precisely, I was not the one who did the leaving. I'll say more: In resigning, I wanted to help him save the cause. How we make use of the chances that fall to our lot is another matter. Sometimes I think a man has no more dangerous enemy than himself. Before finding friends around you, you must find a friend within yourself. People have varying degrees of success with this.

On January 26, 1991, when he came to the U.S.S.R. Foreign Ministry to install the new Minister in person, Gorbachev said many kind words about me. I recall one thing in particular: "He was always by my side, my closest comrade in all the most difficult situations and, most important, in making the choice."

Yes, that was really the main thing—the choice. It was the choice of a path, a line of behavior, an ally, a friend. It was not only a personal choice: It was made by the times, the idea, the principles, the cause. They place their limits on the choice. After all, choice is not a unilateral act. You choose, but also are chosen, and if the choices coincide, everything is fine. If they do not, then you must make another choice.

[7] Alexander Pumpyansky, "What Is Left Unsaid," *New Times*, no. 2, 1991.

I made my choice, and I do not regret it.

Among many words of farewell, Gorbachev said the following: "For me, it was strange that he didn't seek my advice. I told him I would never forgive him for that." To which I replied in a joking tone that I accepted everything he said as applicable, except the words "I will never forgive him."

Later, in a private conversation, Gorbachev said that he could understand me, personally.

Well, I understand him as a person, too.

Lately, I have been troubled by an idea in Vaclav Havel's recent book:

> The system serves a person only up to the point necessary for a person to serve it; everything that is "above that," i.e., when a person exceeds his already limited standing, the system views as an attack on itself. And it is right: Every time someone steps out of line, it really does negate the system as a principle. . . . Despite the enormous power that the centralized system bestows upon them, its leaders are often nothing more than the blind functioning of the system. Experience teaches us that the "autonomous movement" of the system manifests itself as stronger than the will of an individual. If anyone still possesses a definite individual will, he must hide himself behind the ritually anonymous mask, in order to obtain a chance at the hierarchy of power. And if he still manages to get something for himself through the hierarchy and realize his intents, then sooner or later the "autonomous movement," with its enormous inertial force, will gain the upper hand, and he will be expelled from the structure of power, or forced to renounce his individuality gradually, to merge with the "autonomous movement" and become its servant, almost indistinguishable from those who went before him, or those who will come after him.[8]

I apply this idea to myself, but I did fulfill my intentions, did not renounce myself, and did not let the system beat me.

I ask people to believe me: This is not arrogance, but a statement of fact, which is too significant for my future life for me to remain silent.

∎ ∎ ∎

[8] Vaclav Havel, *Moc bezmocnych* [The Power of the Powerless], as quoted in *New Times*, no. 16, 1991, pp. 42–43.

Repentance ends with a brilliant metaphor. An old woman asks the film's heroine whether or not the road she has chosen leads to the cathedral. No, the heroine replies, this street bears the name of the tyrant, and therefore does not lead to the cathedral. That's strange, remarks the old lady. What good is a road if it does not lead to the cathedral?

In one of his interviews, Tenghiz Abuladze called me his "coauthor." Of course, this is a very magnanimous exaggeration, but now I suppose I must accept it so as to avoid a charge of plagiarism for using that image so dear to my heart.

Can we attain a high aim using low, unworthy methods? In search of truth, is it permissible to lie? Can justice be achieved through unjust means? These questions are as old as the world, and the argument around them has been going on forever. The immutable reply—if you must, you may—seems to prevail. Then why does the figure of the lone hero, preserving his faithfulness to the idea of a righteous path to the cathedral, remain so indestructible? At every turn, life tells him that it is impossible to follow that road, but he continues along it anyway.

I am not a saint, not a hero, but neither am I alone. I am not alone because a time has come when more and more people in our country are seeing that the only road that leads to the cathedral is one that is worthy of it. Once they are convinced, people live and act accordingly. Thus an exceptional mode of thinking requiring self-denial and sacrifice becomes a generally accepted norm for human existence. Politics has to come to terms with this sooner or later.

Journalists love to say that the most noble punctuation mark is the period. I would place a period here, but I sense it is too early. What has begun must be continued. We must live, speak, write, and act for that cause.

This book is an appeal to the future. Beyond its narrative are many days and years, events and people in the past which I should tell about. But since books are written for the future, only the future can tell the true worth of what has been done and said. I hope that I will live to see that time and will be able to accept whatever judgment it may offer.

The Coup: The "Shadows" Come to Light

In truth, I wish this epilogue had not been necessary. Four months ago, as I was finishing this book, I wrote that only the future would determine the real value of my words and deeds.

Now the future has arrived, and their value is established.

I have little of the politician's pride in correctly forecasting events. Nor is it my style to smugly declare, "I told you so!" Quite the contrary, after my resignation, I reassured my friends and family again and again that I would be happy if my prediction did not come true. But it has, and I am anything but glad.

Like everyone else, I am deeply shaken now as I reflect on these last days and nights.

The events of August 18–21, 1991, cast a harsh light on remembered events and highlight many things in a new way. This glaring light is very bright, but does not blind. Instead, it sharpens one's vision. Now all the disconnected facts, observations, thoughts, guesses, sudden insights, emerging and disappearing doubts, these shards of life that had wounded my heart and mind

Epilogue translated by Catherine A. Fitzpatrick and Joel Golb.

and which compelled me to act in one way rather than another, have merged in one complete mosaic. Now, I understand.

During the past two years, from April 1989 on, a feeling of depression never left me. I was depressed about events in the country, by what was happening around me and within me. My sense of an imminent explosion grew stronger all the time. Although I could not find a name for it, one word came increasingly to mind: "dictatorship." Finally, at dawn on August 18th, I was awakened by the voice of an announcer declaring that a state of emergency was in effect.

Everything I'd feared and that I'd warned about had come to pass. But strangely, I felt nothing but relief, as if the great weight that had burdened my heart for so long had been lifted. Everything that tormented my soul and gave me no rest—that drove my thoughts around in an endless labyrinth of questions such as "who?" "how?" and "why?"—dissolved and vanished at that moment, like fog dissipates with strong wind. I felt an astonishing clarity within me. Everything was now manifest and open: names, intentions, deeds. Former secrets were no longer secret, and murky shadows took on the distinct contours of concrete figures and people. The balance of forces was now clear.

I felt—it was almost a physical sensation—how every cell in my brain was working, how every aspect of my being had been liberated and was already connected to other energies which were no longer shackled by previous bonds.

No less surprisingly, my fear was subdued by a sudden clear insight. This was a conspiracy of losers, whose instigators, organizers and participants would not succeed. The media announcers solemnly read their declarations and decrees, but it struck me that these words were addressed to an audience that no longer existed. Their archaic words were like echoes from the dark caverns of our history. But the listeners had found an exit from those caverns long ago, and such macabre appeals would never touch their hearts and minds.

My wife went with me to the elevator that first morning. We said good-bye and hugged each other. "I know you are ready for anything. So am I. So go, and may God keep you!"

Yes, I was ready for anything. I had been ready for a long time, even when I lived and worked in Georgia, and all the more so since my resignation on December 20, 1990. The day after that, the phone rang in my apartment on Plotnikov Lane. My wife lifted the receiver: "This is a friend and well-wisher of your husband. After his speech yesterday, anything is possible. Warn him that he should not speak out anymore." Then the line went dead.

I informed my aide, Taimuraz Stepanov, about the call. Later on, several trusted friends and acquaintances informed me, on the basis of so-called "reliable sources," that my life was in danger. Everything I knew about the system's mores and methods, the events and indications of recent years—the mounting smear campaign in the newspapers *Glasnost, Sovietskaya Rossiya* and other publications of an imperialist and chauvinist slant—not to mention the obvious signs that someone had broken into the apartment in our absence, convinced us this was not an empty threat.

But these attempts to intimidate me were 20 years too late. I had already done and said everything possible. Only a few details remained, which had not seemed very significant at the time of my resignation. But by the summer of 1991, everything, even the tiniest detail, took on new weight. Now all that frightened me— besides, of course, the possible fate of my family—was the thought that if the worst should happen to me, no one would completely understand why.

My wife would know, but I needed some insurance lest she meet the same fate. In June 1991, as I flew from Vienna to Moscow, knowing already that the Party had issued an order to investigate my recent statements, I dictated a testament to my friends and aides, Stepanov and Sergei Tarasenko, and brought to their attention that they could only make it publicly known in specific circumstances.

The tone of this epilogue, a report on the dramatic events of August 18–21, is different from much of the rest of the book. This is not surprising, and I ask the reader's sympathy. The book was written for another time, and from another perspective. Today I am writing under the very strong impression that the last few days have made on me. I am writing in Moscow to the sound of funeral marches and requiems for the three young men who died defending Russia's White House. The evolution of the reform process culminated in a revolution, and this applies to me as well.

And one thing more: The upheaval we experienced and the avalanche of information, the faster pace of change and the uncertainty of the general situation will obviously stifle the strictly analytic element of these remarks. A tide of feelings flooded over me; I am fighting against them and can only control them with effort. I don't want my emotions to get the better of me, but don't intend to hide them. May everything that ruled us in those days and nights belong to you, honored readers. That's no less important than analysis based on cold and clear understanding. That will come in its turn. Everything is still to come.

One and all, I knew the signatories to the document issued by the "State Committee for the State of Emergency," from Baklanov to Yazov. With some exceptions, I had already counted them all among the enemies of our policy. But mistrust and speculation over the possibility of a looming dictatorship is one thing. It is another to have precise and irrefutable proof. I didn't have such proof until the coup. Still, a politician is justified in guiding himself not only by sober analysis but by his intuitions. He must reveal his fears at every opportunity to his colleagues, his society and indeed to the whole world. This I had done.

But what had I left undone? On the morning of August 19, there was no time to think about that.

At nine o'clock in the morning, I sat in my office on Yelizarov Street, calling all my allies in the Democratic Reform Movement. I do not have a *vertushka*, one of the special direct communication lines, but only a regular telephone, which is to say one that worked poorly. I dictated to my aides the draft of an appeal to our political movement. At 11:15, I managed to reach Boris Yeltsin.

"I am virtually isolated here," he said. "Almost all the lines have been cut." In unison, we said, "This is fascism." We agreed to meet at the first available opportunity.

"If such an opportunity arises," I joked, "if we're offered one . . ."

"We'll offer it to ourselves," responded Yeltsin. "Today it probably won't work. Too much to do. But tommorrow, absolutely."

By noon, the journalist Galina Sidorova had somehow managed to fight her way into our Foreign Policy Association building and had brought me the text of Yeltsin's appeal to the citizens of Russia.

The fax was still working and calls started to ring on this number. There was a call from the French Embassy: "What's happening with Shevardnadze?" My secretary said that I was at my desk. Journalists called from *Komsomolskaya Pravda, Izvestia,*

Georgian newspapers, and American television companies. Alexander Yakovlev[1] called. "I'm at home. I can't get out. The exit is blocked by a detachment of soldiers."

On Saturday, August 17, at a meeting of our movement's Political Council, we had drafted a statement concluding that the threat of a right-wing coup was imminent. Now we regretted that we had not managed to distribute the document.

Then the news came that tanks and armored personnel carriers were moving around Moscow. People were lying down as living barriers in front of the tanks on Tverskaya Street. At the Likhachev Auto Factory, a rally was assembling. Later, I learned that the auto workers had been sending several thousand people each day to defend the White House. At the time, I did not know this. There was a lot I didn't know. What was happening to Gorbachev? Alexander Vladislavlev and Mikhail Minasbekyan, leaders of our movement, came and reported: "No one can get a phone call through to the President. Either he has been murdered, or he is in jail."

We started editing the text of our appeal, communicating with our friends by fax. We used the same method to send copies to Interfax News Agency, to Italy, and to reporters at Novosti Press Agency. We ran off as many copies as we could and continued to send them out until we ran out of paper. (A Moscow firm called Astep brought us more.)

At 2:00 p.m., I went to the Movement headquarters. I absolutely had to be there, in order to cheer on the Organizing Committee and help facilitate various matters. Astonishingly, I was able to drive right up to the building. It was already clear which way Moscow itself was going to vote. The mass of people that has now become a nation had already jammed the tank treads.

At 3:30 p.m., there was a press conference at the Association. Along with Vladislavlev and Minasbakyan, Academician Yuri Ryzhov, Vorontsov, a member of the Cabinet of Ministers, and other friends took part. They announced that the defense of the White House would need to be organized that night.

We all knew that the plotters would stop at nothing, having laid their own lives on the line, and we agreed that when the

[1]One of the initiators of perestroika and a former member of Gorbachev's Presidential Council who had warned of a Stalinist takeover two days before the coup—Trans.

arrests began, not one name of those taken would be forgotten.

About four dozen journalists had managed to find us. I was glad to see the familiar faces of Soviet and foreign reporters. A great deal depended on them, and they did everything they could so that the country and the world would receive our interpretation of events. On the following day, however, I learned that our appeal had not reached the Soviet media because the publications themselves had been closed down. That was when I dictated my "Cry in the Wilderness," in order to have my final say, and leave at least some trace.

At 5:50 p.m., Kazimiera Prunskiene[2] called.

"I'm flying out of the country. If I manage to get out, how can I help you?"

"We need the support of the entire world, both moral and political. We need to organize a resistance to the massive abuse of human rights."

We also spoke of Gorbachev. I said, "I am uncertain of his role and of his fate. If he is still alive, he should go on television immediately and explain why this has happened. If he is not able to do that, then we must demand that he be given the opportunity. We have to sound every alarm."

Regarding the plotters, I said, "Tell them that their action is so mad that it cannot succeed."

Then the Russian Interior Minister called.

"I have placed guards outside your home on orders of Boris Nikolayevich Yeltsin."

Thanking him, I said that I did not need guards, but that it would reassure my family. And not only my family. For this phone call implied if not the coup's collapse, at least a premonition of it. The legitimate authority, derived from the will and support of the people, had taken the initiative.

The democratic press ignored the censorship. We gleaned information from the reports of the station "Moscow Echo." The publications banned by the junta joined forces to put out illegal editions of a so-called "collective newspaper." Workers from *Izvestia*'s printing facility copied various Russian governmental documents with a manual press. With its spiritedness and courage, its inventiveness, and its contempt for the conspirators, this inde-

[2]Former Prime Minister of Lithuania.

pendent journalism illustrated the triumph of ideas long suppressed by the system: freedom of information is an inalienable aspect of freedom and democracy.

Praised be information technology! Praised be CNN's reporters and announcers. Anyone who owned a parabolic antenna able to receive this network's transmissions had a complete picture of what was happening. Meanwhile, Leonid Kravchenko's servile television broadcasts emitted murky waves of lies and disinformation. I had feelings of guilt toward the young people from the Vaglyad station: at one time they had made a film about the work of our "team" which they paid for later by being banned from further activity. According to the television people, the head of the Union network had forbidden any mention of my name and had prevented my advisors from having access to the cameras.

Now those same young producers made a film called "The View from Illegality." Their colleagues from Vesti discovered an honorable man in the Minister for Long Distance Communications, who placed at their disposal a satellite channel. In this way, Russia, from Moscow all the way to the Kamchatka Peninsula, received truthful information. Such people were also to be found in the Union network. In this manner, the ghoulish voices of the plotters were coupled with the actual events of the day: Boris Yeltsin on a tank; barricades at Kutuzovsky Bridge; an enormous rally at Mariinsky Palace in Leningrad; Sobchak[3] at a podium and banners saying "Fascism Will Not Prevail!"

People who had apparently been stifled by the system were transformed into heroes. Courage and devotion to the truth became the norm. The electronic media also served the truth. The plotters were clearly in a great hurry and did not consider cutting off all of our communications with the outside world.

That day I had already heard the voice of Hans-Dietrich Genscher on the telephone, had answered his questions and told him what we needed. Fogel, the head of the Social Democrat Faction in the Bundestag, informed me of the possible arrival of a delegation from the Socialist International.

In times of need we recognize our friends. A day later, Jim and Suzy Baker phoned me from their ranch in the Rocky Moun-

[3]Anatoly Sobchack is the mayor of Leningrad and a founding member of the Democratic Reform Movement—Trans.

tains. Small gestures take on unexpected force when they occur in moments of confusion and uncertainty.

I spent a sleepless night. In the morning, with great difficulty, I shouldered my way through to the City Council building. There, despite a ban by the junta, a rally was already in progress. Gavriil Popov,[4] Alexander Yakovlev and others spoke, as did I. "We are seeing the eruption of a volcano that has been rumbling for a long time. They want to bury our democracy and freedom under tons of ash and mud. The dictatorship, the shadows I have spoken of, have come out in the open to fight. It is the end of democracy and the beginning of civil war; the resumption of the arms race and a new cold war. Do we want this? No! Therefore, we must unite and stand in the way of the dictatorship, in order to overthrow it. . . ."

The Democratic Russia movement, our own movement, and the democratic parties formed a united front. I do not like the word "enemy," but now I was seeing him up close, and I knew who our friends were in this struggle.

We then moved towards the White House and linked up with officers and troops of the resistance. And we made further speeches there, because we sensed that words were acquiring the force of actions.

After the demonstration I had a meeting, along with Alexander Vladislavlev and Mikhail Minasbegyan, with the president of Russia. Boris Yeltsin told us that he had just had a conversation with George Bush on the phone. That was a very important and, above all, timely signal of support.

We dealt with a whole list of questions related to foreign affairs, as well as key domestic problems. Now this white marble building on Krasnopresnenskaya Street along the Moscow River had become the center of Russia's political life: the center for the defense of democracy, constitutional authority, and the country's legal president. The White House was transformed before our eyes into a fortress. In the vast spaces of its basement, a transmitter for Russian radio began its work. Vice President Alexander Rutskoy, a professional soldier, Hero of the Soviet Union and a veteran of Afghanistan, Premier Ivan Silayev, and Russian state advisor Burbulis described how life was being maintained in the White House. Simultaneously with the organization of its

[4]Mayor of Moscow.

defense, decrees and rules from the president of Russia were explained.

I was expecting the German Ambassador to come to my home at 7:30 p.m., so I went there to meet him and we spoke for awhile. The French and Italian Ambassadors also honored us with their attention and support during those days, along with Robert S. Strauss, the new U.S. Ambassador, who paid me a visit as well.

After my meeting with Mr. Blech, the door bell rang: at the threshold were Eduard Sagalayev, the Chairman of the Union of Journalists, and his deputy, Nugzar Ponkhadve. My old friend Guram Mgeladze arrived a half an hour later. I understood why they had come. Guram said that rumors of my imminent arrest were already circulating, and if that was going to happen, they wanted to be with me.

We went out on the balcony. Tracer bullets streaked the night sky. Suddenly, an explosion was heard above the New Arbat district and a white cloud of smoke arose.

"We should be over there," I told my friends. But my wife, Nanuli, stood in the doorway and refused to let us go. Nugzar resorted to a "military" trick and staged a phone call to the apartment. A voice ordered us, "Go into hiding for several hours!"

"Get out of here!" said my wife.

I have never lived through anything like what I would experience in those hours. At the approaches to the White House, soldiers let us through without hindrance. A young fellow in a khaki uniform embraced me and, swallowing a lump in his throat, whispered, "We will defend you!" A colonel shouted after us, "Tell Yeltsin we won't let them storm the White House!" Young men who had linked arms pushed a path for us through the heavy crowds. Some women wiped the rain off my forehead with their kerchiefs. One of my fellow countrymen ran alongside me, crying, "Eduard, we Georgians love you very much!"

Oh my dear Russians, Georgians, Armenians, Jews, Uzbekis, Lithuanians, Latvians, Ukrainians—how I love you! How grateful I am that you were there, and always will be. How thankful I am that through you I have felt myself truly a part of the people!

An atmosphere of calm determination reigned at the White House. Young people with Kalashnikov rifles were posted at strategic sites. Colonel General Kobets was giving out orders from a central command post in the building. I am not a military man, but

I could see that everything was being done in a highly professional manner.

Among those in the building I saw Mstislav Rostropovich[5]; an exhausted soldier had fallen asleep on his lap. I also saw the economist Grigory Yavlinsky[6] and compared notes with him.

"This is it! They've lost."

I left the White House at 5:00 a.m. when I was convinced that the expected attack had been thwarted.

Dawn broke in fog and rain. The fog soon burned off and the rain stopped. The Supreme Soviet of Russia convened in the White House. The President announced that Mikhail Gorbachev and his family were alive; he had spoken with him. In a little while, there was fresh news: the plotters had fled. Where to? In an hour, there was a report that they had flown to the Crimea. But why there— why there precisely?

Then I saw Mikhail Sergeyevich Gorbachev on television, alive and unharmed. I also glimpsed Chief of Staff Mikhail Moiseyev among the crowd of greeters, and I had further thoughts about the president's entourage.

■ ■ ■

Meanwhile, my thoughts can't help wandering back to Mikhail Sergeyevich Gorbachev, his odyssey and destiny, his transformations, and to the turns and zig-zags of the last months and days. After all, his destiny is mine as well. Who is to blame if our paths diverged? Am I at fault in any way?

No, no matter how sternly I judge myself, I can't feel guilty for my part in these developments. I did everything I could. But could I perhaps have done more, even if it meant risking a complete loss of his trust? Not now, during these days, but much earlier?

Perhaps, but what should I make of the fact that more than a year ago, I shared with him my suspicions that ultrareactionary forces were consolidating, clearly moving towards a suppression of perestroika? What of the fact that all throughout 1990, I had been issuing warnings, with facts in my hand, with analyses of state-

[5]Celebrated emigré conductor—Trans.
[6]Author of the rejected 500-day Plan for economic reform who resigned from the government in 1990.

ments, actions, and writings, both overt and covert, by various officials, some of whom later turned up in the self-proclaimed Committee for the State of Emergency? Had I not spoken out from the podium of the Congress of People's Deputies, after exhausting all personal opportunities and resources, to say that a dictatorship was coming? I did speak out, but what came of it? I should have stated that the President is deaf and blind, that he cannot see or hear anything. Instead I let all the punishments of heaven and earth descend on my head. Probably it would have been naive to think that the president would use my "self-immolation" in order to arouse the country and the people to resist the reaction. On December 20, 1990 I already knew very well that Mikhail Gorbachev is extremely choosy in his response to things that happen without his knowledge or agreement. With some he may be unusually patient or indulgent. With others, on the contrary, he may be intolerant or irritable. Some destroy his life's achievement virtually before his eyes, and he seems not even to notice. Others attempt to save this achievement, but encounter only lack of understanding.

In my case, he made a display of iron self control. The president came forward and said that he saw absolutely no threat of dictatorship.

But the junta sprang up right under his wing.

Whether Mikhail Sergeyevich intended it or not, his statement at that time dovetailed perfectly with the chorus aimed against the former Foreign Minister and the steps he had taken. Phrases were used like "political spectacle," "fear of responsibility," "threatening a dictatorship," "he is tired," "his nerve has failed," and other such comments. Anatoly Lukyanov, Chairman of the Presidium of the Supreme Soviet, was among the authors of these slanders, as were some of the plotters, including the self-proclaimed "president," Gennady Yanayev.

Now not only I but many others understand that all this was a smokescreen for the future midnight "bonapartistes," hatching their own "18th Brumaire." But this realization does not give me any satisfaction or relief.

A word about Lukyanov and his friends: In mid-1990, I sent to the Supreme Soviet a draft resolution on the renunciation of the treaty of union with the GDR. If memory serves, it was September 15-16. In light of the approaching unification of Germany, it was absolutely necessary to present me with a final document for my response. But Anatoly Lukyanov only produced the draft on October 3. In other words, on the same day that the German Democratic Republic ceased to exist as a legal entity.

I don't doubt in the least that this delay was planned. It was a signal agreed on by the "Union Group" to attack the foreign minister and his colleagues along with the country's foreign policy.

That is, in fact, the way it happened. Lukyanov had scarcely announced—directly before the end of the session, as if by chance—the last point of the agenda, when this promptly followed: "What's going on here? At the very last minute, Shevardnadze foists upon us a question of the highest importance! For how much longer will parliament and the interests of the country be scorned in this manner?"

Then all hell broke loose. Everything played out beautifully, according to a scenario written by who knows whom? But the austere, steely, politely military regime was transparent. Behind the backs of the men with epaulets we could divine other figures.

I have been told that the draft of the resolution circulated for two weeks around the offices of the Presidential staff. Instead of blaming Boldin, the Kremlin Chief of Staff, and publicly admitting the oversight, the President praised my stunned deputy for keeping silent about the fact. And I committed the error of also keeping silent because I wanted to protect the dignity of the President.

I well recall October 15, 1990, the day when the announcement was made that Gorbachev had been awarded the Nobel Peace Prize. In the hours when Gorbachev was accepting congratulations, his Foreign Minister was at the podium in the Supreme Soviet, fending off attacks from the Soyuz group, which condemned him for the very thing that had motivated the Nobel Committee to make their award. Knowing this, Supreme Soviet Chairman Lukyanov kept silent.

The next day, I called Gorbachev and congratulated him on the well-earned distinction. He thanked me and said that I shared it with him. I had no need of this private recognition or of any public tribute to my merits, whether real or imagined. The only thing I needed, wanted and expected from the President was that he take a clear position: that he rebuff the right-wingers, and openly defend our common policy.

I waited in vain.

Let us recall the army units and weaponry that were placed around the Kremlin with the ridiculous excuse of having to protect seven deputies after supposed threats from "so-called democrats." Who on earth convinced or forced the president to make such a decision, which powerfully destabilized the situation in our country's capital? And why did he—the guarantor of our country's safety—thus visibly fall under the ominous influence of one of his advisors, while the reasonable advice of others fell on deaf ears?

I am remembering a great deal now, and see things in a different light than earlier. In the course of the present tragic circumstances, much has come to the surface.

In the old days, people would either say only good things, or nothing at all, about the dead. A person departed from life had thus removed himself from the judgment of the living. Still, there is another kind of justice, other norms, tied to the fate of our country and our people, and we ignore them at our peril. This is especially the case when the deceased has brought such judgment on himself. The news about the suicide of Marshall Sergei Akhromeyev shook me. He was a man of duty, and I respect that in him. We were not friends. He said that himself. We were colleagues, and could not be more than that. But he never left me indifferent. He was a fighter with an open visor.

I spent many hours alongside him at the treaty table, and in explaining our positions to each other. He was the co-author of many very important decisions regarding armament. But in the process, he didn't hide his views from us—or almost never. He knew how to underscore his disagreement with a look, with an expression, with a gesture.

One could immediately see that he was a dutiful soldier. To be sure, sometimes people were taken aback that he could deviate from the demands of honor in the name of duty. For example, he could wrap himself in a veil of silence when we were savagely criticized on account of decisions that he himself had helped to make. Or he could claim to have opposed the dispatch of troops into Afghanistan, even though he had simply in fact advised a delay.

On reflection, I would say that the following sort of statement was most typical of him:

"My father disappeared during the period of collectivization. But I don't hold that against the Soviet state, because collectivization was a historical necessity."

Feelings of duty that are set above moral sentiments fill one with horror. What duty instructs you to exterminate your own father, along with thousands of others, in the name of "historical necessity". . . ?

The accomplices in the August conspiracy may have been planning something similar. On my desk there is a copy of a directive from the high command concerning preventive detention—but detention of whom? Of anyone whom the junta considered it necessary to seize? The space for names is blank. Include whomever you want. With totalitarianism, this "whomever" has no limits. There are just as few limits when it comes to executions, deportations, and reprisals. A mass of tanks is worth more than human lives. In the scales of "history," the latter means nothing.

Speaking of tanks, when the Ministry of Defense and the General Staff hid thousands of them behind the Urals in circumvention of the Paris Charter, I lodged a protest with the President. He instructed his advisor, Marshall Akhromeyev, to clarify the matter. Sergei Akhromeyev submitted a memorandum completely justifying the move. My protest withered under the metallic gleam of his argument, along with my distress that the reduction of tanks was accomplished by deceitfully repainting them with Marine Infantry colors.

The country has paid dearly for all of that. The treaty on strategic arms, the trust reposed in us by others and the politics of new thinking, the future of Soviet-American relations and the new world order—all of this was placed in doubt. That's how Akhromeyev fulfilled his duty. Was it fulfilling his duty to serve the President and the top military commanders even though he disagreed with them?

But there is another more pressing question. How could the President bring such people into his circle—people who so unmistakably opposed his policies? Was this generosity? Breadth of vision? Tolerance for those of different viewpoints? Those are magnificent qualities, as long as you do not have to pay the price with plots and putsches. The shadow forces had made themselves at home alongside the legal powers, not even bothering to hide themselves, and undermined their partners.

From time to time, people called for "measures of salvation." The press and television gave reports about meetings in which decisive measures from the center were proposed. The chief argument here focused on the threats of the separatists against Party members, the repression of the military and of the Russian-speaking population. In the parliament, delegates of the republics refuted such arguments, upon which new ones were thrown at them. We can now shed light on these reports and proceedings: they reveal that the hidden layer of opposition had risen to the surface and was trying to cloud the picture. In such a situation, anything could have happened. Explanations of some of the delegates to the effect that the events of January 1991 would be subject to serious examination should make us take notice.

Meanwhile, the anxiety mounted. In November 1990, after the notorious "Declaration of the Fifty-three," it became unbearable. On one occasion I couldn't stand it any longer and called Gorbachev. I was told that he was on his way to work. I phoned his car.

"Acts of violence are the end of perestroika, and of your reputation. . . ."

"What are you thinking?," said Gorbachev furiously. "How can it even occur to you that I would allow something like that to happen?"

I believed him. I had to believe him, just as I had to both earlier and later, when Mikhail Gorbachev said that the puppet-masters who were behind the events in the Baltics were unknown to him. But I began to suspect that there were certain hidden forces that were prepared to take criminal actions, lurking behind the President's back. Soon my suspicions began to be certainties.

In my own mind, the events of April in Tbilisi represented the dress rehearsal for a totalitarian anti-utopia. What I had experienced in December 1989 was still sharp in my memory: a powerful chorus raised their voices in support and justification of the organizers of this slaughter. The directors remained hidden, and no one did anything, as if nothing had happened.

This lesson was useless. The President allowed more blows to land and was thereby made all the more vulnerable. Now they dictated their demands to him and imposed ultimatums. I am not speaking here of deputies with epaulets, but rather of men of the highest rank.

Everyone in Moscow remembers the "mutiny" in the national parliament when Prime Minister Pavlov demanded extraordinary powers for himself. This happened at a closed session. But who closed it, and why? Why wasn't it shown how Defense Minister Yazov, KGB Chairman Kryuchkov, and Interior Minister Pugo supported this demand? Why were these speeches quoted on the Leningrad television program "600 Seconds"? This film should be shown now, today. Only when the President found himself in an atmosphere of complete, hopeless frustration, did he make a resolute statement in an effort to defend our common policy, saying that not only had he and Shevardnadze conducted it, but a large number of high-ranking and now silent experts, who also shared responsibility.

A day later, Gorbachev said that he had no disagreements with the Prime Minister.

Thus surrounded by two-faced partners that he himself had put in power, the President was left unprotected against their perfidy and ill-will. The glowing coals of reaction suddenly flared up in the Supreme Soviets of the USSR and Russia, in the ruling structures of the Soviet and Russian Communist Parties, and among the Army's leaders.

I have already written about the large movement of tanks and the Paris charter, and about Gorbachev's prize. With the support of Party bosses (including Oleg Baklanov,[7] a candidate for dictator, the Soyuz group,[8] and the right-wing press) the General Staff erected yet another obstacle by breaking the package agreed upon in Houston into separate issues. Finally, when after seven months the two sides returned to the agreement they had reached before, it was touted as a grand success for the military establishment. The same people who half a year earlier had branded me a traitor were now posturing as victors.

On the day the START treaty was signed, one of the TV channels showed a film taken in the "secret city" of Arzamas-16. The secrecy turned out to be imaginary. People had managed to scale a high wall that even a bird could not cross, and wailed on television that the country's nuclear weapons program was being ruined. A notorious Colonel appeared on camera periodically, shouting "Treason!"

Who let those people in there? Who timed this broadcast to the signing of the Soviet-American treaty? At that moment, I knew the names of the authors of this provocation, and now I know their inciters and backers. No direct proofs, however; only indirect ones,

---

[7]One of the eight members of the coup committee—Trans.
[8]The Soyuz, or Union group, is a right-wing caucus in the parliament—Trans.

only suspicions, and these based on unhappy personal experience.

August 3, 1990: I had already reached an agreement with Baker about a common Soviet-American declaration opposing Iraq's aggression in Kuwait. I had the agreed-upon wording of this declaration in my briefcase. We set out on our way to the Vnukhovo II Airport, from where the Secretary of State wished to fly, when someone called me on behalf of a competent authority: "Today the US attacked Baghdad." I didn't believe that, but asked Baker: "Is it true? Tell me the truth. It is a question of my honor." He looked at me with hurt and regret.

Then the President called me. "Just look at this now." What he meant was, I'm holding you responsible. And I accepted the responsibility, offered up as a sacrifice to the caprice of our own internal Saddam, somewhere in the background. It is now clear that the campaign directed against me in the press and in the Supreme Soviet was a part of this conspiracy: the psychological preparation for the coup.

On July 23, 1991, a little article with the headline "A Word to the People," appeared in the newspaper *Sovietskaya Rossiya* which in my view was a call to rebellion. Among those who signed this incendiary manifesto I found the names of all those who had for many years overtly or covertly acted against the legitimate government, organized smear campaigns against us, slowed down the execution of the decisions we had made, and had called Gorbachev, Yakovlev and myself "the Knights of Malta[9]." Heroes of the Soviet Union and Heroes of Socialist Labor, generals from the infantry and writers of a chauvinistic bent proposed an overt plan of action. The article even mentioned people who were willing and able to seize the reins of power. Two of those who signed this piece wound up on the list of dictators, and a third went to Gorbachev in the Crimea with an ultimatum.

The increasingly visible reactionary front, which had united everyone among the ultras from the Party apparatus, the military, and the chauvinist press, was now preparing direct attacks.

What did the President do? He went on vacation.

What did we do, his former friends and comrades who did not want to conceal the activities of the gang surrounding him?

[9]A reference to the Soviet-American summit in Malta, where conservatives believed Gorbachev had made compromises—Trans.

Everything, even resigning from the team, was in vain. The President always remained deaf to the advice of the people genuinely loyal to him. Thus in June 1991, I thought it necessary to call for the unification of the country's democratic forces, and for a legal and constructive opposition. I was motivated by this simple thought: an organized democratic opposition should form the political base for the few reformers still active in the country's government. The elbow with which the President tried to prop himself up on the right was obviously slipping out from under him.

How did he reply to me and my friends? How did the reactionary leadership of the CPSU respond? With threats of a Party inquisition and punishment. New insults and insinuations. Persecution of the most prominent members of the Party devoted to democracy, Alexander Yakovlev, Alexander Rutskoy, Vasily Lipitsky, Nikolai Stolyarov and others.

But the Democratic Reform Movement which we had founded in spite of the President's wishes (and I also knew that for a fact), and even with his frank opposition, did not weaken; on the contrary, it grew and spread. And the right-wingers, seeing it as a threat, concentrated their fire on its initiators and leaders.

We were pummelled from the right, but he was silent. We were supported by those whom he branded as "so-called democrats"—Democratic Russia, and other parties in the RSFSR and other republics.

To be sure, he was busy with the drafting of the new Union Treaty. Yes, he himself suffered attacks and humiliations. But even so, with amazing stubbornness, he refused to see that the circle of the coup was closing in on him.

Did he not see it? Did he not want to see it? Or was it something else? I don't know. Numerous questions are raised for which I don't have any answers. On August 20, upon finding the French TV reporter Ulissa Gosse on TV1, I gave him my "Cry in the Wilderness."

In the interests of truth, it is worth quoting:

"The events of August 19 were not unanticipated. They were foreseen and forecast publicly, not only by me but by my comrades. Both I and they warned the President of them in personal conversations, and warned the country and the world in public statements from the parliamentary tribune, in newspapers, and on television."

"At the moment we know nothing about the fate of President Gorbachev and his family, so we are refraining from any speculation about the degree of his complicity in the plans of the coup plotters. For now, only one thing is clear: We have repeatedly warned of the shadow government operating at cross purposes to the legitimate authority and behind its back. Now this anti-Constitutional underground is out in the open. More, as has often been the case in our history, it is claiming its actions are lawful. But there is nothing further from the law than these actions. Under the law, a state of emergency can only be declared by an act of the Supreme Soviet, and only strictly in agreement with the legitimate authorities of the localities where the emergency is to be declared. Attempts to legalize an unlawful action after the fact is nothing more than a deception of the public at home and abroad. A parliament cannot make responsible decisions under the rumble of tanks and machine guns."

"If the President of the country is not well enough to perform his duties, he must himself, immediately and freely, under conditions monitored by democratic institutions, inform the people of this and order the procedure for the transfer of power himself. Although I have not had personal contacts with Gorbachev for a long time, I am still certain that his physical and mental state would not deprive him of the ability to perform his functions and executed powers. The natural fatigue that the President experiences given the weight on his shoulders would hardly prevent him from making coherent statements on television and in the press, which he has never refrained from doing, even before his ill-fated vacation."

" Therefore, it can only be a question of someone else, not him, preventing him from taking this opportunity, and preventing him by force. He is being blocked by these same midnight coup plotters, the majority of whom he himself has promoted to the heights of power."

"This can only be a question of an outrageously illegal, anti-Constitutional removal of the lawful President, actions not subject to rights and morals. The group which has seized power is now trying to 'bless' the actions with the name of the President. They are trying to create the illusion that they are defending his interests and the succession of power. . . ."

"I maintain that regardless of possible statements still to come from Gorbachev and the junta that has replaced him, the President is not sick. Rather, the junta's actions show symptoms of a chronic ailment that perestroika had tried to heal; a deliberate plot behind the scenes, in secret from the people; the removal of disliked leaders by unlawful methods and under false pretexts; hypocrisy and a double standard in dealing with the people; the projection of an enemy image and the setting of popular masses against disliked or inconvenient persons. . . ."

This is what I said and wrote in the hours before the storm in Russia's parliament, when all its defenders, all the advocates of lawful authority—along with our President—were threatened by something far worse than attacks in *Sovietskaya Rossiya* or the CPSU's newspaper *Glasnost*.

After Gorbachev's fortunate release from arrest in the Crimea, he was asked by one journalist at the press conference in Moscow to comment on my personal statement of August 20. How did Gorbachev answer the journalist's question? He said that he had not read my statement, but if I had really said that, it should be on my conscience.

Well, let it be on my conscience. He ought to have analyzed recent events. He had so little idea of what was going on around him that I could simply not be free of all suspicion.

As a man, as a father, as a husband, finally as his former comrade-at-arms, I lived through the 72-hour nightmare of Gorbachev's confinement in the comfortable palace jail of Foros.[10] He was a prisoner of the junta. But when he returned and spoke at the press conference, I saw that he was still a prisoner—of his own nature, his conceptions, and his way of thinking and acting. And now I am completely certain that none other than Gorbachev himself had been spoon-feeding the junta with his indecisiveness, his inclination to back and fill, his fellow-travelling, his poor judgment of people, his indifference towards his true allies, his distrust of the democratic forces, and his disbelief in the bulwark whose name is the people—the very same people who had changed thanks to the perestroika he had begun.

That is the enormous personal tragedy of Mikhail Gorbachev, and no matter how much I empathize with him, I cannot help but say that it almost led to a national tragedy.

That is precisely how the Democratic Reform Movement's

[10]Gorbachev was detained at his decha in the town of Foros in the Crimea—Trans.

Political Council characterized the right-wing coup on August 19. In just this way, simultaneously with the Appeal to the Citizens of Russia signed by Boris Yeltsin, Ivan Silayev[11] and Ruslan Kahasbulatov.[12] Without waiting for the failure of the coup on August 21, as many others did—including the "leaders" of the Communist Party—we immediately asked what was happening to the President and persistently tried to get answers.

That is precisely how Gavriil Popov spoke and acted in Moscow, and Anatoly Sobchak in Leningrad, and thousands of their fellow citizens and supporters throughout all of Russia.

In the final analysis, the people who defended the President were those he had betrayed, mistrusted or seen as enemies: Boris Yeltsin, the people of Russia and Moscow, the democratic movements and parties, his former comrades. And in this, despite the tragedy of the situation, I take enormous personal satisfaction, because the outcome of the August events confirmed the correctness of my chief principle: only the policy that is morally right will be victorious; only the political idea which takes human freedom as the measure of all things is invincible.

For some—and I would like to believe that they are very few—these were days of shame. For others, the majority, they were days of glory and great happiness achieved through common effort. And now I know that the people, armed only with the faith that they are right, carried the victory.

The plotters took many things into account, except the most important: the years of perestroika had rid us of fear, and we were different people now. And since we were different and they had remained the same, they could not conquer us. I am certain that the end of the coup will be the beginning of a new country, a new community of proud, strong and free people and a new world community. For during these days, I was convinced anew how many of us there are in the world, and how we are united in the thirst for honor, dignity and truth.

Since anything is still possible, we cannot succumb to euphoria. Everything may still turn out differently. Anything can happen in the death throes of a system pitched in final battle. And

---

[11]Prime Minister of Russia appointed by Yeltsin as chief of the economic reform committee after the coup —Trans.
[12]Chairman of Russian parliament —Trans.

eight conspirators is not the whole conspiracy. They are not the entire dictatorship. They could not have succeeded in launching their sinister plot if they had not relied on a fair number of supporters. I am not calling for a "witch-hunt," the settling of political scores or political revenge, but only for justice. "Mercy to the defeated" must be part of a moral politics. But we have no right to forget how many "defeated" there still are among us. Only then will the politics of conspiracy be doomed, just as its champions and adherents are doomed. I'd like to think that Mikhail Gorbachev has also become a different person. It cannot be otherwise. He endured a hard trial—standing at the edge of death, betrayed by his colleagues, and fortuitously saved. Such events leave their traces—and they must do so.

I wouldn't want my prophecies to be confirmed yet again. But I must say the danger is great. The conspirators brought about a chaotic, irrational development of events. They've set a fateful pendulum in motion which now threatens to wreck a wall already full of cracks. They must be stopped at any cost, so that the country and the world can be saved, and further human suffering avoided. Law must speak, not arbitrary will. We cannot take the enemies of democracy as our models.

This book was written in defense of democracy and freedom. I do not know whether it fulfills this intention or not. No matter how the readers of today or tomorrow will judge this book, no matter what verdict on its author both people and time will deliver, I can say one thing: if I had not told all of this, I could not have gone on living.

Moscow, August 24, 1991

Resignation Speech

Comrade deputies: I have perhaps the shortest and the most difficult speech of my life. I did not ask for the floor, but because certain deputies have insisted—the reasons, what it is about, are known to me, why this particular group has insisted on my speaking—I have drawn up the text of such a speech, and I gave it to the secretariat, and the deputies can acquaint themselves with it. What has been done in the sphere of current policy by the country's leadership, by the president and by the Foreign Ministry, and how are the present conditions shaping up for the development of the country, for the implementation of the plans for our democratization and renewal of the country, for economic development and so on? A certain amount has been done, and this is spoken of in the speech.

I would like to make a short statement, comprising two parts.

The first part: Yesterday there were speeches by some comrades—they are our veterans—who raised the question of the need for a declaration to be adopted forbidding the president and the country's leadership from sending troops to the Persian Gulf. That was the approximate content, and this was not the first or the

Speech by Foreign Minister Eduard Shevardnadze at the Fourth Congress of U.S.S.R. People's Deputies in the Kremlin Palace of Congresses in Moscow on December 20, 1990. FBIS–SOV–90–245, December 20, 1990, pp. 11–12.

second occasion. There are many such notes and items in the press, on television, and so on.

These speeches yesterday, comrades, overfilled the cup of patience, to put it bluntly. What, after all, is happening with the Persian Gulf? On about 10 occasions both within the country and outside the country's borders I have had to speak and explain the attitude and the policy of the Soviet Union toward this conflict. This policy is serious, well considered, sensible, and in accordance with all standards, present standards, of civilized relations between states. We have friendly relations with the state of Iraq. They have been built up over years. These relations are being preserved, but we have no moral right at all to reconcile ourselves to aggression and the annexation of a small, defenseless country. In that case we would have had to strike through everything that has been done in recent years by all of us, by the whole country, and by the whole of our people in the field of asserting the principles of the new political thinking. This is the first thing.

Second, I have been repeatedly explaining—and Mikhail Sergeyevich spoke of this in his speech at the Supreme Soviet— that the Soviet leadership does not have any plans—I do not know, maybe someone else has some plans, some group—but official bodies, the Defense Ministry—and they are now accusing the foreign minister of having such a plan, a plan to land troops in the Persian Gulf, in that region. I have been explaining and saying that there are no plans like this, they do not exist in practice. Nobody is planning to send even one serviceman in a military uniform, even one representative of the Armed Forces of the Soviet Union. This was said. But someone needed to raise this issue, this problem again. I know what is happening in the corridors of the congress.

The third issue. I said there and I confirm and state it publicly that if the interests of Soviet people are encroached upon, if just one person suffers—wherever it could happen, in any country, not just in Iraq but in any other country—yes, the Soviet Government, the Soviet side will stand up for the interests of its citizens. I think that deputies should back up, should back up the Soviet leadership in this. I would like to raise another question. Excuse me, is it all accidental? Is it an accident that two members of the legislature made a statement saying that the minister of internal affairs was removed successfully and the time has come to settle accounts with the foreign minister?

This statement has been circulated literally throughout the world press and in our newspapers. Are they such daredevils, these lads—I will call them that, age permits me to because they are really young, in a colonel's shoulderboards—to address such statements to a minister, to a member of the government? Look in the newspaper, I will not name a single name today. What is surprising, I believe one must think seriously about this: Who stands behind these comrades, and what sort of thing is this? Why does no one deny it and say that this is not so, that there are no such plans? Perhaps there are such plans?

In this connection permit me to say a few words about the personal worth of the man, about his personal sufferings, because many people think that the ministers who sit there or the members of the government or the president or someone else are hired, are being hired and that they can do what they like with them. I think that is impermissible. In this connection I remember the party congress. Was this really a chance phenomenon? Because at the congress a real struggle developed, a most acute struggle, between the reformers and—I will not say conservatives, I respect the conservatives because they have their own views which are acceptable to society—but the reactionaries, precisely the reactionaries. Furthermore, this battle, it must be stated bluntly, was won with merit by the progressive section, by the progressive section, by the progressive members, delegates, by the progressive-minded delegates to the congress. I would like to recall that it was against my will, without being consulted, that my name, I, my candidacy, was included for secret voting, and I had 800 against; 800 delegates voted against. What then: Is this random, or on purpose? Is the Foreign Ministry's policy not good enough? Or am I personally undesirable? This is a serious matter, more than serious. I say that, all the same, this is not a random event. Excuse me, I am now going to recall the Supreme Soviet session. At Comrade Lukyanov's initiative, literally just before the start of the sitting, a serious matter was included on the agenda about the treaties with the German Democratic Republic. As it happened, I was on my travels, and they called in deputies, and people found themselves in an utterly stupid position, and the issue was a flop. I myself had to speak the following week. How did it turn out? Those same people who are now speaking as the authors came out with serious accusations against the foreign minister, of unilateral concessions, of incompetence, lack of skills, and so on and so forth. Not one person could be found, including the person in the chair, to reply and say simply that this was dishonorable, that this is not the way, not how things are done in civilized states. I find this deeply worrying.

Things went as far as personal insults. I endured that, too. Comrades, a hounding is taking place. I will not name the publications, all manner of publications, the Pamyat society—I add the Pamyat society to these publications—what expressions: Down with the Gorbachev clique! They also add Shevardnadze and several other names. Who are they, the so-called reformers? I will put it bluntly; comrades: I was shaken; I was shaken by the events of the first day, the start of the work of our congress. By the pressing of a button, the fate not only of the president but of perestroika and democratization was decided. Is that normal? Democrats, I will put it bluntly: comrade democrats, in the widest meaning of this word, you have scattered. The reformers have gone to seed. Dictatorship is coming; I state this with complete responsibility. No one knows what kind of dictatorship this will be and who will come—what kind of dictator—and what the regime will be like.

I want to make the following statement: I am resigning. Let this be—and do not respond, and do not curse me—let this be my contribution, if you like, my protest against the onset of dictatorship.

I express profound gratitude to Mikhail Sergeyevich Gorbachev. I am his friend. I am a fellow thinker of his. I have always supported, and will support to the end of my days, the ideas of perestroika, the ideas of renewal, the ideas of democracy, of democratization. We have done great things in the international arena. But I think that it is my duty, as a man, as a citizen, as a Communist; I cannot reconcile myself to the events taking place in our country and to the trials awaiting our people. I nevertheless believe, I believe that the dictatorship will not succeed, that the future belongs to democracy and freedom.

Thank you very much.

Index